SAGE was founded in 1965 by Sara Miller McCune to support the dissemination of usable knowledge by publishing innovative and high-quality research and teaching content. Today, we publish over 900 journals, including those of more than 400 learned societies, more than 800 new books per year, and a growing range of library products including archives, data, case studies, reports, and video. SAGE remains majority-owned by our founder, and after Sara's lifetime will become owned by a charitable trust that secures our continued independence.

Los Angeles | London | New Delhi | Singapore | Washington DC | Melbourne

THE
WOMEN'S WAR

THE WOMEN'S WAR

A Female Soldier's Account of Her Time in Afghanistan

Anne-Cathrine Riebnitzsky

Translated from Danish by **Martin Aitken**

ʃ YODAPRESS | **⑤**SAGE | **select**

Los Angeles | London | New Delhi
Singapore | Washington DC | Melbourne

First published in 2021 by

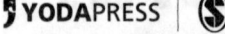  

SAGE Publications India Pvt Ltd
B1/I-1 Mohan Cooperative Industrial Area
Mathura Road, New Delhi 110 044, India
www.sagepub.in

YODA Press
268 AC Vasant Kunj
New Delhi 110070
www.yodapress.co.in

SAGE Publications Inc
2455 Teller Road
Thousand Oaks, California 91320, USA

SAGE Publications Ltd
1 Oliver's Yard, 55 City Road
London EC1Y 1SP, United Kingdom

SAGE Publications Asia-Pacific Pte Ltd
18 Cross Street #10-10/11/12
China Square Central
Singapore 048423

Published by Vivek Mehra for SAGE Publications India Pvt. Ltd. Typeset in 10/13 pt Bembo Std by Fidus Design Pvt. Ltd, Chandigarh.

Library of Congress Control Number: 2020947005

ISBN: 978-93-5388-630-1 (PB)

SAGE YODA Team: Arpita Das, Ishita Gupta, Tanya Singh, Amrita Dutta, Satvinder Kaur

Say thank you to the mothers who sent
their sons to help us. They will never fully
understand how much it has meant to us. But
hopefully they will understand just a little.

Gulaley Sherzad,
Leader of the Women's Centre in Gereshk

While it is estimated that women perform
two-thirds of the world's work, they only earn
one-tenth of the income, and own less than
1 per cent of the world's property.

**UNICEF, 'Gender Equality
The Big Picture' (2007)**

Thank you for choosing a SAGE product!
If you have any comment, observation or feedback,
I would like to personally hear from you.

Please write to me at **contactceo@sagepub.in**

Vivek Mehra, Managing Director and CEO, SAGE India.

Bulk Sales

SAGE India offers special discounts
for purchase of books in bulk.
We also make available special imprints
and excerpts from our books on demand.

For orders and enquiries, write to us at

Marketing Department
SAGE Publications India Pvt Ltd
B1/I-1, Mohan Cooperative Industrial Area
Mathura Road, Post Bag 7
New Delhi 110044, India

E-mail us at **marketing@sagepub.in**

Subscribe to our mailing list
Write to **marketing@sagepub.in**

This book is also available as an e-book.

CONTENTS

PART II

NARGISS AND THE GUNS

The first time I meet Nargiss, she comes with another woman I've known for some time. Together, they have driven thirty kilometres through an area crawling with highway robbers to meet with me at a military base.

Nargiss is young, pregnant and beautiful. She is also afraid of the Taliban. She covers her smile with her hand because she is unhappy about her teeth, and she says almost nothing at all. She drinks my tea, eats my cake and sneaks leftovers into her pocket.

The second time I meet Nargiss, I understand why she has sought me out. Some months before, Nargiss gathered the women of her village and formed a cooperative to manufacture handmade jewellery. The colourful beads they use come from Pakistan. They weave the yarn themselves. For the first time, these young women are earning their own money. The Taliban don't want women to work. But the men in Nargiss's village are supportive.

'I would like you to help with my project, just as you help the other women. But that is not why I am here,' she tells me.

Nargiss is still shy, yet the way she speaks indicates that she is a strong woman determined to take care of herself. She makes it clear to me that she is not dependent upon my help, but that she is here to tell me something.

The Taliban have begun running arms through her village and Nargiss wishes to pass on the information. Nargiss wants the Taliban out. Later, her opposition to the Taliban will cost her dearly.

Nargiss is one of a score of women I get to know during my first tour of duty in Afghanistan's Helmand Province. The women will end up changing my life, and I theirs.

This book has been written because I promised the women of Gereshk to thank the mothers of the Danish soldiers stationed there, but also because I feel something important is missing from the domestic debate on Afghanistan, something that cannot be encapsulated in a three-minute story on the evening news.

Afghanistan, and Helmand in particular, have been part of my life for more than four years. In 2006, my then partner was sent to Helmand with ISAF 1. Being left behind was hard. Support for the soldiers was almost non-existent and politicians were indecisive.

In August 2007 I went there myself as an officer with ISAF 4. My personal hope was in some way or another to be able to help Afghan women. During six months I formed bonds with women who were very often alone. Surviving as a widow and a mother of six is no mean feat when you're forbidden to work or mind a shop.

Following my tour and a short period at home in Denmark, I was asked by the Danish Ministry of Foreign Affairs to return to Helmand as a civilian adviser. I jumped at the chance. This time, I stayed for eight months.

With this book I hope to be able to pass on the thanks of women I know and for whom I have developed profound respect. I hope, too, that my personal experiences as described on these pages will provide insight into what may seem distant but which nonetheless impacts heavily on families in Denmark and elsewhere every time a son, daughter, brother, sister, friend or partner travels to Helmand to do a job of work.

The book represents my own experiences. All the incidents described in it are true and occurred in the chronological order in which they are set down. In the interests of the personal safety of some of the women involved, a few names have been changed or left out completely. Other women appear under their own names. These are women whose faces have already appeared on electoral posters and who for this reason already live under the threat of death at the hands of the Taliban. Publication of this book will neither heighten nor lessen the experience of those threats.

My book is of course by no means the whole truth about Afghanistan. But it does describe a part of that truth otherwise seldom told by domestic media.

Anne-Cathrine Riebnitzsky

PART

1

1
FROM HOME TO HELMAND

'I'm going to take sixteen X-rays now inside your mouth.'

The woman in the white coat in the dental clinic of Denmark's Varde military base bends over me to explain.

'For identification, if anything should happen and more than one of you get hit at once. Armoured cars going over landmines, roadside incendiaries, that sort of thing.'

I nod, unable to say anything with my mouth full of plastic. It takes over half an hour to X-ray my teeth. The teeth my dentist finds worthy enough to send to Helmand.

I mull over what she has said. They'll need to identify me among other bodies blasted to pieces. That's what she has said, only in a nicer way.

It's August 2007. I'm driving my sore mouth back across Denmark to Copenhagen. The occasional combine harvester crawling up the gentle hills, devouring corn. I sniff in the scent of summer and fresh straw.

My parents never argued during harvest. The year's earnings were rolled in, and in the smell of it all was a sense of hope and opportunity. Now, again, it's a smell that fills me with a profound sense of happiness, and yet somewhere beneath it all is a tinge of sadness. Harvest doesn't go on.

Beyond the yellow fields, the sea is clear blue. I grew up by the sea, am struck afresh by its changeability. I try to take in all the blue with my eyes so I can remember it forever.

I'm looking forward to leaving. At the same time, everything else becomes more sharply defined, because I know I have to leave it.

Back home in my apartment in the capital's multi-ethnic Nørrebro district, I begin to fill in the standard form: my last will and testament. They need to know what I want to happen in case of severe injury, and how my funeral should be organized if I get killed.

The last point urges us to write to our next of kin: a last goodbye in case we never see each other again. I think about my parents, my mother in particular. I think about my younger brother for a long time. I think about my girlfriends and my ex-boyfriend, with whom I'm still in love.

I think about my funeral. Inside the church is a coffin, and on the pews are all my friends and my parents. I see their faces before me. Some of those who have turned up are people I haven't seen for a long time. My girlfriends are overcome with grief and can't understand why it had to be me who died.

I cry. Tears fall on to the forms. I don't want to die. I really don't want to die.

Yet amidst it all is a sense of calm. I think through my life. I think of all the things I have achieved and all the people I have known. There's a sense of satisfaction there. Few regrets. Not much I wanted but never got round to doing. The only thing I need is more time.

'Take care of me, God,' I whisper. 'Take care of my mum and dad, and my brother.'

I take a deep breath. I still feel it's the right thing to do. I'm going to Helmand.

So far I've enjoyed a brief and intense career as a language officer in the Danish Armed Forces. I've done interpreting at home and abroad, but have never been on a real mission. For some time now I've found it frustrating to teach soldiers about managing meetings, body language and cultural understanding without having taken part myself in the things they do.

Visions of burkas and an increasing knowledge of the aims of Taliban made me think my male colleagues weren't the only ones who should go to war.

I got exactly the job I wanted. The army's human resources command offered me everything from Kosovo to Kabul. But I got what I wanted. I'm going to Helmand to help rebuild. They gave me a position as one of ten soldiers in a CIMIC unit. CIMIC stands for Civil-Military Cooperation.

Soldiers and civilians working together on small-scale rebuilding projects. The criterion is that projects benefit the military task at hand, but may encompass anything that creates better contacts between the military and locals. I'm going to be on patrol a lot of the time, on foot and in vehicles.

The unit is headed by Lars, a major in the Danish Army. He's happy there's a woman on the team. We share the same hopes, the same ideas. I'm going out to make contact with the women and hopefully do something good for them.

I begin my first letter of farewell:

Dear Mum

You gave me life and have taught me so much.

I know the most natural thing would have been that you died first, but since you are now reading these words, it was not to be. Hopefully, my death was sudden, and if there has been pain I ask you to recall that I always faint when pain is too strong, so I have almost certainly been spared the worst. If I was captured and taken hostage, remember that I have my faith and have been trained to endure and to hold on to my hope until the last.

I have written a lot of things about my funeral and how I see it, so here I will simply tell you how much I love you. I ask you to hold on with all your might to the thought that even though I have often been away from you, sometimes very far away in physical terms, I have always loved you and carried you with me in my thoughts and in my heart. We have, both of us, looked up at the Plough in the sky and thought of each other ever since you first began to teach me how to go out into the world.

You should know that I have always loved you, even at times when our lives have been troubled. And I have done so even when you have been unable to love yourself. I know that you supported me in my decision, even though at times it must have been difficult for you to be without me. Please know how much it makes me happy when you cast caution to the wind and do something nice for yourself. You, more than anyone I know, have carried such huge burdens, and you deserve all the pleasure and happiness you can find in your old age ...

It takes more than three hours to write the letters. Afterwards, I'm all cried out, but at the same time it's a relief.

Down on the street below, people are protesting about the Youth House, a kind of headquarters for the anarchist movement, which the authorities are trying to close down. There have been clashes with the police. The newspaper informs me that two kids have been killed in road accidents.

Three or four hundred people each year lose their lives in traffic accidents here. Small notices here and there. When a soldier gets killed in Iraq, they clear the front page. The first was killed in Helmand, wounded by shrapnel during combat, then flown home to the Rigshospital, where he died. Soon, more will follow in Helmand.

I push the thought from my mind. I still feel lucky. I pack my stuff. Go through the checklists. Almost nothing more to do.

'Isn't it dangerous living where you do?' my mother's friends sometimes ask.

My mother sidesteps the question.

'We see it on the news and in the papers. The most awful things going on there ...'

When my mother tells me about it on the phone, I sometimes lose patience: 'Oh, for God's sake. Life is dangerous. Don't they know they'll die themselves one day?'

Now the same people ask about the situation in Helmand, which is basically the same as where I live, just as far away, just as incomprehensible, and only a tiny bit worse. My mother hasn't the heart to tell me what they say. Only that she tells them: 'She could be run over by a bus just around the corner.'

I've lived here in the Nørrebro district for some years now. I lived in Moscow once. This is safe by comparison. During riots sparked by the closing of the so-called Youth House, one of my Russian friends called and asked how many protesters the police had killed, because the television reports hadn't said. When I told him no one had been killed he was amazed. How could that be?

Another friend called me from Ecuador. She didn't think she could come and visit me in Copenhagen after all, she was too afraid. CNN showed images of pillars of smoke rising up over the district from the many fires the anarchists had started. Three weeks before, I had visited my friend in Ecuador and narrowly avoided being shot by police who were chasing a young man for stealing two T-shirts from a shop.

'Parachuting's dangerous,' say the well-meaning people of my childhood's rural paradise.

Sometimes I think my mother was put into this world for the sole purpose of defending me against narrow-minded people who are so satisfied with their lives that they willingly die of the usual ailments: arteriosclerosis and boredom.

The evening I'm due out, my mother, my brother and I enjoy a meal together in my apartment. My dad's too old to make the journey from Fyn to the capital. We said our goodbyes back home on the farm.

We eat sushi. It's something I'm hardly likely to get in Afghanistan. I keep looking at my younger brother. Beneath the close-cropped hair and grey-blue eyes there's usually a wry smile that keeps appearing. Now, though, his lips are tight. He's been in Afghanistan twice himself, once in Macedonia.

Last time he went out, my boyfriend at the time had just gone to Helmand with Unit 1. It was hard to see him go, but the day my brother went was worse. It was like they had both left me all at once. I felt abandoned.

'What is it, Martin?'

He's distressed, almost in tears.

'It's just sinking in now that you're really going. Promise me you'll take care of yourself. Helmand's the fucking pits!'

We give each other a long hug.

My mother's crying because we are. My brother's going to Lebanon as a UN observer in only a month's time.

We make a pledge that night. If anything happens to me or my brother or our family, the most important thing is to convey the information right away. Better a quick phone call than holding off out of consideration. It's a deal that turns out later to be necessary.

We hail a taxi down on the street. The driver squints at my khakis.

'Where to?' he asks.

'Afghanistan.'

'That'll be expensive!' he says.

My mum smiles through the tears. My brother laughs.

I say he'd better make it the Sports Centre behind the Central Station instead.

Servicemen and families trying to say goodbyes. Sniffling girlfriends and mute, disciplined fathers. Tearful mothers and children too young to know what's going on. My closest girlfriends are here too. Some are proud, others concerned.

A black-clad demonstration approaches with carts, bikes and loud music.

The escorting police officers kindly ask if we'd mind standing back. They're afraid the sight of soldiers in khakis will provoke the supporters of the Youth House anarchists. I watch the demo go by from a distance and listen to the slogans they shout. It's the last I see of Denmark: police politely escorting a march.

Twenty-four hours later, tired, I'm sitting clutching the pillow I've taken with me. I'm looking out from the window of a plane. We're on the tarmac at Tbilisi, Georgia, a country whose government controls the capital city and not much more.

In the bright afternoon sunshine I can see a couple of men leaning against brooms made of bundled twigs. There are one or two old fire engines of Soviet manufacture. Along the runway are planes and choppers I've seen pictures of during my training as a military interpreter of Russian. Most of them are falling to pieces.

The French cabin crew are standing outside under the tail, smoking, but we're not allowed off the plane. The smokers are going out of their minds. A slightly built steward stands in the aisle, blocking the rear exit. One of the staff sergeants, a brick shithouse two metres tall, glares at the little fellow, then shakes his head.

'I could use him as a toothpick if I weren't so well behaved.'

Everyone bursts out laughing. It's an absurd situation: being sent to war, possibly to shoot people, and not being allowed to go outside for a smoke.

Many hours later, a snow-clad mountainside passes by my window. The pilot takes us down into Kabul. I'm exhausted now and looking forward to a bed to sleep in. It's been more than twenty-four hours since I grabbed two hours on the floor at the Karup military airport back home. But they won't let me sleep yet. Along with twelve other soldiers I'm being sent on right away to Camp Bastion in Helmand.

In the waiting area by the gate, a bunch of Afghan men stand around dressed in a mix of threadbare uniforms and civilian clothing. They stare at me. My guess is they're with the ANA, the Afghan National Army, of which I've heard good reports. The men are black-haired, dark-skinned, and all of them have long black beards. Most have bright green or grey eyes.

They keep staring.

I'm a good ten centimetres taller than most of them and glad of it. I made sure to dump a combat vest demonstratively on to the concrete floor alongside my other gear, just to show I knew the score.

My gaze falls on the only other woman in the room. She's in Western clothes, but with a scarf over her blonde hair. All of a sudden I want to look her in the eye. She turns out to be a British journalist living in Kabul and profoundly taken up with the plight of the Korean missionaries kidnapped by the Taliban, who are now threatening to cut off their heads unless Korea gives up its presence in Afghanistan.

A British serviceman shouts out that our bird has landed and we're to get our gear on.

We file out in a long line, out into the night air of Kabul. I pull back the bolt of the carbine and a soldier shines a light into the chamber to make sure my gun's not loaded. In the beam of his torch I can see he has freckles. His eyes are blue as ice and hard. Perhaps he sees all of us off as novices, secure in the knowledge that in a couple of months we'll be back, worn out and wounded, like all the others he's sent out before us.

'Next,' he says mechanically.

I let go of the bolt and it snaps back into place with a harsh, metallic sound. It's not the first time I've heard it, but it's the first time its true meaning becomes salient. It's easy to hear how all the pieces work together.

It sounds like forcing the jaws of a large predator apart, then letting them snap shut, only to discover the teeth lock together perfectly. Precise and lethal. It's the sound of one's own defence, of a chance to do something.

I hope I never have to shoot. That's not what I'm here for. I'm here to talk to people. But there are no guarantees. I'll be lucky to avoid combat.

Long lines of Afghan, British and Danish troops move out towards the Hercules transporter. Despite exhaustion and the gravity of the situation, I find myself suddenly grinning at the sight of the four engines as they turn, and the open tailgate ready to consume us. I shield my face against the hot airstream and step on to the ramp like so many times before. It's a plane from which I've done many jumps. A plane I've always connected with holidays and parachuting.

In the ribbed interior I settle down alongside the Afghan soldiers. We sit on the red nylon straps that are meshed together to form primitive seating and backrests against the fuselage and up through the middle axis. Shortly afterwards, the blue-eyed Brit with the freckles steps up on to a box.

'Lady and gentlemen, may I have your attention …'

His voice is weary. He reels off brief instructions about manoeuvres in case of our coming under fire and informs us of the capabilities of the plane to respond. Then we thunder off down the runway. Once in the air, the lights are turned out and people fall asleep.

I'm sitting by one of two small portholes and can see the stars in the sky. We're flying directly south. Twice we change course, banking sharply to the right, then shortly afterwards to the left, as though there's something out there we need to avoid.

The wheels touch down. We step out on to the ramp, down on to the uneven soil and into the darkness. Further ahead, someone follows a pair of yellow snap lights, small plastic tubes that can be bent so as to allow the two chemical solutions inside to combine and give off fluorescent light. We fall in behind two sheltering walls, three ranks. Our names are called out and one by one we climb on to the backs of three trucks and are soon on our way to Camp Bastion.

Above me, the most unbelievable firmament unfolds. The Milky Way extends from the horizon, dissecting the heavens and arching on behind me. I've never seen a night sky like this, never seen so many stars. Powdery sand flies up behind the trucks, the starlight turning it into a shimmering haze of icing sugar. The night is so incredibly beautiful. I sit with my legs stretched out in front of me against the cold metal of the truck's platform and lean my head back as far as my helmet allows. I'm here.

2

THE FIRST PATROL

My alarm rings in the middle of night. I turn it off immediately and lie awake in the dark. It's Saturday, 25 August 2007. Four in the morning. I'm in Lashkar Gah, Helmand's biggest town, Brigade HQ, home of the supreme military authority in the Province. I arrived by helicopter four days ago from Camp Bastion.

CIMIC is directly under the brigade, so the ten of us work out of Lashkar Gah rather than from Camp Price at Gereshk, where the rest of Danish company is to be based. The brigade has divided Helmand Province into North, Centre and South. The Danes are to be handed control of Centre in a month's time, while the British are to cover North and South, where HQ is.

I climb out of the bunk and put on my clothes. I haven't slept well. Hazel, one of my three British room-mates, whispers in the darkness to say I can turn on the light if I want. I don't. There's a bright full moon outside, shining in through our little window.

'Be safe,' she mutters, and turns back to sleep.

My locker clicks open. I take out my carbine and put it down on the bunk. Then comes the heavy fragmentation vest, or body armour as we call it. I pull it towards me on the bed. Three litres of water are heavy, but I'll need every drop in the heat of the afternoon, when temperatures soar to forty degrees Celsius. The vest is further weighed down by loaded magazines, a first-aid kit, snap lights, radio equipment, a harness for pulling away the wounded, fragmentation goggles, morphine, a tourniquet kit and disinfectant.

'Look after yourself, darling,' Hazel whispers. She talks a lot in her sleep and I'm not sure if she's talking to me or to her husband back home.

I walk through the sleeping camp and feel remarkably awake. Today is my first live patrol. This is what six months' training was all about.

The mess tent is quiet. I grab a plastic plate and pile on bread, butter and fried eggs. Around the tables sleepy, dishevelled Brits shovel in their baked beans. Torben, CIMIC second-in-command, is here too. He'll be with me along with the British lads. Torben's in fine fettle.

I sit down next to Bash, a strapping staff sergeant with no hair, brown eyes and dark skin. Bash, as in strike or hit. He's second-in-command of the British company who'll be escorting us. Bash seems likeable enough, but rumour has it he's a stickler for authority.

On a patrol some days before, a couple of his men mouthed off at some local women. Bash had them shifting sandbags before they knew what had hit them. From one end of the camp to another. When they were finished, he ordered them to move them all back again. After a whole day of meaningless toil in the baking sun, the hapless squaddies were told they had also been docked a month's wages. But everyone loves him. And we've heard he has a way with the Afghans.

Bash's plate is piled high with eggs and toast and baked beans. He folds his enormous hands over the plate to pray: 'Dear God, please keep me Christian in this Muslim world. Amen!'

I eat my breakfast with a strange tranquillity inside. As though I've lived all my life in an aquarium and in a minute I'll be removed from it and thrown into a reality I have observed only through glass, without ever knowing how it feels.

The first couple of days in the camp have been hectic. A thousand new things to take into account. The heat, the people, finding one's way around in the labyrinth that is the camp. Getting to know our British colleagues.

Just finding a place to sleep in the overcrowded Brigade HQ was a problem in itself. And now I'm finally going out on my first patrol. I'm nervous and excited, dying to get started. And yet it all seems so unreal.

We'll be going off into the rural districts south and west of Lashkar Gah, moving north-east in a curve cutting through Lashkar Gah and Gereshk.

Passing through desert, villages and the Green Zone, the verdant cultivated belt along the Helmand River and the big irrigation ditches.

While coalition forces and the Afghan government have a major say in Lashkar Gah, their influence outside the Province capital is minimal. To the north, British forces in Gereshk and Sangin are squeezed. In Sangin, troops can move only some two hundred metres from their base before the Taliban shells rain down on them. In the north-west, Musa Qaléh is in the hands of the Taliban and in the north-east Kajaki is the scene of constant exchanges.

The arrival of the Danish Battle Group in Helmand provides much-needed reinforcements. The British are stretched to the limit and are suffering many losses. The Danes are still at Camp Bastion, training before being handed Helmand's second-largest and most violent town, Gereshk, whose mayor and his son are at present being held captive by the Taliban, and where suicide bombings occur every week.

The battle group are to go out and fight to secure areas of land before development projects can be started, but the ten of us in the Danish CIMIC unit at Lashkar Gah have plenty on our hands. The provincial capital has been outside Taliban influence for more than a year and is relatively quiet. Occasionally a suicide bomber will strike, or there'll be threats to the local population, but generally the Afghans regard Lashkar Gah as fairly secure. CIMIC has kicked off a number of different projects there, and civilian aid organizations are present too. One of CIMIC's major forthcoming projects is to survey all schools in order to map pupil and teacher numbers and assess needs for teaching materials and equipment. In between tasks we'll be patrolling in the rural districts where the Taliban have the upper hand.

The area between Lashkar Gah and Gereshk is called Babaji. It's a wedge-shaped area of about three hundred square kilometres, bordered by the Helmand River to the east and two major irrigations channels in the north and west. It's in the Green Zone, lush agricultural land with many dwellings and small villages nestling between maize fields, irrigation ditches and tall trees. The Taliban prefer to fight in the Green Zone, where they are able to creep up on the enemy and come in close.

Until six months ago, Babaji was a base for some three hundred Taliban warriors. They were challenged by the Afghan army, in whose wake corrupt Afghan police conducted purges among local clans. After twenty-four hours, the Afghans ran out of ammunition and the British came to their aid. It took three days of battle to liberate the area from the Taliban.

Unfortunately, neither the British nor the Afghan army possessed the resources to hold the area permanently and after a few days forces pulled out again despite protests from the local population.

This morning, as we make ready to go on patrol, none of us knows if the Taliban have returned to Babaji. Two patrols have carried out sporadic visits there since March, but information on local feeling and Taliban influence is sparse. The Green Zone is the perfect hiding place and the worst-case scenario is that the Taliban channel supplies through Babaji to the fighting in Musa Qaléh and Sangin, as well as sending suicide bombers into Gereshk and Lashkar Gah.

I get up from the breakfast table. Bash is still munching happily away. None of us knows what's going on in the Green Zone between Helmand's two largest towns. It's our mission to find out. I toss the carbine over my shoulder and stride across to the interpreters' quarters. I've been assigned a good interpreter, but rumour has it that he can't get up in the mornings.

Above the roof the full moon casts down its light and a thin layer of silver is spread over the grey buildings. I knock on the door of the interpreters' building. They're just a bunch of young lads who sleep together in a heap on their blankets, mess around and dream of finding a girlfriend. But they provide for their families and run a considerable personal risk by collaborating with the foreign forces and the government against the Taliban.

'Pajan,' I call out.

A sleepy sound issues from within. A young man sticks his head out. 'Who are you looking for?' the young man asks.

'Pajan.'

'Are you going on patrol?' 'Yes.'

Pajan knows this. He may not have known the exact time, but he knew he'd be getting up in the night.

'OK, I'll wake him. He's a heavy sleeper.'

I nod. It seems to be the accepted truth about Pajan. The young man disappears inside. I stand outside in the middle of the yard, looking up at the moon. I'm tense—not afraid exactly, but still. I listen to the sounds inside the interpreters' building. The other interpreters are displeased with Pajan and are having difficulty waking him. Curses fly through the air in Pashto, Dari and English. Eventually he appears.

'Good morning, Miss AC.' He smiles, seemingly unaffected by the displeasure of his colleagues.

'Morning, Pajan. Where are your helmet and your vest?' 'Everything in the car. Major Torben took them yesterday.'

I nod and start to make tracks. Typical of Torben. The man has an eye for detail.

I halt suddenly at the convoy of vehicles parked two abreast, headlamps dimmed and engines running. Pajan walks on. He's seen it all before.

The so-called light vehicles, 4x4s with a minimum of armour plating and heavy weapons on top. We won't be able to take on a mine, but we should be all right in a minor war.

Trails of ammunition belts glint in the weak light beneath every roof—except one. Eventually, I find our Toyota Land Cruiser and Pajan jumps into the back, pulls on his vest and promptly falls asleep. Our car is the only one without external weaponry. On the other hand, it's better-armoured than those of the British.

CIMIC commander Lars has got up in the middle of the night to see us off. I've a feeling he's a bit worried as to how my sensitive being will cope. I'm more relieved than he realizes. Premenstrual, sleep-deprived and ratty in the few days I've been here at the camp, I really need to get out and show what I can do.

We stand there for a moment, three Danes in the still cold of morning, watching the Brits running around in general confusion. Their men are younger, their system more hierarchical.

I get into my body armour, sensing its immediate weight, then buckle my combat vest on top. I go over to the loading bay, click a magazine into the carbine, jam it into place with the butt of my hand, load and see the first cartridge disappear into the chamber. With a bit of luck it will remain there, I think to myself. Then I load my pistol and put it back in the magazine pocket of my combat vest.

'Well,' says Lars solemnly, 'if you don't come back, your fucking arses are going to be in trouble. And I mean it!'

I look into his big green eyes. His eyelashes are a thick mesh. Lars is a major in the reserves with an impressive civilian career as a lawyer. A highly intelligent man. I don't want to let him down.

He glances over his shoulder. 'I don't know if the Brits can see us, but what the hell …' He spreads out his arms and gives me a big hug. Torben gets the same bear-like treatment and a friendly pat on the shoulder.

It's a wonder we get the door of the Land Cruiser shut. I feel like a Sunday roast, corseted by bulletproof vest, radio, ammunition, a helmet on top and the carbine between my legs.

Torben, who must be one of the most talkative people ever to come out of Esbjerg, says in his West Jutland drawl: 'Best go easy on the desserts with all this gear we have to have on …'

We laugh. Actually, he has a point. I noticed it the first time in the mess tent and was quite taken aback. The combat troops are seldom over twenty-five; they work like horses and need all the calories they can get. But the desserts were clearly a major threat to anyone whose work did not take them outside the perimeter.

At last, the call is given, an informal 'Let's rock 'n' roll!' over the radio.

The patrol leader goes by the name of Boss, a young, slightly built guy straight out of Sandhurst, the British Army officers' training academy.

We roll out through the gate, directly into Lashkar Gah, where only a few people are up and about. The occasional trader on his way with his donkey cart or moped. I scan the little market stalls, all empty or boarded up in makeshift fashion, all knocked up in a combination cardboard, planks and sacking. The grey buildings are interspersed with occasional whitewashed houses decoratively striped in bright colours. This, then, is the capital of Helmand Province. Not a single building is more than two storeys, and most are made of grey-brown clay.

The patrol zigzags through the town towards its first challenge. The Bolan Bridge is a long, two-lane concrete construction. Patrols have been hit here on several occasions by suicide bombers and roadside incendiaries. We stop.

I sense Boss's hesitation over the radio. This is the only crossing over the river. On the bridge, a few locals are on their way into town. Small, inconspicuous figures pulling donkeys and carts or carrying wares on their shoulders. It's about a hundred metres to the other side. At this time of year, though, the river is a slow-flowing stream flanked by rocks, sand and small trees.

The order comes and the first vehicles edge their way on to the bridge with Bash at the front. We follow on behind.

On the other bank we pass by a bazaar that has yet to wake up to the new day. The town stops suddenly and fields unfold before us.

We investigate a number of blind alleys. The many ditches and channels that cut through the area mean we continually have to turn back. Now and then I catch sight of men making the best of the early hour to work in the fields. Often they are helpful, pointing and waving to show us where the road ends. Other times they stop for a moment and look up before carrying on their work with their hoes and other primitive utensils.

The nine vehicles, with our green Toyota number three in line, push on through the landscape. Each time we make a turn I see those in front and behind as a dark outline shrouded in dust.

The Brit in front, a jeep with top cover, turns his machine gun to the side to cover our flank. His movement reveals his black skin to be encrusted in a thick layer of dust. He's wearing goggles to protect his eyes and a bandanna pulled up over his nose and mouth.

Most of the armaments carried by the convoy consist of heavy 12.7 machine guns with a range of up to one kilometre. They're fixed to the vehicle and can be turned 360 degrees. A 12.7-calibre bullet is the size of a large finger and will tear a man to pieces a kilometre away. Presupposing, that is, that we see him in time. We're already a long way from base and will have to fend for ourselves if we run into an ambush.

I concentrate on scanning the way ahead through the clouds of dust. Via dirt tracks riddled with potholes, we approach a small village.

3

TALIBAN LAND

Pajan suddenly straightens himself up in the back seat. He wakes every time we stop, or so it seems. My radio crackles and I press the earpiece to my ear.

The voice belongs to Boss: 'OK, CIMIC, let's see if we can find anyone to talk to.'

Torben gives me a nod. I jump out and Pajan follows suit.

The name of the village is Shesh Kaley. The patrol has stopped by a man who looks to be in his forties, weather-beaten, slightly built, with intelligent eyes and a long beard. His turban is grey, like his traditional tunic and trousers. He's flanked by three young men, one of whom seems to be intellectually disabled. From our briefing the evening before I know the leader of the patrol has questions to ask about the cultivation of opium poppies. Sure enough, Boss pulls a list out of his pocket and starts at the top. The directness of his approach astonishes me. Surely this isn't the way to go about things? As though we were the colonial masters bossing the peasants about. It makes me feel ashamed.

As Boss reels off his questions I study the man's face. It's plain to see there are certain things he doesn't want to talk about. He would prefer not to talk about opium. The peasants here grow mostly wheat, he claims. He has heard about the agricultural market that's just been held at Lashkar Gah and he knows the government demonstrated alternatives to opium.

When Boss gets to the end of his list he turns to me to see if I have anything to add.

I ask the man politely who the young men are and he proudly introduces me to his sons. I repeat their names slowly and put out my hand. No

Afghan man would ever dream of shaking the hand of a woman unless she was the one to take the initiative. Anything else would be an affront to her honour.

'Do your sons attend school?' I ask.

The man listens attentively as the interpreter translates.

'Sadly, no,' he says. 'The school is no more. We had one here, where a hundred or so boys were taught.'

The school was a tent and a teacher in the field behind us. Teaching was split into morning and afternoon school, fifty boys at a time. The tent was burned down a year ago and the teacher threatened by the Taliban. A small group of villagers have gathered around us and a strange silence passes through the little crowd when the Taliban are mentioned. Some glance over their shoulders, as though the man had invoked an evil spirit.

'Do you still have problems with the Taliban?' I ask. 'Not very often.'

'What about the schoolteacher? What happened to him?'

'He is still here in the village, but he won't teach any more. He is afraid.' 'What does he do now?'

'He works in the fields. It's a waste. But it's not safe to have a school here.'

The Taliban still have a say here, I conclude. Not to the extent that no one will talk to us, but enough to make people scared to let their children go to school.

'Did the children like school?' I ask. I sense they find my question odd.

'Of course. To read and write is the most important of all.'

The man explains that schooling is a privilege and that too few in the village are able to read. Children and adults alike crane their necks to see my notebook, in which it seems I am writing down all that they say. Some jostle for a better look.

Suddenly I understand, sense it almost physically: illiteracy is not merely a concept but a fate. Those who cannot read or write are 'unskilled' and will never be able to hope for any future other than the one their parents had before them: hard work, a lot of children, limited means.

The villagers who have gathered round follow our discussion and pitch in with ideas of their own. They point and gaze at me intently as they talk among themselves. The man explains that they have never had a teacher for the girls of the village.

The village has about five hundred houses, the man believes. The figure seems somewhat exaggerated, but it's a common thing to exaggerate the size of one's village or clan. The bigger the better.

Just outside the village is a checkpoint manned by local police. It was attacked by the Taliban only three days before, but the police were able to repel the assault. People comment on what happened and explain. They seem satisfied with police efforts.

At no point does the man comment on the fact that I am a woman. He is polite and attentive. I'm very much aware I could just as well be a traveller from outer space. An armed woman, seemingly spokesperson among a group of men.

We thank him for his time and drive on along the track to the next village, which according to an old Russian map is called Loy Hagh. Four men standing by the road lift their heads in astonishment. One is bareheaded, the others wear turbans, grey, white and black. We climb out to say hello.

Quite spontaneously, the men tell us they're glad for our stopping by.

They have heard about the ISAF forces but have never encountered any of us until now. It's strange for us to know that we're the first international troops they've seen. I glance over my shoulder and pray that everyone will behave themselves and act politely.

'Where do you come from?' one of the men asks. 'Are you from America?' another is keen to know.

We tell them we're from the UK and Denmark. They nod. A man sporting a long white beard suddenly introduces himself in English. He's an engineer and tells us proudly that he worked with the Americans when they dug the irrigation ditches.

As early as 1910, the governor of Kandahar hired German engineers to construct channels for irrigation. Work continued up until the Second World War with the aid of Japanese as well as German engineers. After the war, collaboration with the losing side was out of the question. Among the victorious allies, the British and the Russians were regarded as enemies of

Afghanistan. Therefore, the Afghan king brought in American expertise in order to develop irrigation systems in the southern provinces. Without artificial irrigation from the river, the land could simply not be cultivated and Afghanistan found itself facing hunger on a number of occasions. The United States seemed to be appropriately distant in geographical terms and without historical ties to Afghanistan. The Idaho company Morrison-Knudsen's work initiated what was dubbed the Helmand Valley Project.

The expansive network of straight irrigation channels cutting through the landscape still means that here in the desert relatively large amounts of wheat, cotton, vegetables and fruit can be grown—as well as opium poppies.

With the advent Cold War, however, the US developed a strategic interest in Afghanistan. When the Soviets invaded the country to secure the interests of a teetering Communist government, the United States began to support the resistance movement that in time became the Mujahedin. To begin with, assistance was in the form of agricultural support, but it quickly turned into a more wide-reaching alliance against a common enemy.

The Afghans were the only ones persistent enough to openly resist the Soviets over a period of years, and the US supplied the Mujahedin with weapons capable of taking out Soviet choppers. When the Soviet Union eventually withdrew, leaving the Mujahedin triumphant, internal strife soon became the order of the day. The Mujahedin were warriors, not politicians. The country wound up in a civil war only the Taliban proved capable of bringing to an end after much bloodshed.

In this village the United States is remembered neither for the Mujahedin nor for arms. We have stumbled upon a whole society whose relative wealth can be attributed to the irrigation channels. Here what is grown is not merely maize and the usual cereal crops. All along the channels delicate, pink oleanders flourish. The village elder proudly tells us that Loy Hagh—literally 'the great garden'—is home to no fewer than thirty-six different clans. To the men here we are guests, descendants of those Americans who helped them all those years ago.

A couple of soldiers report that they have found a mosque further along the road. We drive there in the hope of being able to speak to the mullah.

The children run after us, crying out and pointing at our jeep. On the back seat, Pajan begins to laugh.

'It's you they're telling everyone about, Miss AC. They're shouting: "Look, a lady!"'

We stop outside the mosque, but there doesn't seem to be anyone there.

Down an alley I catch sight of a woman in black. Because she is old, her face is uncovered. She beams when I mention the Americans, but is otherwise shy and reticent. I ask if she thinks the mullah will speak to me even though I am a woman.

'Yes, of course,' she replies, and points towards a slim, white-clad figure coming along the road.

The lean, dark face seems proud and full of dignity. He has appeared out of nowhere, like people in deserts are suddenly just there. He does not extend his hand and he politely avoids looking at me on account of my gender. As is the custom among some of the clans, he has brown pencil marks around his black eyes. I find it distracting. Mild-mannered and eloquent, he tells me how much it disturbs him that the children cannot go to school. The Taliban burned it down a year ago and people have been too fearful to have teaching resumed. In the future he would like girls to be taught too, if it would be possible to convince some of the women teachers to return to the villages.

As we climb into the vehicles and get ready to leave, the village elder steps forward and taps on the window.

'We would like to know if there is anything we might do for you?' he asks.

I'm stunned. This is the exact opposite of anything I had imagined. I explain to him that we are gathering information and hope that one day the government will implement its policies in the villages too. The old man shakes his head.

'That will be after my time,' he says, and wishes us a safe journey.

Radio communication soon becomes intensified. We are now on our way into an area in which the Brits have previously engaged with Taliban forces.

I've really no idea what to expect after such friendly encounters in villages only kilometres away.

We are on our way towards a fair-sized town called Nad-e-Ali in which crime and corruption are rife. The police are strongly involved. The police chief is just as much on the side of the Taliban as on the side of the government, depending, so it would seem, on the circumstances. Brigade reports say he is unreliable, corrupt and uncooperative. The ISAF cannot get rid of him, the position of police chief of a district being an internal matter for the Afghans alone.

Suddenly a soldier reports a man photographing the patrol with his mobile phone.

'Stop!' Bash yells.

He and a couple of Brits leap out and wrench the phone out of the young man's hand.

Bash shouts angrily at him: 'Why were you taking pictures of us?'

I can't hear the reply, and all I can see is a couple of scared young men staring down at the ground. I hazard a guess they're avoiding the question. I've seen it before in interrogation exercises. People with a guilty conscience and a poor capacity to lie. But is a snap on a mobile phone really worth getting so worked up about?

'Why were you taking pictures of us? Answer!' Bash thunders.

The young man has almost been swallowed up into the ground. Bash takes hold of his phone and starts pressing at the keys. I catch myself wondering if he's quick enough to check for some of the numbers that were mentioned in our briefing as being those of known Taliban leaders.

The local people lining the road are reticent, suspicious of what we're doing. I don't blame them. I wonder what kind rumours circulate about us here?

Boss and Bash roll into the police compound looking well pleased. I feel I'm being observed from all quarters. Some of the police are clearly out of it on opium. They keep grinning like fourteen-year-old kids and follow me everywhere. I don't like it. I'm getting angry. Until now I've been met only with respect. Now I'm a whore to be ogled and salivated over.

I follow Bash and Boss inside the station that reminds me of a fort on two storeys. I pass by a couple of empty offices containing dilapidated furniture and a few official-looking photos of politicians and policemen. There are holes in the walls and litter on the floors. I'm disappointed. No one could possibly have respect for a bunch of drugged and barely uniformed police officers purporting to be representatives of the government. If only half the rumours of corruption are true, then the police here must be an affliction worse than the Taliban, who, although they may be violently oppressive, at least crack down hard on crime.

I begin to realize that some police are simply playing a game with us, the international forces. If only they say they're fighting the Taliban, we'll support them enough to look the other way with regards to their lack of discipline and widespread corruption.

The chief of police isn't in. Boss and Bash must abandon their enterprise.

Bash buttonholes a couple of officers and gives them a dressing-down for being stoned on hashish and opium. The sheer size of the man and the noise he makes at least ensure that they look as though they have some respect.

After the visit, we agree that I can go on foot patrol through the bazaar. 'Don't go too far,' Bash advises. 'I'll give you two men to accompany you.'

He calls over the radio. The first is a black guy called Sunshine, the other a stumpy little lad they call Trigger, hardly a day over the limit of seventeen and a half. He's really not much bigger than the weapon he's carrying, a pasty young chap with freckles and spiky blond hair. But the determination on his face says he'll blow anyone away if needs be.

Just to make sure there's no misunderstanding, I tell Trigger that if they feel uneasy at any time and would rather I didn't stop to talk to people, then they should say so.

'You stop where you want, Ma'am,' the lad replies.

I take off my helmet and say hello in Pashto as we move through the bazaar. I've got my eyes peeled for an opening, a friendly smile, someone with the will to talk. Many turn their backs on me. Occasionally, someone will respond to my *salaam aleikum* and say a couple of sentences in kind, basic salutations I can understand without an interpreter.

The bazaar is just a row of pent roofs extending from the buildings in the street. Almost all of it is taken up by makeshift moped and motorcycle workshops. In a few places fires have been lit in discarded oil drums. The whole street is on edge. I can sense the distrust in my stomach. A moped comes close, then speeds off. Trigger shouts something at the driver.

Another moped comes in through the crowd from the other side. Trigger and his partner keep cool, making hand signals for people to stay clear. The moped shoots close by and turns to come back. It's pure harassment, and they keep on. Sunshine and Trigger raise their weapons to make them more visible. It feels as though we're on the edge of war.

Further down the street I meet a man willing to talk. He seems inquisitive and a wee bit overindulgent. At least fifty Afghans gather around to listen. I ask him about his shop and about the school.

'The school's closed,' he says. 'Too dangerous.'

'Why's that?' I ask. 'You've got the police just around the corner.' 'They never lift a finger. When our things get stolen they do nothing.' I'm surprised the man has the courage to criticize the police.

'Who steals around here?'

'I don't know. It happens in the night.'

His gaze becomes distant, and my thought is that he knows more than he's willing to let on. This is becoming dangerous for him.

'Who causes you problems?' I ask, sending an enquiring gaze to the gathering of men.

They stare at the ground.

'Rumour says the Taliban and the chief of police are best pals,' I suggest. 'There are too many people here. It's unwise to talk anymore,' the man mutters.

All of a sudden, a man in snow-white garb steps in front of me. He clearly doesn't fit in here in this filthy garage environment.

'What you say is not true,' he says angrily to the crowd. 'The school will open again soon. Everything is peaceful and well here. You must not tell these soldiers such lies.'

I sense Pajan is on his guard. I am too, but decide to engage him anyway. 'Tell me how you see the situation here,' I ask.

He looks me directly in the eye and replies defiantly: 'We have no problems here!'

I ask him a couple more questions, but the man ignores me and shoos away those who have gathered. They turn and amble off reluctantly, and the man disappears into the crowd.

Is this al-Qaeda? Is this what they do? I've heard about their aid to the Taliban. They supply cannon fodder and strategists who can lead groups of warriors and advise on planning. But they make their mark on the Taliban and the local inhabitants in other ways too. Suicide bombing, for instance, is an al-Qaeda speciality, though loathed and feared by the Afghans.

Bash calls me over the radio: 'CIMIC, I've got you in sight. Don't go any further. Turn back!'

I withdraw the same way I came in, inviting people to talk, though no one will.

As I come closer to the convoy, I realize how tense I've been. I may be good at sounding relaxed, but inside it's another story.

Trigger reports briefly to Bash, who is sitting on the bonnet of the jeep.

He looks down at me.

'Yeah, a fucking ugly place, this is.'

'Don't they have anything but motorbikes in the bazaar here?' I ask. 'Further in, yeah. But we need about thirty men with us to go that far. You were right on the edge there. Did you get anything out of them?'

I shake my head.

'Nothing we didn't already know. People feel unsafe. The Taliban have got their spies everywhere. The police are incompetent, and we met this weird guy who definitely didn't belong.'

'On loan from al-Qaeda, most likely.' Bash grins. 'Give it to intelligence when we get back. We were here and we didn't kill anyone. That's as good as it gets in this area.'

He raises his voice: 'OK, lads, let's get the fuck out of here!'

We head north-east towards Babaji. On the outskirts of a village we stop in the middle of the road. Bash wants to see a local doctor a number of people in the area have mentioned.

I peer out of the side window. Behind us is a little compound surrounded by trees. There's a man in a white coat. He raises his hand cautiously to say hello.

I click the radio: 'Boss, I've got one here who wants to talk.' 'Roger that.' A click and then: 'Trigger, move out.'

I jump out of the car. Twenty seconds later, Trigger's with me again to cover my back. Boss comes striding.

'Might as well, while we're at it,' he says, and waves his sheet of opium questions.

Sheltered by the trees, the man greets us. His brown eyes are wary. I can sense he wants to talk, but opium's the last thing on his mind, and when Boss receives a call on the radio I jump at the chance and quickly win the man over. I go straight to the safety issue.

'That's exactly what I want to talk to you about,' the man says. 'Just the other day, the Taliban were here outside my house kicking up a fuss. They are going to kill my brother and I am afraid.'

I take notes and ask questions. Two of the man's brothers, a soldier and a policeman respectively, have been killed in engagements with the Taliban in Kandahar, and a third, who also wants to join up, has been receiving threats.

Behind him, the gate of the compound opens and four beautiful women in colourful robes look out at me. These are the first young Afghan women I have seen up close. I hold my breath. They smile and whisper to one another as they gaze at me. Their eyes are brown, their hair jet black and covered only by bright red or green gossamer.

I pluck up the courage and ask if I can enter. The man declines, turns and shoos the women back inside. I could kick myself. Why couldn't I just hold back?

A few minutes later I notice a pair of pretty brown eyes peeping through the slats in the gate. Then another. Soon, all four are there. I leave it at that. They're looking at me, a woman soldier, a vision from another time and place.

Our man is full of information, all of which fits with what I was told at the briefing. I'm given names and places. But I sense there's more. I just don't think he's ready to tell me yet. I flick through my notes and pick up on a few things I'm not sure about, but then Trigger pulls gingerly at my sleeve.

'I think they're waiting for us, Ma'am.'

I smile to myself at the honorific. I always think the British lads are saying 'Mam', as though they're talking to their mothers, at once formal and a bit silly. His blue eyes are nervous. Something's not right.

I haven't got my headset on, wanting to concentrate on our man and what he's had to say. I must have missed something.

I thank him and say goodbye as Trigger tugs at my sleeve. 'We really have to go now, Ma'am.'

It's hardly fifteen seconds since he first said it. I pull on my headset again as we stride down the path. I'm wondering if the others have encountered fire. But I've heard nothing.

Trigger escorts me back to the Land Cruiser, then breaks into a trot as he continues along the road. Torben gets going even before I've closed the door.

'We've got a bomb squad on our arse,' Torben says grimly. 'They've been following us for almost three hours. Ever since Nad-e-Ali.'

4

THE DESERT SEA

Torben tightens his grip on the wheel.

'What do you mean, bomb squad?' I ask him.

'No idea. The Brits just heard on the radio. That's why Boss disappeared when you were talking to that bloke. HQ reckons we were tagged in Nad-e- Ali, maybe before. And they're pretty sure they're going to chuck an incendiary, a prefab dressed up as rubbish they just chuck into the road.'

The information leaves me cold. I feel nothing, but my heart rate increases noticeably. I stick my notebook inside my vest and start scanning the road outside the window so I can help when the convoy turns and needs to find a way back that won't lead us into the arms of those who want to chuck a bomb in our lap.

'How do they know we're being followed?' I ask. 'Probably a drone with a camera.'

This comes as a complete surprise to me. How can I be so naïve?

Torben's been through it all before in Iraq. It takes moment for it to sink in that we're being observed without being aware of it. The base keeps an eye on anything that moves, things we're unable to see ourselves. But resources aren't that plentiful, so someone must have reckoned there was a risk here. Or maybe we were just lucky to get that extra bit of help.

'Wrong way, you bloody tea-drinker!' Torben shouts suddenly, as the car in front turns.

All the focus now is on swinging the nine vehicles round on the narrow road between ditches, trees and houses.

'I got some good stuff out of our man back there,' I say.

'Well done,' Torben says. He's chewing gum and looks totally concentrated. A moment later he exclaims again: 'Don't these bloody Brits know where they're going, or what?'

We speed along the narrow roads, past houses where smiling people wave, unaware of what's going on. We wave back as we tear by, past local graveyards with their strange decorations of fluttering plastic strips.

We don't stop until the last houses and fields are out of sight, pulling in on a little ridge in the landscape. There's no one in sight, nothing but sand and stunted vegetation blown awry by the wind.

Emptiness. That's what desert's called in Russian, I suddenly think. And it's true. Where the irrigation channels stop, the desert begins, like some desolate sea without an end. It's as though we form our own little island, floating around with no land in sight. Like nomads, we make camp in the middle of nowhere to find a moment's peace.

The guys light a fire with the rubbish they've gathered from the cars.

They pull out empty ammo boxes, fill them with water and put them on to boil.

I'm starving and I'm soaked with sweat. I grab a couple of boxes of rations out of the car and carry them over to one of the young guys who's putting sachets of ready meals into the boiling water.

'Can you tell me what tastes best out of these?' I ask.

'Yes, Ma'am.' He rummages around a bit in the two cardboard boxes and tells me how the rations are organized. I ask him to roughly sort them out for me. I don't feel like experimenting much on the culinary side for the next three days. He chuckles a bit awkwardly at my directness.

'No problem, Ma'am. When we get to dinnertime you can come to me with what you want and I'll heat it up for you.'

'Brilliant. Thanks a lot.'

I make sure Torben knows too and tell him I now know that no one in the British Army cares for caramel pudding. Milk chocolate at forty degrees Celsius isn't exactly popular either.

'Food was never a strong point of those windswept islands,' Torben says, smiling.

We pull off our combat vests and body armour and store the carbines in the car. It feels great to walk around in just these light khakis with only a pistol at the hip. Within minutes my jacket's dry again. The sun is harsh, but the wind cheats us into thinking it's not as hot as it actually is.

I go around to the various vehicles with my camera and take pictures of the lads. They put their lives on the line to ensure our safety. Maybe they'll appreciate a CD of photos of themselves.

Watching them, I realize that many are sons of miners and factory workers. They're the ones who got away. Good at their jobs, professional soldiers with a sense of community that comes only from working the line between life and death. They would lay down their lives for one another, and for their senior NCO, their strict yet always cheerful father. Few have the opportunity of doing what they do, and their professional pride is enormous.

I look out on this bunch of warriors. Some are asleep in folding chairs, others are kicking a ball around or chucking stones. One or two are tidying up inside their vehicles. It's a sight that would surely surprise their mothers. One has his head inside a metal box, then straightens up clutching a mix of spices, perhaps just the one to give the food that perfect edge. A couple of hours pass under the baking sun. The wind caresses us and makes the adrenalin go away.

'Briefing in five, lads. Ready in fifteen!'

Bash waves a map in the air. The lads nod and finish their meals, draw their games to an end. One has rigged up a hammock between two cars. Above him hangs an army-green tarp like a shade sail. He turns and pulls his cap down over his eyes. I don't know what his job is, but I'm in no doubt he can be packed and ready in no time.

Boss and Bash spread the map out over their car bonnet. Torben and I amble across to join them. Soon about a dozen of us are gathered.

'OK, no need to go blasting into the arms of our friendly neighbourhood bomb squad, so we're heading straight for Babaji now. You all know the score. We need to assume the Taliban are in the area and we need to be prepared for combat. It's Green Zone, densely populated, perfect for ambushes. Standard procedures. Wide irrigation channels all over the area. They can be crossed at these points here.'

Boss points at the map.

'There may be mines. Be on the lookout for fresh mounds and all other indicators. If it looks suspicious, we stop and sweep.'

We nod. All this is normal. Everyone's done it before. Everyone except me. No one seems afraid and I feel safe.

Bash turns and bellows out his orders: 'Right, let's get a move on, then. Two, three, four, CIMIC, myself up front and the rest of you girls tag on.'

The patrol kicks up a cloud of dust that can be seen miles away. On our right, the gravel track falls sharply away towards a canal which is about ten metres wide. On the left, it's bordered by houses, walls and fields. Then the desert unfolds.

To all intents and purposes we're shut in on the road. It must be the easiest thing in the world to eyeball us and call your cousin up the road to say we're on our way. There's nothing we can do about it. This is the road. People know half an hour in advance there's a convoy coming.

Torben sits at the wheel and tells me about his time in Iraq. I gaze out of the window at people fetching water from the canal, children splashing around in the gentle blue-green flow. Herds of mottled goats driven along by little kids with sticks. Wild and tame camels loping steadily through the desert. Most are light brown or sand-coloured. Some are almost white.

Sometimes they just stand in the road gawping.

Eventually, we cross the road that leads us over the canal and into Babaji in one long, tight convoy. I spotted the crossing a while back. Three big pipelines lead the water under the road. On the other side is a fair-sized village. I look out at the men. They stare back at us with suspicion.

'Not exactly pleased to see us, are they?' says Torben, and initiates a full-scale waving campaign.

I do likewise. Not one waves back.

We drive slowly through the village. Boss and Bash aren't stopping and I figure there must be a reason.

We ease out again into all the green, following minor roads. Tall deciduous trees shade the sun. Fields of maize and marijuana interrupted by traditional high clay walls enclosing houses or fields. For a long time we see not a single soul.

The patrol pulls over on a winding road. We're hemmed in on both sides by walls. From a security perspective it's not good, yet it feels safe here. I can hear birds.

Boss comes on to the radio.

'CIMIC, do you want to get out and have a look? I think there's some people in the field over there.'

'Yeah, thanks.'

I climb out of the Land Cruiser and make my way up a track with two men accompanying me. The lads are on their guard. The thought occurs to me that they have only a couple of months to go before being sent home. They've seen their fair share of fighting and now they want to get home in one piece.

Boss has spotted three men on the edge of a maize field. One of them is intellectually disabled and sits leaning against a wall, staring perplexedly. There's nowhere for the sick or disabled to go here. They're put to work according to the best of their abilities.

Boss asks his standard questions about opium. I listen, then when he's finished I try to approach subjects of more interest. It's a method that seems to work. Sometimes, Boss stands and listens. He's already getting a feel of how the Danes work.

We know that many have heard of the alternatives to opium growing that are being offered by the government. The problem is the cost. The people here know that opium finances the Taliban, but at the same time they can't do without the money they earn on the illegal crop. It's not for lack of will. It's about need.

The three men are brothers and have inherited the field from their father.

One of them knows a small amount of English from a school providing adult education before the problems with the Taliban. He tells us that the Taliban engulfed Babaji and forced people to give them food and shelter. They were a plague and a burden. After the major Anglo-Afghan operation in the spring, people now are trying to keep themselves to themselves.

The hope was that the Afghan army would secure the area and make it safe, but instead the local people had to set up their own militia. The elders held assemblies, so-called *jirgas*, and decreed that each family should pitch in to the effort by supplying men according to the decisions of the council of elders. This is new to us. Moreover, it is indicative of a wish to wrestle free of the Taliban. For now, the Taliban come only in small groups and only in the night. There has been no fighting so far.

Before we go, I ask on an impulse what the young man would like to do if he didn't have to tend the land. He lowers his gaze and smiles sheepishly.

'I would like to be a doctor.'

I wish him good luck. He thanks me and lifts his hand to say goodbye. My two bodyguards rise up from their kneeling shooting positions and we make our way back to the car.

I have the same feeling I've had a number of times before on this patrol. I am a kind of alien from outer space, landing in its spaceship, asking questions, then disappearing again. I only hope the Afghans aren't too frightened by all my tentacles and my strange weapons.

'Doctor,' I say to myself and smile.

Our worlds are so different, yet still we recognize each other's dreams and ambitions.

We pull out of the area. We've done enough for today. We've been on the go for twelve hours and all of us are tired. On our way through the little village by the canal we smile and wave stubbornly to those we see. They stare and walk on or go back inside.

We drive out, far into the desert, and light fires. It feels good to get hot food inside us again. We gather around the patrol leader's jeep. Boss briefs us with precise instructions for the night. We don't want anyone to see where we bed down, so as soon as we've eaten we turn off all lights and drive further on into the darkness. Torben and I nod in agreement.

'Probably not such a good idea with those camp beds. They make too much noise,' Torben says.

He's right, of course. Sound and light regulations mean we can forget all about putting our beds up. It makes us laugh. They take up so much space in the car.

The sun goes down as we eat. Blacked out, we roll through the night until we stop somewhere in the desert. Cautious, we open the doors and climb out. The tearing of Velcro on our body armour makes a hell of a noise, but it feels great to finally be able to take it off.

I lay out my self-inflating mat and unfold my sleeping bag. Then I brush my teeth using bottled water, pull on a clean T-shirt and chuck my jacket on the front seat. Boots go next to the sleeping bag, socks pulled over the top to keep out yucky camel spiders the size of your hand.

The ground is hard, but the firmament is just incredible. I find the Plough, which looks all wrong here. Imagine if my mum could see me now, on the ground next to my carbine. I lie awake for what feels like a long time, gazing at the stars. I think about the four women peeping through the gate.

What were they thinking about me?

I close my eyes and see the shimmering desert pass by behind the irrigation channels, children bathing, herds of goats trotting along the road. I hear a pair of boots going about on watch. I fall asleep.

When we return to the crossing at Babaji the next morning we're surprised to see the men who were so distrustful yesterday now waving cautiously to us. Some even want to talk. From what they say, I gather they've spoken to some of the men we chatted with yesterday. They know we're here to ask about opium, schools, education, problems with the Taliban and life in general.

At one place we stop by a cluster of houses to speak to four young men. Ducks paddle about in a nearby stream. It could just as easily have been a village pond back home. The young men are nervous. They giggle. One plucks up the courage to say he'll never be able to afford a bride like me. Our chat provides valuable information.

Like so many others, the four young men will inherit land and divide it between them. With time, the lots become smaller and smaller. The price of a bride has gone up as opium growing spreads. An ordinary run-of-the-mill bride costs ten thousand dollars now. One of the men says a good-looking girl from Herat who can read and write and who comes from a good family can cost up to seventy thousand dollars. Just to marry an ordinary girl takes years of opium growing on the small lots to save up the money. And all the young men want to get married.

At another place we meet a teenager who has sprained his arm. He has come running because he knows we can sometimes help the sick. We're in the middle of Babaji, hardly fifteen kilometres from Gereshk as the crow flies. Even so, the boy tells us, it will take him two hours to get to the hospital on a borrowed moped. He won't risk the journey, though, because the town is unsafe. I examine his arm and put on a bandage. He's grateful for our help and runs around after us in the neighbourhood for the next half-hour. Every time we stop, he raises his arm, jumps up and down, and waves.

On a break, we eat watermelons one of the soldiers has bought from some of the locals. Again, water is boiled in the empty ammo boxes. No British patrol without tea. Another soldier has bought flat bread. It's been baked in an earth oven and tastes fantastic. Another has got his hands on some grapes. I've no idea how they do it, but gradually it dawns on me that while I'm talking to the Afghans, the lads are pointing to what they want and offering a few Afghani, a dollar or a couple of cans of Coke in return. Sometimes people just want to give them fruit and bread for nothing.

Whoever we are, we certainly won't be allowed to leave with a bad impression of hospitality.

We move on through the rural areas, through the villages. I speak to more than a hundred Afghans in the three days we're on patrol, and we drive some three hundred kilometres through sand, water, stony desert, maize fields, villages, bazaars and even an old fort that's on UNESCO's World Heritage list, but which primarily functions as a rather primitive prison.

I find myself growing used to the absence of women and to the age in which I have landed, a kind of Middle Ages with a sprinkle of mobile phones and rocket launchers.

We spend our last night in the desert south of Lashkar Gah. This is enemy country and we wouldn't be here at all if it could be avoided. We don't really know what's going on but hazard a guess that the Americans or the Brits are involved in operations and don't want us getting caught in the crossfire. We have to stick to the coordinates given to us by HQ and bedding down for the night everything's hushed as a church. The next morning we find out that helicopters have dropped supplies for

Special Forces close by in the night. We were put where we were so the choppers would know we weren't enemy.

On our way home two of the British cars break down. For two hours I sit with the doors open, scanning the landscape outside while the mechanics toil in the dust.

The sky is pure and blue. The landscape extends almost as far as the eye can see. I breathe in the sharp, clear air. Over the last couple of days a strange contentment has settled inside me. Together, we are free and strong. The patrol feels like a family. The lads are funny when we take a break, professional when we work.

I flick through my notebook. It's a mine of valuable information now and I know that much of it will be of great benefit to the brigade when we get home. I've passed my first test. I was tense about it, but it panned out as I'd hoped.

Some hours later we slowly cross the Bolan Bridge with the two cars on tow. We feel winged and cross our fingers that nothing else happens. We reach the camp unharmed.

Many things change during the next few months. But the feeling of being happiest on patrol, closest to what this is all about, remains the same.

5

THE GIRLS' ROOM

Hazel sneaks quietly into the CIMIC office where I'm writing my report from the patrol.

'Hey, I heard you got home safely. Pleased about that!'

I laugh and Hazel gives me a big hug. My hair's still wet from the shower and my body's tingling from exhaustion and energy all at once. I know now that I've got a talent for conversing with the Afghans and sniffing out opportunities, sensing the air and coaxing out information.

It's a week since I arrived in the camp, but it feels like a month already. I've slept out in the desert as much as I've slept in the room that's going to be my home in the months to come.

Brigade HQ is slap bang in the middle of Lashkar Gah and space is therefore tight. It's only one and a half kilometres around the perimeter wall, but even so it's home and work for eight hundred soldiers and civilians. Tents have been erected all over the place between the few existing concrete buildings. My nine male colleagues have taken over the three rooms formerly inhabited by their predecessors, while I'm in one of the girls' rooms. Getting Hazel as a room-mate was sheer good fortune.

'Can you slip away for five minutes, or should I make an official request to your boss to borrow you?'

Hazel's blue-green eyes sparkle beneath her head of thick, dark, straight hair. Mostly, she looks like a suburban English housewife. Which is what she is. Thirty-six years old, married to a fireman and living just outside London. But Hazel's also a major in the British Army and heads up the bomb-disposal units in Helmand. She's highly intelligent and methodical, one of the select few to have passed the test in bomb disposal and who knows how to keep a cool head in an extremely tight situation.

Behind the CIMIC office is a little arid patch of earth in which the interpreters grow vegetables. A pent roof provides a shady spot to hold meetings if there's no room indoors. We sit down on a dusty bench. Hazel's eager to hear all about the patrol and anxious to make sure I'm all right. I'm warmed by her obvious concern. We agree to see if we can get off a bit earlier today so we can sit and talk in the evening.

Getting up to go, she says: 'See you half seven unless the war gets in the way.'

I beam at her. I don't know her that well yet, but I'm already very fond of her.

Fortunately, the war leaves Hazel alone. No mines to be detonated tonight.

I'm impressed by what four tours of duty in hot spots around the world have taught Hazel about being good to yourself. With a cosy quilt over her bed and a pillow at her back, she's all ready to hear about what I've been up to. My bed is the one next to Hazel's, but looks anything other than a comfy sofa. I sit on my duvet and tell her as vividly as I can about the landscapes, the sense of freedom and the hospitable Afghans. It's the people who have made the biggest impression on me. Amazingly resilient and welcoming.

'Do you know what, I actually envy you your job,' Hazel says. 'You get to meet all these people and talk to them. I know that myself from Africa. I was in Eritrea with the UN as head of the engineering troops, and I learned the most incredible things. You know, half the time we were building compost toilets for the troops. They were full of these grubs that turned pooh into compost. It wasn't exactly what I'd imagined I'd be doing. But the great thing was working with the local people. This was long before they invented CIMIC, but we were doing a lot of things then that you're doing today. My lads couldn't bear to see all those schools that were falling apart, so we repaired them and made furniture for them out of leftover timber. They were so grateful. And of course they'd come and tell us about the fighting going on, who was doing it and why. Which of course was a bonus.'

I nod my agreement. She's just outlined CIMIC's whole raison d'être.

Hazel clears her throat and continues: 'In the job I've got now, I feel I have to be careful not to get cynical. I work with mines and roadside incendiaries all day. Some of them are really horrific constructions. If you don't watch out you could start hating the whole country. But the people who are responsible for these things aren't your average Afghans.'

'No, you're right,' I say.

I think of all the people I met on patrol and try to find some common denominator of all the many impressions I gained.

'Hazel, I don't believe the Afghans would hesitate to praise the Taliban for a second if they really thought they were fantastic. But they don't.

They're afraid of them. They believe the Taliban wage war, wreak havoc and bring violence with them. People are genuinely distressed by their children not being able to go to school. They're sick and tired of being threatened and having to defer to the warlords who push them around. But sometimes they've no choice.'

My thoughts wander off into my own world of landscapes, children and hardened peasants, when Hazel interrupts my chain of thought.

'Do you believe in fate?'

She pulls her hair back behind her cute little ears and looks at me intently. I don't know what she's getting at.

'I do. I believe in fate,' she says. 'I don't think about the danger that much. I mean, if your number's up, it's up, isn't it? Does that sound daft to you?'

'Not really, no. It reminds me of that sort of fatalistic approach to traffic, I think. My brother lived in Cairo for a year and he said that people just wander out into the traffic when they want to cross the road, because if it's Allah's will you're going to die, then there's nothing you can do about it anyway.'

'No, that's not what I mean. You have to take care, but if it happens, it happens. Fate is often cleverer than us. And I think it was meant to be that you and I got to share a room here.'

I nod again. When I arrived at the camp I was actually down for two other rooms first, but they turned out to be occupied. The first night,

I ran into a young blonde girl in the showers, and since one of the girls from her room had left a day early, she offered me her place. So landing in North Block, Room 7 was really fate. Either that or divine intervention.

Hazel and I sit looking around the room. All of a sudden, we burst out laughing. Our room has holes in the plaster, mould in the corners, a tiny little window, a buzzing fluorescent tube on the ceiling, loose electrics, a mishmash of different colours, four old iron beds with heavy mattresses, one desultory bedside table, a bookcase, piles of clothes, and cardboard boxes filling up the corners.

'We really need to get this place sorted out! And as soon as the other two have gone home we need to find a couple of good room-mates,' Hazel says firmly.

She hasn't said a thing about the snoring girl who is due home in a couple of days. The other girl, Chloe, who offered me the room, seems quiet and keeps her chin up, but she'll be off too in just a few weeks. With two empty beds in an overcrowded HQ, we'll soon have room-mates whether we like it or not. In that respect, Hazel is intending to lend chance a helping hand. I'm with her, though I've no idea how to expose a snorer beforehand without breaching British rules of politeness.

Hazel becomes my best friend. She picks me up a million times when I'm down. She insists on bringing out the positive things in life, and with her enormous wealth of experience from other tours of duty, she's able to help me with practical matters and to cope with the emotional side of life as a soldier doing service in one of the hot spots of the world.

There's another thing about Hazel. While always forthright and present in the now, she maintains an irresistibly hilarious, very British aloofness towards just about everything. She can put on this exaggeratedly posh accent that turns everything into a stage set, a play in which we are merely appearing for the day.

I spend the next two days writing an eighteen-page report based on more than a hundred encounters. It doesn't adhere to the British standards for such reports, but it does receive praise. I've a lot to learn and the camp is still new to me. The heat is exhausting and the sheer number of people here and all the new impulses I'm having seem at times to be overwhelming.

Unable to go out, there's only one place to seek peace: your room.

One afternoon when I come into the room, Chloe is sitting on her bed with her face to the wall. Her shoulders tell me she's crying. I think she expects me to go out again and leave her alone. I sit down beside her. Her face is puffy. She lowers her gaze and looks away, clutching a tissue in her hand. Gingerly, I put my arm around her.

'What's the matter?'

Chloe bursts into tears. I stroke her gently. After a while, she says: 'I'm just so tired. I want to go home. I can't cope anymore.'

'What can't you cope with?'

'It's Andrew. He's on my back the whole time. Nothing I do is ever good enough. But then today … He's postponed my going home indefinitely. I was supposed to be leaving in two weeks. Now he's changed it all around. And the way he goes about it too … he just leaned over and said: "I might keep you here permanently." I hate him. I really hate him!'

'Chloe, he can't keep you here permanently. Not even your system allows for that.'

'I know, but why does he say it, then?' 'Because he likes to make you feel afraid.'

'Yeah, he's such a jerk,' she says, wiping away tears. 'Did you cry when he told you?'

'No. That's the only self-respect I've got left. I've never let him see me cry.'

'You're tougher than me, then,' I say. 'I cried after two days. Right in front of my boss. He asked if I could cope under pressure and I started crying.'

'Shit,' she says.

We sit for a while. At first, she seems relieved, but then she doubles up and clutches her stomach. All her pluckiness falls apart.

'I miss him so much. Oh, I miss you,' she whispers, suffering. 'Who do you miss?'

'My boyfriend.'

'I understand,' I say gently. 'No, you don't,' she says.

I'm thinking about the man whose heart I was unable to win. It wasn't always an easy relationship, but I miss him every day.

Chloe gasps out: 'He's dead.'

I'm devastated and have no idea what to say. Chloe's in her mid-twenties.

The man in the picture above her bed isn't even as old as me. 'When did it happen?' I ask cautiously.

She weeps uncontrollably. I imagine all sorts of scenarios. Maybe he was killed in action, maybe he stepped on a mine.

'He died four days before I left.' 'At home? In England?'

'Yeah. He died in bed in the night. Right next to me. I woke up and he was dead.'

'But ... what did he die of?' 'Diabetes.'

I look up at the photo above her bed. Chloe reaches out with her hand and gazes despairingly at the image of the young man.

'Do the others know about this?' I ask.

'Yeah. I spoke to the brigadier about it. They said I could decide for myself if I wanted to go. I put it off a week until after the funeral. And then I came out here.'

Chloe wails, grieving from deep within. Her face is a mess of tears, snot and mascara.

'Am I a terrible person? Am I terrible for coming here?'

'No Chloe, you're not a terrible person at all. Of course, you're not. This is so awful for you. I'm so sorry about your ex—'

I said her ex and I can't take it back. I could bite my tongue off. 'He's not my ex, he's still my boyfriend. I love him and I can't ever imagine being with anyone else!' Chloe bursts out angrily.

'I know that. I'm so sorry. I'm the one with an ex,' I mumble to myself.

While I soothe Chloe, the thought hits me that a person cannot possibly survive being here for six months without having anyone to talk to.

Everyone needs someone to talk to. Perhaps women have more need of it than men, or maybe we're just more used to it.

Eventually, Chloe is all cried out. My ex isn't dead. We just couldn't make things work. Deciding to split up from each other means there's a long and arduous withdrawal process lying ahead.

That evening I tell Hazel about my talk with Chloe. Hazel nods.

'I knew her boyfriend was dead. I didn't know how and I didn't like to ask. We all need someone to confide in. The girls Chloe has shared with haven't been there for her. Now it's different. I want to share with good people. Chloe's time here, the time she's got left, is going to be good for her. And you and I are going to make sure of it.'

Later the same evening, Hazel establishes 'The Lashkar Gah Star Gazing Club'. She's brought along a book on astronomy so we can become familiar with the Afghan firmament. To start with, she and I are the only members, but more are soon to come.

When the Star Gazers meet that night, we stand on the gravel outside the women's showers with our toothbrushes and sponge bags. All two of us.

Leaning back, we gaze up at the astonishing stars of Helmand.

I think about Chloe. Every time I feel sorry for myself I think about Chloe.

6

TWO WOMEN OF GERESHK

The gravel crunches beneath my boots, the dust puffing into a cloud around my legs before settling on my clean new uniform. Nicky and I are on our way over to the main gate to meet two women of Gereshk.

Nicky's training as an interpreter in the UK and has been working for CIMIC for five months. She's one of the first soldiers to have established contact with women in Helmand.

I think of the four young women I saw peeping through a gate far from Lashkar Gah. The women are there, but getting to speak to them is almost impossible. Great courage is required of them. They must go behind the backs of their husbands and they must pluck up the nerve to speak to us and believe that it will be worthwhile. They need to have reached the conclusion that being caught by the Taliban is a risk worth running in order to make steps towards a better society that can provide a better life for their children.

I'm awestruck walking there across the compound with Nicky. She's the one with experience. I'm the new girl, tagging along. The first woman soldier to make contact with women in Helmand was another British girl attached to CIMIC. She always wore lipstick on patrol so everyone could see she was a woman. She went back home a month ago and only two others have attempted to carry on her work. One is Nicky, the other is Rebecca.

The women we are to meet are two of five with whom we have made contact in Helmand. I find myself thinking that if they don't like me, the whole thing could go belly up. Nicky's returning home in three weeks, Rebecca in just over a month. This *has* to go well.

Nicky asks at the gate and the guards point towards an old shipping container between the outer and inner gates. The guy in charge is broad cockney, which for me is hard to understand. But what he said sounded like a question.

'No, no, I'll do that,' says Nicky in her South African drawl. 'What did he say?' I ask.

'It's the search. They always assume they've got bombs in their burkas.

It's quite ridiculous. These women are putting themselves at great risk coming here to see us and all we want to do is search them.'

Nicky trudges over towards the container. She's angry. It's no easy thing either for the women or for those of us who want to help them. On more than one occasion I've overheard male colleagues asking what good it's supposed to do in a country in which women have no say anyway.

Fortunately, my boss, Lars, is convinced. The women are a force.

Inside the container are two blue burkas waiting for us.

'*Salaam aleikum*,' they say cheerfully. They lift up the fabric in front of their faces and lay it down on top of their heads, the rest hanging down their backs like a bridal veil. The women are genuinely pleased to see Nicky.

'*Waleikum salaam*,' Nicky says, bending forward and exchanging kisses on the cheek.

Nicky says their names: Fatima and Gulaley. They say hers and stretch the vowel at the end: Nick-yyy.

Fatima has raven hair and a shaded complexion. Her dusky eyes observe me. She looks to be in her early forties and has a sharp, piercing voice and strong-looking hands, her fingernails painted orange with henna. Her forceful laughter and the punch of her voice make her anything but what I'd imagined finding underneath a burka. Fatima is a lady who expects to be heard and who is used to getting what she wants.

Gulaley appears to be the exact opposite. She's older and more rounded.

Polite, friendly and most of all hesitant. Her complexion is paler, she's wearing make-up and her hair is fine and coloured a reddish brown.

Instinctively, I know she's grey underneath the dye. There's a sorrowful expression in her eyes, but kindness too. It's something I notice a lot in the eyes of the Afghans. I've begun to see it as being along the lines of: 'Thank you for coming. By Allah, we are tired of this war. You are not always able to understand what is going on here, but you are the only hope we've got.'

Nicky introduces me in Pashto. I recognize the phrases from my week's crash course. I tell them my name's AC. Fatima looks me straight in the eye and rattles off a whole bunch of words ending in something that sounds like a question.

'I don't understand Pashto,' I say. A contradiction in so far as Fatima can hear what's coming out of my mouth as Pashto.

Nicky has to stop her and explain that I only know a few phrases. I hazard a guess she asks Fatima to speak more slowly too.

Nicky searches the two women and looks inside their bags. Fatima and Gulaley seem to know the procedure. When Nicky's done, they pull down their veils again.

On our way over to the conference room, Nicky and the two women talk quietly. Mostly it's Fatima doing the talking. She has a lot of questions to ask, especially about me.

The few soldiers we meet on our way don't know what to do with themselves and look away. Everyone knows you're not supposed to look at the local women. As soon as we're past I sense their stares in my back. Do Gulaley and Fatima feel it too?

Fatima and Gulaley are both in worn high-heeled shoes. The shoes are the only things visible under the burkas. High heels and sequins.

We unlock the door of the conference room. Fatima pulls back her burka with a look of relief and liberation. Gulaley is more polite resignation. They sit down at the big table as though they've been here before.

Nicky goes out to fetch an interpreter. She's heading the meeting herself and interpreting is a very fatiguing business. The women cast inquisitive glances my way, exchange a few words and laugh. I smile and feel awkward. Fatima breaks the ice.

'Are you married?' she asks. It's one of the questions I know. 'No, I have no husband,' I say.

The two women look at each other, clearly unsurprised. 'You have no children?' Gulaley asks.

'No, I have no children.'

Gulaley sends me a long, pitying look. More words are exchanged.

Nicky comes back with one of our regular interpreters, whom the women have met before and seem to trust. They give friendly nods and ask after his family.

I need to tell them about myself. Apparently, it's impolite to ask my age.

They think it's odd that I'm not married, but say they understand we do things differently. They're sorry Nicky will soon be going, but glad to make the acquaintance of a new girl. And they're very excited about how things are going to turn out with their first projects, which hopefully are going to help the women earn their own money.

Nicky has applied for funding to the Helmand Executive Group (HEG), a British development board made up of various officials that administers funds provided by the British government. Around thirty civilian experts are stationed at the Lashkar Gah HQ, along with a number of advisers and specialists on contract. Together, they make up the Provincial Reconstruction Team, or PRT. As yet, only one Dane has been involved in an advisory capacity.

The HEG funds projects ranging from wells to new schools and staff training within the provincial administration, the aim being to get more lasting civil development under way. More than 80 per cent of projects are concentrated in Lashkar Gah. Helmand's second-largest town, Gereshk, where Gulaley and Fatima live, accounts for only a tiny proportion.

One of the projects the two women are involved in aims to provide a hundred poor women with ten hens each. The women can use the eggs they produce either for their own consumption or to sell for income at the bazaar. The second is a sewing project whereby ninety women are to be trained to make clothes and ten to machine-embroider.

When Nicky goes home, the idea is that I take on responsibility for the projects and pay the women's wages, control expenditure and generally monitor progress.

More ideas are coming in all the time: vegetable gardens, a beauty salon, a weaving shop. These are projects that have been successfully run by humanitarian organizations elsewhere in Afghanistan. Experiences from around the world show that it pays to back women. Women think about their children and of the future. Men tend to spend income on themselves, either in the form of status symbols or for their own short-lived pleasure.

Gulaley is the one with all the ideas. I try to draw my own picture of how she is as a person while she quietly tells me about her background. Gulaley was born and brought up in Kabul, where she trained as a nurse and midwife. She worked in a big hospital and enjoyed the relatively free conditions the Communist government and Soviet influence provided for women. Hers was an Afghanistan in which women made up the majority of the country's schoolteachers and almost half of the service sector.

She married a traditional Pashtun from Helmand, but speaks little of her husband. I soon learn that when Gulaley has nothing good to say she holds her tongue. Her husband took no fewer than four wives. When he died, the other women remarried. Gulaley, however, had had enough. Her husband had forbidden her to work, despite a marital agreement stipulating otherwise, and she wanted desperately to return to nursing.

The Taliban came to power while she was still married and the hospitals lost forty per cent of their staff in one fell swoop. Gulaley witnessed how women were prevented from seeking medical attention because of the Taliban's ban on their being attended by male doctors. There were some exceptions, but women were still dying in childbirth or from ailments and diseases left untreated.

Gulaley began working secretly as a doctor. She attended both women and men, witnessing human decay on a scale she had never thought possible.

She still goes to Kabul once in a while when it's safe. She has a house there. One daughter is married and lives in Germany. Another lives in the country's cultural capital, Herat. As a result, Gulaley's perspective is broad. Despite her ties with Kabul, though, she feels she can do most good in Helmand.

Gulaley and Fatima's destinies were linked by a bizarre incident of domestic violence. Fatima's husband is fiercely jealous and regularly beats his two wives. Though admitting to being beaten brings shame upon a woman, Fatima has repeatedly sought the help of Gulaley, who is known in Gereshk to be a skilful doctor, despite her lack of formal qualifications.

One day, Fatima's husband climbs down into the well to repair it. Fatima and his other wife decide to teach him a lesson. They fill the well bucket with stones and cast it down upon the man, who besides the shock he experiences also suffers injuries requiring medical treatment.

Fatima's husband duly goes to Gulaley for help, only to be turned away with the words: 'May it teach you not to beat your wives.'

Fatima is the first-born of a renowned and respected mullah who has spoken out against the Taliban. She trained as a teacher and collected money herself to build the girl's school where she teaches today. If anyone ever were in doubt as to the Qur'an's view of girls going to school, Fatima would quote her father, who was a champion of schooling for all. Fatima soon won support for her school, though many consider her hot-tempered and too vociferous for her own good. Airing strong opinions in a public place is not considered appropriate behaviour for a woman.

Both women see themselves as leaders of their own women's groups.

Fatima meets with her women at the school, whereas Gulaley runs a centre for widows in a couple of buildings in the middle of Gereshk. She's been given the land by the government, which has donated plots specifically for use by women, and the buildings were erected with funds provided by the HEG.

When Gulaley learned from her network that women in other places in Afghanistan keep hens and sell eggs in the bazaars, she decided to do something similar in Gereshk. Poverty hits women and children hardest. Many widows have need of a source of income in order to provide for themselves and their families. The moment they end up begging on the streets they're expelled for good, never to be taken in by their families again. I've seen these sad blue burkas sitting by the roadsides begging in Lashkar Gah, so I know what Gulaley is talking about.

Many of the women who are now going to keep hens are either widows or so-called drug widows, she tells me. The fortunes of the latter are particularly horrific.

The husband of a drug widow is still alive. He is a drug addict and unable to work. He lies around at home, calls for food and must be obeyed, though he no longer contributes to the family. He may have worked the opium fields. The field workers score open the immature seedpods of the poppies so the latex inside can seep out. It dries into a raw opium residue that can be turned into heroin. During work in the fields, the workers absorb some of the latex through the skin and become addicted.

Drug widows must provide for their families. The government supports women entering the labour market, but in the southern provinces the Taliban often intimidate and threaten those who try. Women are prevented from setting up businesses and accepting employment anywhere. Some are fortunate enough to be trained teachers and sufficiently courageous to take on work at one of the three schools for girls in Gereshk. Even then, the pay of some sixty dollars a month is far from enough to support a family of six children, the average for the women of Helmand. The three hundred women who use Gulaley's centre and the hundred and fifty or so approached by Fatima live in extreme hardship. The chance of becoming trained as a seamstress, or of being given ten hens to keep, is an opportunity they have yet to fully comprehend as true.

American aid organization USAID has analysed import and export activity here and points out that Helmand imports some two hundred thousand eggs a week from Iran and Pakistan. Clearly, there would seem to be a basis for more widespread production. Hens don't appeal to men and are therefore well suited to giving women an income. Few men would forbid their wives to keep hens in the yard or in an outhouse.

The big drawback, though, is that we're unable to go out in our vehicles and knock on the women's doors to see if the project's working. First, we can't go on patrol just to check eggs; second, we'd be sending a pretty clear signal out that the woman in question collaborates with us, which could put her life in danger.

The projects are a gamble. We need to trust the reports of the two women and otherwise rely on photographic evidence they've agreed to supply using borrowed cameras. Eight thousand dollars for a thousand hens delivered by truck is worth a shot, even if there have been difficulties persuading some of the civilian advisers.

The sewing project is rather more costly. On the other hand, the women learn a skill and are provided with a hand-operated sewing machine, obviating reliance on haphazard power supplies. Gulaley explains that the Taliban allow only male tailors, who of course would never make clothes for women. At present, clothes are imported from Pakistan, but the women want to break into the market. It is almost impossible to do any market research here, so we're putting thirty thousand dollars into the project in small amounts against receipts for equipment and fabric. My only guarantee of success is the enthusiasm shining in the two women's eyes.

Fatima and Gulaley promise to bring me some samples of their work. If all else fails, I think to myself, at least they'll have learned something about working on a budget. The first envelopes of dollars change hands and the two women sign the forms.

After our two-hour meeting, I escort Fatima and Gulaley back to security and we exchange kisses on the cheek as a means of farewell. I am in awe and feel truly affected by the situation. This exceeds by far anything I'd ever imagined. I've met two women today with whom I shall be working for some considerable time if all goes well. I intend to do everything in my power to help them and their invisible friends.

I stand for a while watching them as they trip towards the main gate.

They have called a driver they trust, a male family member who is waiting for them outside. He is but a small pawn in this maze of secrecy that is necessary in order to survive and create something new in the face of the Taliban's fierce opposition to women who move beyond the realm of the home.

My gaze falls on their delicate shoes. The Taliban forbade high heels, make-up and perfume and ordered that all women go clad in the burka. But inside the burka is still a woman. A woman who wants to smell nice, who wants to look good and to wear high heels.

I look down at my own uniform. All women of the military dress the same. Nonetheless, all of us endeavour in some way to stand out. We arrange our hair, beautify ourselves discreetly and wear earrings. Hazel has decreed that we wear red undies on the weekends—just so we can get the sense of time elapsing. She's also made a rule that red toenails are obligatory in combat boots. Perhaps we have more in common with Fatima and Gulaley than we realize.

The guard opens the outside gate on to the street. The two burkas turn. A hand appears and waves goodbye. They pass through to the other side, back into Afghan life.

7
SUICIDE AND POVERTY

The stench of shit and urine rises up from the dust-ridden streets. There are no sewers here and excrement seeps from cracks in the walls directly out on to the street to form a dark stream hugging the lowest part of the road. The walls lining the road have the same grey-brown hue everywhere, whereas doors are painted bright green and blue.

We're on patrol in the poorest part of Lashkar Gah. The children know the sound of the 4x4s and come scurrying to see what the soldiers are up to. I wave at a little flock as they run alongside the car. They beam and wave back, jumping up and down to get a view inside. Often, the adults too stop and raise a hand in greeting.

We pull over in a little square where there's a water pump. I climb out to the kids. They're so cute with their raven hair, dark skin and big eyes. The boys wear the same discreet colours as the men: light blue, dusty green and brown. The girls are brighter: red, green, blue and pink. Even four-year-olds often wear make-up, their eyes accentuated with dark eyeliner. The adults say it keeps flies away from the eyes.

The boys are full of go and eager to answer our questions. The nearest school is a long way off. One little chap points to one of the girls and says that she goes to school. The three girls stand shyly in the background, like girls always do. I approach them cautiously. They're not afraid of me, it's my interpreter they're worried about. As usual, Pajan is wearing his favourite CIA cap. A black scarf covers his nose and mouth, and his eyes are hidden behind a pair of sunglasses. Like the other interpreters, he's scared of being recognized. Pajan isn't his real name. If the Taliban find out who he is, they'll track down his brothers and sisters or his parents and threaten them.

The schoolgirl is afraid of Pajan because he's a grown Afghan man. If he should become interested in her and make a deal with her father, her childhood will come to an end, her schooling will be terminated and with it the sense of having some opportunities open in life.

I settle down next to her on my haunches. I tell her my name and ask hers. The girls are almost always named after flowers. This is a country populated by delicate blooms deprived of their will, waiting obediently to be plucked.

This little buttercup answers demurely: she's twelve years old, a good age for a suitor. I ask if she likes going to school. Pajan translates discreetly from behind me. I imagine him standing slightly removed, desperately trying to avoid looking at the girl.

She nods.

'How long do you think you'll be allowed to continue there?'

She bends down to one of the younger girls and whispers something. The little girl says: 'It depends how long her father allows it, but she hopes it will be for a long time yet.'

I smile and say I hope her wish comes true. Her eyes sparkle as though she has just been given a blessing.

An adult man has appeared in the background. I get to my feet to speak to him. The youngest of the three girls clings to me and takes my hand. Her little fist is rough and calloused. I have a new friend, a little curly-haired girl in a dirty orange dress.

The man's name is Khaled. He is friendly and polite. Like so many others in this part of the town, he has come here because Lashkar Gah is relatively peaceful. He and his family fled from a rural district because of the fighting. His voice is without regret.

'It was no longer safe. Besides, I want my children to go to school here. The school in our area closed.'

I've a feeling I needn't ask why, but do so anyway.

Khaled shrugs: 'The Taliban. They threatened the teachers. Surely you know that by now? It's the same everywhere. They do no good for us, at least not where I am from. I have heard there are places where they ensure justice, but not where I am from.'

I ask about the quality of the water, opportunities for work and general living conditions in the neighbourhood. We already know the mayor is unwilling to acknowledge his responsibility to the poorest neighbourhoods, which are growing at an alarming rate as people move into the town from the rural districts. Just about everything here is lacking.

A new urban district is being planned. Some of our interpreters have bought plots there and are building. But to live there you need an income. The mayor has decided to follow an old Soviet model. There's to be a school and a police station of a size to match the number of inhabitants. But the poor areas in the old town here are left to their own devices and there's no planning here at all. New families put up lean-tos of cardboard and planks wherever there's room. I ask if the Taliban ever come here. Khaled just shakes his head.

'If we could do one thing to help here in the area, what should it be?' I ask.

He lowers his gaze.

'If I had a job, I could provide for my family. That's the only thing I really want.'

The patrol leader signals for us to move on. I thank Khaled for the information he's given us and jump into the back seat.

'Driving Miss Daisy,' quips my Danish driver, Warrant Officer Winther.

His birth certificate says he's forty but he hasn't found out yet. 'Why do you keep calling me that?' I ask.

'You look like the Queen the way you sit there waving at folk,' he explains.

Back home in Denmark, Queen Margrethe is known by all and sundry as Daisy.

'You see, you're doing it again!' Winther's bright blue eyes sparkle as he begins to laugh.

Of course, I know the film, but the respectable old lady in it certainly wouldn't give her driver the kind of treatment I do when Winther suddenly jumps on the brakes as we turn a corner. We find ourselves in the middle of a flock of sheep being driven slowly along the street. Hundreds of the creatures jumping, lolloping and braying.

The radio crackles: 'OK lads, we seem to have infiltrated a flock of sheep here. Suggest a right turn,' comes the message from the front vehicle.

'Great country, this,' Winther mutters to himself as he tries to manoeuvre us through the flock.

We turn down yet another street we've never seen before. Winther and I talk for a while about the unemployed men. They make an impression on us, these sinewy men up to their ankles in shit, yet so unwilling to complain. They expect nothing of us, would never dream of begging for favours from the soldiers. All they want is the chance to work for their food. We've long held them in respect for their efforts to provide for their families in this extraordinary hardship.

We stop a few times to chat to traders, unemployed, old and young. The streets grow narrower. Here and there a gutter has been dug to lead away the sewage. Winther has his work cut out behind the wheel. Our Mercedes GD is a lot heavier and wider than the British 4x4s. The streets narrow still more, the houses closing in on us. We drive more and more slowly and eventually stall. We've landed in a blind alley amid a maze of increasingly narrow, labyrinthine streets.

Some way behind us is a triangular area just about big enough for a car to turn. I look out at the people gathering around us. We look like what we are—strangers lost.

I remember the briefing before we set out. The security update is like the weather forecast for us. At the moment, two, perhaps four suicide attackers are thought to be in Lashkar Gah. Two on foot, two in cars. Those on foot are only dangerous to the extent that we're on foot too. Against an armoured car they would have little effect. Car bombs are much worse. I scan the street outside. We're sitting ducks for a suicide attacker here. If they hit the vehicle at the rear, we'd never get out.

Winther berates his fellow motorists and others—a donkey cart and the poor Brits struggling to turn the cars around. Those on the street follow our efforts with interest.

I click the radio: 'Do you want me to get out and distract them a bit with some questions?'

'Bloody good idea. Get out there,' comes the enthusiastic reply from the patrol leader.

I jump out with my interpreter and a back-up, so for the locals this suddenly looks like it was the plan all along. The people here are happy to answer our questions and the information they give us helps with our efforts to gain an overall picture of what's going on in the town.

The method becomes standard whenever we get lost, which is a lot. The streets here are a maze of blind alleys when you look at aerial photos of the town. There are no street signs and we never know when people are going to start driving their goats and sheep down whatever street we happen to be on.

Back in the camp, Fatima and Gulaley have come to visit Nicky, who's going home in a few days. They've brought gifts with them and a crumpled envelope from a photo shop. I find myself wondering about who actually develops photographs in the middle of a war.

The envelope's on the table waiting. Faintly lilac colours, richly decorated. But first there's something the two women want to tell us.

'Do you remember you called and warned us about a woman suicide attacker on a moped?' Fatima asks. She leans across the table eagerly and lays her hand on Nicky's bare arm.

Both Nicky and I remember it well. It was only a few days ago. HQ received a call from Camp Price at Gereshk, where some Brits on patrol had encountered two burka-clad women acting suspiciously. They were alone on a moped, which in itself is highly unusual, and it seemed as though they were trying to get away from the patrol.

Brigade intelligence issued a warning about female suicide bombers.

Nicky and I discussed it between ourselves. I found it rather implausible, but extremely dangerous if it were true. Nicky called to warn Fatima and Gulaley.

Gulaley begins to laugh, her hand to her mouth, as though trying to control herself.

'That was us,' says Fatima, wiping away tears of laughter with her sleeve.

'You? How could that be?' Nicky asks.

Fatima explains at rattling speed. The interpreter gives up.

'Fatima, you're prattling away like a machine gun!' I laugh and imitate her: 'Da da da da da … da da da da da.'

Gulaley splutters with mirth. It's true. Fatima talks fast. But this is the first time anyone has compared her to a machine gun. Gulaley catches her breath and wipes her eyes with a tissue.

'Enough, Fatima, enough,' she pleads, giving her friend a gentle nudge. Fatima, though, isn't for stopping. She's doubled up now from laughing.

Gulaley turns her back slightly on Fatima and makes an effort to regain her composure. A smile twitches in the corner of her mouth and her eyes sparkle with laughter.

'We were trying to meet up with some other women in a place we didn't know and we thought there were Taliban spies watching us. We went from one place to the next, then knocked on the door of one of Fatima's cousins and had tea. Then we changed burkas and put on different shoes, but still we were followed. Then Fatima got the ridiculous idea of borrowing her cousin's husband's moped. I didn't have the nerve to drive, but she did, and all of a sudden we were off and away. That must have been when your soldiers caught sight of us.'

'The whole brigade's been at sixes and sevens,' Nicky says, laughing.
'Yes, and we'd like to apologize.' Gulaley smiles back.
'The important thing is you weren't suicide attackers,' says Nicky.

'Oh, I haven't laughed so much in ages,' says Gulaley, only to hit a more serious tone: 'I was frightened when you called. I thought how terribly dangerous it would be if some women really had become so deranged as to side with the Taliban and were going to blow up one of the schools. But that evening after we'd spoken to you, Fatima suddenly said: "What if it was us the soldiers saw?" Then we realized that was actually what had happened.

We were trying to get away and had been seen by your soldiers, who of course couldn't understand what two women would be doing alone on a moped.

'And Fatima was going very fast,' she adds quietly.

I smile. Basically, it's slapstick. But it's great to see Gulaley and Fatima have such a good laugh. It's a mad world.

'Seriously, Gulaley, have you ever heard of women actively supporting the Taliban?' I ask.

She leans back in the chair and thinks.

'In all my time, I have only ever heard of one woman who sided with the Taliban and she didn't mean it seriously. She had argued with her husband and had left home. She sought out the Taliban in Musa Qaléh. But I think she was only there for a very short time, perhaps a couple of weeks at the most. She and her husband got back together again.'

'What about female suicide bombers?' I ask. She shakes her head: 'Never.'

Fatima picks up the lilac-coloured envelope from the table and opens it. She hands the photos to Nicky, who passes on to me one by one. They are grey and somewhat blurred, but it's easy to see what they show—hens. On one, many women are gathered in a yard as Gulaley passes out hens from a truck. On another, a little girl sits on a red mat with a white hen in her lap.

Gulaley points at the girl: 'She was so glad to get that hen. Strokes it all the time like this.' Gulaley pretends she's holding the hen in her lap, stroking it over its back. 'The girl lives with her grandmother. The mother died in childbirth. The hen is her responsibility now, and the grandmother looks after the others.'

'This is from Gulaley's women's centre,' says Nicky, pointing out a yard between whitewashed buildings. 'You must go to Gereshk and visit them some time.'

The women nod their approval, eager for me to come and visit them. I know it's impossible for the time being. I have to stay in Lashkar Gah. The threat of suicide attackers in Gereshk is too great for foot patrols in the bazaar area. Only a few weeks before, a suicide attack killed more than forty civilians and the risk is still high. The women are uneasy about the situation, but it seems that they've found a breathing space. Once they've got here and can sit down with tea and cake, they can dream themselves away for an hour or two.

I'm relieved about the misunderstanding. A burka-clad suicide attacker blowing up a school or a women's centre would most likely put Gulaley and Fatima's work back several years.

Stepping back into my own breathing space, the girls' room, the first thing I see to my surprise is a big cable drum in the middle of the floor.

'Give me a hand, would you?' says Hazel.

Chloe has finally been allowed to go home and Hazel is rearranging the furniture. We get the cable drum manhandled into place and cover it with a tablecloth. Four big red cushions form seating around this new coffee table, and before long we've got candles going and a bowl of potpourri in matching colours. 'Colour coordination' enters my English vocabulary and becomes an absolute minimum requirement of all interior decoration. Our room quickly turns into the cosiest room in the camp and new British girls queue up to move in.

Hazel chooses wisely. Our new room-mates are Andrea and Sarah. Andrea is an exceptionally well-trained girl with straight dark hair and green, cat-like eyes. She is a press officer with a fiery temper and an ability to empathize. Besides that, she has this amazing aptitude for acting the goat and generally having us in stitches.

Sarah is a major, head of J2, an intelligence unit gathering information, forecasting and analysing Taliban plans. Her delicate appearance could easily make you think she was frail and rather vague, but Sarah has risen to her high rank in no time and without compromising her opinions. She's a girl who says what she thinks about wasting human life and about the necessity of good intelligence and analysis before rushing in, even though it's a standpoint that doesn't always improve career opportunities in an army that's pushed to get results.

With Hazel, head of bomb disposal, Sarah, head of intelligence, press officer Andrea and myself from CIMIC, our room is now complete. We span the field, both professionally and personally. Our room is our home, and we become each other's saviours.

8

THE WIDOW OF LASHKAR GAH

Fatima and Gulaley bring in the first samples of clothes. I lay my palms on the fine gossamer and the thick velvet. I turn the embroidery in my hand.

I'm impressed by the work. Glass beads, tiny mirrors and bright colours seem to be popular. All that glitters and sparkles. My own mother is a good seamstress and she would be proud of these women.

In Gereshk, a hundred women split into groups are now learning to make clothes. I still don't know if they will be able to sell their work, but they're completely committed and insistent that things are going to work out.

Another issue has cropped up during our meetings. It's always seemed strange to me that Fatima should speak so often about problems of security and that Nicky would gloss over this as she might a girlfriend's complaints about sore feet. Now, though, everyone from the old CIMIC unit has gone home bar Rebecca. The women are mine now. Having been trained in intelligence myself, I find it hard to shrug things off when Fatima tells me about the Taliban, the widespread corruption and suicide attackers. I choose to take her seriously. I ask questions.

It's as though Fatima has been waiting for a chance to get a load off her mind. In me she finds an ally, someone who can use the information she passes on to get back at the Taliban. There are women in all families, even Taliban families. Women who serve tea wait politely in the background while men talk. Often, the men act as if the women weren't even there.

Trust between us has grown and sometimes the most chance events serve to enhance my status in the eyes of the two women. One late morning, for instance, I'm walking Fatima and Gulaley back to security as usual after one of our meetings. I'm a couple of steps in front of them on the thick gravel of the compound outside Charlie Company's building, where some of the lads are relaxing in the sun.

Out of the corner of my eye I become aware of a small figure trotting along behind. One of the locals we employ for cleaning and cooking seems to be following me. He's overtaken Fatima and Gulaley and is now right behind me.

'Hello, you very sexy body,' he whispers, loud enough for me to hear. I wheel around, livid.

'Who the fuck do you think you're talking to?' I yell at him. The hapless little man backs away into a wall.

'I am an officer and you are not to speak to me in that way!'

I'm effing and blinding away at him, threatening him with the sack and a whole lot more. He has hit me on the wrong spot and everything I learned on my course for interrogation officers comes back to me in a flash. This is a kneejerk fifteen-minute bollocking at a volume intended to bring a grown man to his knees and with an appropriate quantity of saliva to underline the point.

But this cleaner is just a little fella with a few libidinous misconceptions about women soldiers. He is gobsmacked and frightened to death to find himself against the wall with a fuming woman in front of him. He's had enough and wishes he'd never set eyes on me. I let him go and he scurries off with his tail between his legs.

I'm still hopping mad, but I achieved what I wanted well before the fifteen-minute standard bollocking even got going. I glare as he disappears from sight and feel certain that flames are visible in my eyes.

The first time anyone ever wolf-whistled at me at army camp, I didn't know what to say. I felt humiliated and stripped bare. I promised myself I would never allow it to happen again. I shake my head. And then notice Fatima and Gulaley. Two burkas who just grew a few centimetres taller.

I wheel round and stride across to security. What have I done? The women follow resolutely on behind. When we kiss goodbye I can see how their eyes sparkle behind their veils. They give my hand an extra squeeze.

I go back to my room to pack for the patrol. I wonder what the women will say when they get home? I pass by the company building again. The lads cheer and applaud.

'Nice one, Ma'am.'

'Way to go, Ma'am.'

'Respect, AC!'

I nod my approval and churn my way on through the annoying gravel.

I'm off on patrol in town and there's lots to do. The scene with the Afghan cleaner will haunt me for a year.

Fowzia is a slightly built woman dressed completely in black. Fine laughter lines edge her gentle brown eyes, and her skin is light and delicate beneath her black hair. She has worked all her life as a teacher and Helmand's sun has not taken its toll on her as on so many others. She bids us welcome in a large house not far from the governor's residence. The house functions as a school. Small girls scuttle into its various rooms, only to turn in the doorways and peep out like curious mice.

Fowzia offers tea and cake. Her polite and reticent way notwithstanding, we sense she is used to meeting with soldiers and officials. Besides her work as a teacher, Fowzia is the official representative of the Department of Women's Affairs (DoWA), under the auspices of the Afghan Ministry of Women's Affairs. As such, she is the government's point of contact with the women of Helmand. In principle, then, women have their own official structure.

All towns in Helmand are supposed to have an appointed woman reporting directly to Fowzia. Regrettably, Gulaley in Gereshk is the only one. Elsewhere, the Taliban remain too strong for women to venture so far as to organize themselves. Gulaley and Fowzia both act as advisers for those women who wish to meet in Gereshk and Lashkar Gah and have the opportunity to do so. Fowzia reports on their activities and the problems of local women to the ministry in Kabul.

Rebecca, the last of the previous CIMIC team, has been the main force behind cultivating official contacts. Together, she and Fowzia recently organized the first official *shura* for the women of Helmand. *Shura* is an Afghan word for meeting but it may also describe a group of people who meet on a regular basis, like a committee. Rebecca's biggest scoop was perhaps to have this first *shura* held at the old Bost Hotel, a traditional stronghold of Helmand men. The women were thrilled to be taken seriously and to have the chance to take part in a proper consultation in the manner of their men.

I've been looking forward to meeting Fowzia and it seems the feeling is mutual.

'I have heard about the sewing project you have been helping Gulaley and Fatima with. A splendid idea,' says Fowzia earnestly.

'I do hope so,' I say, then add: 'Do you think the women will be able to sell the clothes they make?'

Fowzia smiles.

'I believe they have already sold a great many.' 'Really?'

'If they have not mentioned it, I'm sure it is because they are afraid that you expect to get your money back. Do you?'

'No, not at all. My hope is that they can earn money and thereby have a greater say in what goes on in their families. Perhaps they might even get the chance of sending more children to school.'

'It would give them more power, certainly. Now I see that you are interested in other matters besides the Taliban. They could easily lead you away from the real root of evil.'

'How do you mean?'

Fowzia sits gazing into her tea for a moment, stirring figures of eight with her teaspoon.

'I was quite young when I married. Fortunately, I had my education as a teacher. This was before the Taliban. Most of the teachers in the Afghan schools were women. We dressed in Western clothes, long skirts, nice blouses and a scarf to cover our heads. That was all, no burkas. My husband and I had been married for a week when he disappeared. He went to Russia to seek his fortune there. At least, that is what they said. I never heard from him. I don't even know if he is still alive. He is unaware to this day that he has a daughter, that he has four grandchildren.'

Fowzia's eyes glisten for a moment and glaze over.

'We are still married. Isn't it ironic? I cannot be divorced, because my husband must give his consent, and I do not know where he is.'

I stare into my tea as crystals of sugar slowly dissolve.

'There are thousands like me.' Fowzia sighs. 'A lot of things are wrong with this country. The Taliban are only one of them. A symptom, if you will.'

I nod. Fowzia is telling me something I'm not sure I've entirely understood. But I have wondered at the fact that some village people seem to be able to stand together, to resist the Taliban and keep them away from their villages. On patrols in Lashkar Gah I have often found myself wondering if the Taliban would have a chance if there were a system of law that worked, if the young people could get an education, if there were artisans and craftsmen.

Fowzia and I agree that together we will organize a new *shura* for the women, affording everyone the opportunity to hear of the projects that have been initiated for the women of Gereshk. Hopefully, we'll be able to help more women on their way.

9

THE TALIBAN PROJECT

Torben's standing in the office with the satellite phone pressed to his ear. I can see something's wrong. Really wrong. It's one of the first days of September and most of the CIMIC unit, including our boss, Lars, are off on a long patrol.

Torben puts the phone down. A British convoy has hit something, possibly a mine. Right in front of our own colleagues. At least one British soldier is dead and an interpreter has been badly injured.

Some hours later, after a gruesome clean-up operation, the convoy finally approaches camp. We don't know what to expect. Lars and two of the other Danes saw one of the British vehicles run into a roadside incendiary ten metres in front of them. The car was blown into the air and landed alongside them. They've seen badly wounded soldiers, two of them now dead. A local interpreter has been evacuated to a field hospital with serious injuries. The two other Danes saw it all in their rear-view mirror.

We stand ready in the compound as the patrol rolls in. They're worn out, mute. Two dead Brits who should have been going home in a month. Boss is an empty shell. Bash keeps things together. Lars looks ten years older.

Torben is talking to him. Lars shrugs. He wants to be left alone, he can't talk now. He looks up at me and says: 'You fly out tomorrow as planned.

We need that equipment replaced.'

It's been the plan for more than a week now that I am to fly out to Camp Bastion with some encrypted equipment to be carried by hand, delivered and exchanged. I've been looking forward to it because it's Charlotte's birthday. Charlotte's a colleague of mine from when I trained as a language officer and now she's posted at Bastion. Lars has planned it all so I can get there in time to wish her many happy returns.

I don't know what to say. I want to go, but maybe it would be best if I stayed. Some soldiers find it easier to talk about their feelings with women. Maybe all of us should be together here at Lashkar Gah.

The other guys seem to be OK. One snivels a bit. Most are just empty and exhausted. They want a shower, food and sleep. The one who seems most together is a hardened lance corporal who gave first aid to the wounded interpreter. Though the interpreter would die the following day, the lance corporal knows he has done all he can. The others are left with the doubt, the uncertainty of whether they could have done anything differently. Lars is taking it really badly. Responsibility can be devastating.

The next morning I'm sitting in a chopper, listening to the heavy sound of rotor blades cutting through air. We're shoulder to shoulder, with backpacks piled up between us, our carbines pointing down.

All of a sudden there's a flash outside. My brain registers, my body doesn't react. It must have been the automatic flares going off. A diversion the helicopter sets off when its systems think it's under attack. I glance sideways at the gunner sitting at his little hole in the side of the chopper. He tightens his grip on the Gattling and focuses down on the ground. We fly on. A few minutes later we land at Camp Bastion and exit calmly.

I end up stranded here because of lack of helicopters. What was meant to have been a quick exchange of essential equipment turns into a three-day stay.

It's early September and just before the Danish Battle Group sends soldiers into hard combat. They've been cooped up in camp for a month. They spend their time discussing their tasks, wanting to get going, get out there and feel the ground under their feet, to address real dangers rather than wondering about a thousand different scenarios. Some find it hard to call home. What can they say when they're not allowed to say much? How do you mask your thoughts for people who know when you're holding back on them?

In the afternoon I stop by the infantry scouts to say hello and hear how things are going. My ex has trained them, so I've known them for a long time. We chat as they dismantle their weapons, lubricate the parts, put them together again. It's a way of keeping calm. Being sure everything works.

I meet up with some of them that evening at Pizza Hut, little more than a dusty shed in the middle of the camp. All the benches are taken, so we sit on the gravel. The stars are out above us.

Norman is an experienced lance corporal on his second tour of duty here.

René is a sergeant here for the first time. Reese is a young and eager private, a chain-smoker who likes to cook and who's good at drawing. I know him well. We were together on a three-man team back when I did the advanced first-aid course. He makes me laugh. We sit for three hours under the stars, talking about life, death and the risks involved in what we do.

I observe their familiar faces and sip my coffee. They're good professionals, skilled at their work and aware of the risks. Their job is to go out there and clean up. I wish I could put a cable in my head and transfer images and conversations from my patrols directly into their brains. Just to give them that little head start. For each hour you're exposed to the realities outside camp, you gain experience and adapt.

I tell them about how much the Afghans want their children to be able to go to school so the next generation can make a better life. I tell them about that moving moment when a villager asked me what they could do for us—not what we could do for them. I tell them how desperate the people are to be able to live in safety.

Safety comes when soldiers slowly but surely push the Taliban further and further back. It's a mammoth, gruelling task. The soldiers only rarely see the gratitude of the local people when the battles are over and the Taliban repelled. But I do. And it's so grossly unfair that I should receive praise for our soldiers having killed the Taliban.

When I get back to Lashkar Gah, some of the lads from Boss's platoon come to see me. They want more copies of the photos I took on our long patrol. They're the last ones taken of the two dead Brits. I recognize their faces, recognize the car that was blown to bits. The two lads had a furry pink rabbit dangling between the seats. Everything's gone now. None of it is left.

I'm aware that the grief is not mine. I didn't know them that well.

Nonetheless, it feels strange that two soldiers with whom I'd been on patrol for three days are suddenly no more. Two faces missing from the group. But I can't put what I feel into words.

The Brits have been there before and have found ways of dealing with it.

They're pleased about the photos and grateful. One of them tells me how much it will mean for the parents. He keeps saying it. I nod, able only to understand in some abstract, theoretical way what his words mean.

In mid-September the Danish armoured infantry company is involved in heavy combat north of Gereshk. It is a baptism of fire and their courage, determination and raw power come as something of a surprise to the Brits at Lashkar Gah HQ.

From the day the Danish Battle Group engages the Taliban, the ten of us Danes of the CIMIC unit are accorded new respect. Denmark isn't just about talking to the locals and setting up and managing development projects. Now we're seen also as disciplined and formidable fighting machines.

At evening briefings in Lashkar Gah we follow updates on the battles, and the fortunes of the Danes in particular have the CIMIC unit's undivided attention, even though they're based some thirty kilometres away.

At the same time, CIMIC continues its work in and around Lashkar Gah. I've now been given two main areas of responsibility: the women and the rural district of Babaji. In addition, I go on regular patrols in Lashkar Gah, with the aim of providing input into development processes in the provincial capital. My days are full.

A new rhythm emerges, a music of monotony involving sleeping, eating, patrolling, running meetings and writing reports. Everything is mapped. Do people have electricity and access to clean drinking water? Where are the hospitals and what standard are they? What schools exist? When the Ministry of Education says there are 1,300 pupils, is that a true figure? How many teachers are there? Are they paid? What subjects do they teach?

Gradually, piece by piece, patrol by patrol, we're able to gain a view of Lashkar Gah and its needs. All information is gathered in a so-called Base Line Assessment, borrowing directly from various humanitarian organizations. It means that we, the local administration, and the aid organizations that hopefully are to follow on behind us are able to pinpoint clearly the areas in need of targeting. At the same time, it provides us with a constantly updated view of development.

We visit all the schools. We see all the classrooms. We ask the teachers how many pupils they teach, and we document it all with reports and on-site photos of actual conditions. It is the beginning of a database and a foundation on which to build for the special education adviser the Danish Foreign Office will be sending out in early 2008.

One of my colleagues manages to get the mayor of Lashkar Gah to initiate something new: clean-up projects and minor road repairs. The HEG funds the work. A fleet of wheelbarrows and shovels are bought and teams of unemployed are given work for a week or ten days at a time in their own neighbourhoods as the projects sweep through the town. Local police provide security for the teams so they don't get killed by bombs.

The whole thing runs for weeks and is a huge success. Streets are cleaned and money is circulated in the society. For some of the unemployed, the wages they receive are start-up capital for a small business. For others it means being able to stay alive a bit longer. Wages are set so as not to jam market mechanisms. A building worker earns about two dollars a day if he can find work. The mayor's clean-up teams get twice as much, but work only for a week.

The Taliban pay their freedom fighters ten dollars a day, so a Taliban warrior earns more than four times as much as a teacher and three times as much as a policeman. Only our own interpreters earn more.

Each spring when the opium harvest is in, about a million day workers find themselves without a job. They can be directly recruited into the Taliban army as mercenaries. They do as they're told, since only the Taliban can give them work.

The Taliban project begins to become clear to me. As head of intelligence, my room-mate Sarah is a great help in that respect, but my Afghan women are too. Both Fatima and Gulaley have run for the provincial council, which is legally obliged to ensure that four of its fifteen seats go to women. For campaigning openly and uncovering their faces, they have both received death threats. Both are convinced the Taliban will get them one day. They hope to be shot and to escape torture. Terrifying stories abound, probably embroidered a little more each time they have been told.

Fatima and Gulaley no longer live for themselves but for their fellow women and the children. They insist upon a brighter future. Fatima hates her burka, though she concedes that it keeps her concealed from the Taliban whenever she is out and about. The burka is merely a detail that can be turned to one's own advantage. I know how much attention it creates when I'm out on patrol and the men realize I'm a woman. They stare. Burkas, however, walk in peace.

It's hard to see how much power the Taliban actually has. I can hear that the women are scared, yet I can't help but feel that fear of the Taliban exceeds its real power and that it's all part of the Taliban game. By creating and maintaining fear through intimidation and terrorist strikes, the Taliban seek to demonstrate that the government has failed to bring peace and prosperity to the country and that the foreign forces are not in control. It takes an exceptionally fine net and unusual determination to find a man in a crowd with fifteen kilos of explosives, nails, screws and studs taped to his body.

Every time I go out I tighten my helmet, load my carbine and my pistol and put on a smile. I feel no fear at all. I'm beginning to understand what Hazel said: you can't go around being scared all the time. Being scared makes you paralysed. You have to believe everything's going to be all right. Of course you need to keep your eyes peeled, yet the smiles appear on their own every time a happy child waves, every time a child goes to school, even if teaching is done in shifts. The schools in Lashkar Gah are filled to the brim, furniture is dilapidated and books are falling apart. But the children laugh and are full of beams.

I keep the best stored away inside me. The egg project is running well.

One day Gulaley tells me with a smile about something that happened at the home of one of their women the other day. As Gulaley arrives, the husband comes in with one of the hens under his arm. He wants to sell it at the bazaar or maybe have chicken for dinner.

The woman turns on her husband, raises an index finger admonishingly and says: 'You're not selling my hen. It lays eggs, and it will lay eggs tomorrow as well!' Then, showing pity, she says: 'You can have an omelette.'

The story illustrates what I've suspected for a while now. Inside the home, women enjoy considerable influence. They decide on matters involving the children, and their visions for a future Afghanistan rub off.

As Fatima angrily exclaims one day: 'We will not give birth to Taliban children!'

The hardest thing to understand is the bitter opposition of the Taliban to schools. Religiously, the Taliban believe that all teaching other than the recital of Arabic Qur'an verses is dangerous. Politically, they are against every form of progress the government tries to implement. Most Afghans I meet accuse the Taliban of being bad Muslims: the Taliban are often illiterate, they are oppressive and violent, they kills civilians and thereby their own Muslim brothers, and many of them interpret Islam in a way many Afghans do not agree with. We are up against an enormous destructive force and a bizarre imperative of turning back time and returning to prehistoric society.

Until the soldiers have provided security, local Afghans will be unable to find the courage to openly resist the Taliban. That is the context in which we operate. It is a reality that, time and again, catches us off-balance, meaning we are seldom able to avoid falling on our backsides.

Hazel stands rummaging in one of her bags one evening. Her hair's turning grey and she's appointed me *combat hairdresser*. It's a joke she has.

Everything's combat this, that or the other. The British Army even has such a thing as a 'combat field dressing'. As combat hairdresser my job is to dye Hazel's hair once a month in the blinking fluorescent light of the shower room.

There's a knock on the door. Hazel opens it. I only manage to catch snippets of what's said. The tone is hushed and serious. I hear TIC mentioned, troops in contact.

'… find a medic … thought she was with you … two Danes … dead, maybe or …'

The conversation goes on, but I can't hear anything anymore. It can't be true. It's all been going so well. The Danes are in favour, admired. Fierce fighters. The brigade's been so impressed, full of respect. And now their luck's run out.

Hazel turns to me. Her sweet voice says she'll find out what's going on.

She looks all wrong.

10

THE DAY WE BECAME MORTAL

The minutes pass. My brain scans images of faces I know so well. I don't know who's been hit, but it hurts so badly inside.

Finally, Hazel comes back and closes the door. She looks me in the eye. 'I know you heard some of what was said. I'm not supposed to say anything. And there's nothing you or I can do. I don't know what unit it is, but they're Danes, and … there are two T1s.'

She keeps eye contact. T1 is code for fatally wounded.

'Will you still dye my hair?' she asks. 'I know it's a stupid question, but we might as well do something useful. We can talk while you do it. Will you? I perfectly understand if you don't want to.'

I just nod. I know why she's doing it. She doesn't want me sitting around staring at walls.

Another knock on the door: Torben. He clears his throat and looks at me. 'Two Danes killed in action,' he says, composed.

I stare at him emptily and nod. He tells me he's going to inform the others. I feel restless. I need to do something, something meaningful, no matter how absurd.

We go over to women's shower room. Hazel wets her hair and I rub in the dye. I should be out fighting somewhere. I catch myself thinking I must never tell anyone I stood dyeing a room-mate's hair while Danish soldiers were fighting for their lives. I consider my family. What are they going to think when they hear Danes have been killed?

The Brits shut the phones and the Internet down until the families have been informed. They're entitled to be the first to know.

We've already attended ramp ceremonies for six dead Brits. The last two died when the CIMIC patrol hit a roadside incendiary. Next time is for two of my countrymen.

Hazel sits herself down on a big dustbin she's turned upside down. She holds a pink hairbrush in her hand. She has a towel wrapped around her neck and the wet dye smells of chemicals. Everything is wrong and I feel out of place. Hazel takes this little edge of reality and pulls, as though removing a plaster.

'First, I hope it's no one you know. It's really hard when the guys die out there, but the truth is it's easier if it's no one you know. You don't have to go through the personal anguish, the mourning. Second, I know Torben said dead, but it's not official yet. The duty officer said T1. So it's serious. But if they do die I hope it happens quickly. I'm sorry, but I don't believe in suffering. Third, I hope they don't have small children. It's hard and unfair when young men die, but at least they haven't got as far as having wives, children, all those things ...'

Hazel knows what it's like. She has lost people for whom she has been responsible and whose families she knew. As yet, I've no experience that can be put clearly into words. I'm just sad.

I remain quiet all evening, quiet when I get up the next morning.

Something has changed. The idea that maybe we were lucky, that someone was watching over us, protecting us. It's not there anymore.

The next morning, we ten Danes gather in silence in the CIMIC unit's office. It's Thursday, 27 September 2007, and Lars reads out the names in a clear voice: 'Mikkel Keil Sørensen and Thorbjørn Ole Reese.'

Oh, no, not Reese. I pull a chair up and sit down. The name Mikkel Sørensen doesn't ring any bells. I don't realize yet that I know him as *Brille*—Specs. I can only think about Reese. Always smoking. Reese, who loved to cook, was always there to chat, was so good at drawing. Reese, who spent his spare time working with kids who'd got on the wrong side of the law, helping them to find a better path.

Somewhere I hear the chopper that flew me to Camp Bastion. I can smell the dust and recall the evening a couple of weeks ago when I sat under the stars talking with Reese, Norman and René. René and Reese gave me a lift back to our part of the camp. The wheels churned up the gravel, the dust fanning out in our wake. Reese was in the back, the smoke of his cigarette trailing and engulfed by the dust.

In the rush of wind he called out to me: 'You're wearing perfume!' 'I've just washed my hair,' I called back over my shoulder. 'Wicked,' he yelled. 'I don't half miss my girlfriend!'

He laughed.

That's the sound I hear now. The sound of Reese laughing. He was happy. The smell of my hair made him long for a girl I do not know.

I've only one way of coping with my grief. I write. I try to take all my experiences from the patrol, the Green Zone villages, the schools and Lashkar Gah's slum, and relate them to a soldier's death. What does it mean? Why do we keep on? Right now, I feel like I'm one of the few who have seen how the harshness of battle has borne fruit in the town, and who know that it can bear fruit elsewhere too.

I end up writing an article and show it to Lars. He sits down in a corner of the office and reads.

We've all been aware that he's needed to find himself again after recent events. Following the patrol when two British soldiers were killed protecting the Danish CIMIC unit, an investigation has been launched as to whether the Danes are in any way responsible. They're looking at whether there might be technical problems in the combination of electronic equipment used by the Danes and the British, problems that might render protection against roadside incendiaries less effective. Our boss is alone and in the open, vulnerable. He's out fighting his own battle. As a unit we miss him. I miss him.

Lars gets up from his chair.

'It's good,' he says, handing me back the article.

It's the first time since early September I've seen a hint of the familiar sparkle in his eyes.

'I think you should send it in, see if *Jyllands-Posten* will publish it,' he says pensively, then adds: 'Reese's parents would have a chance to see it there. Or someone he knows. He was from Jutland, wasn't he?'

Jyllands-Posten runs the article along with a fine interview with Reese's father.

Days after the names are made public I see the photographs of our dead colleagues. Only then do I recognize Mikkel Sørensen. They called him Specs, because he wore specs and was clever.

Thorbjørn Reese was twenty-two years old. Mikkel Sørensen was twenty-four. With them we have become mortal. Every face is a face that may be gone in the morning.

For three weeks after Reese's death he is the first thing on my mind when I wake in the mornings and the last when I lie down to sleep at night.

11

GARY'S BOMB OFFICE

The Taliban didn't kill Reese and Sørensen, the Brits did. It was a terrible mistake. The unit did everything it was supposed to do, followed procedure, but for some unknown reason the Brits opened fire on the Danish position.

The girls in the room are worried about how I'm going to react and are guilt-ridden, despite it having nothing to do with them. It makes no difference to me. Mistakes occur, even in war. Not as many as in the old days, but not even the most modern warfare is without error. Our vehicles and some of our weapons are packed with electronics. If my gear fails and a British soldier dies, is it my fault?

A long and arduous technical investigation is initiated, and somewhere there are two British soldiers wounded in a way from which they will never recover.

A late evening at the beginning of October and I'm wandering aimlessly around the camp. It's still warm and the moon is bright. I'm restless.

Hazel's got two bomb-disposal teams on the go. Sarah's not usually back before midnight and the same goes for Andrea. The room's empty without them. I feel lonely. I think about going over to see what my male colleagues are up to, but decide I don't really feel like it. Around the corner I hear Rebecca's clear voice. She's the only one from the old team not to have gone home yet.

'Oh, hi, AC,' she says. 'How's things?'

I sense her British politeness, her decent upbringing, the casual aloofness.

I'm really fed up with the way the Brits always ask how you are in that cheery way of theirs, striding by as though they were on a train that can't stop long enough to listen to the answer.

I need company and say it like it is: 'I'm tired and feeling low. In fact, things aren't good at all.'

'Oh, well …'

She looks as though it was the kind of answer she wasn't expecting, and I consider for a moment whether I've committed the fiftieth mortal sin since arriving here in the camp a month ago. Then the tears well up in her big blue eyes and she kicks at the gravel.

'I've had a shit day as well! Fuck it! Let's go and see a film.' I liven up straight away. A film sounds like a really good idea. 'Follow me,' she says, regaining her British control.

We walk through the darkness towards the main gate, then turn behind a container. I'm surprised to realize that the camp opens up on to an area I haven't seen before. The nearest corner is occupied by a big black cube. Rebecca follows its walls, which are made of so-called Hesco bastion, a prefabricated fortification of wire mesh, heavy-duty fabric and sand. She turns the corner and keeps going. I can't see anything there, but then she opens a gate in the mesh.

'Come on,' she says. 'But be careful. There are no lights and we're not supposed to be here.'

It's like stepping into a secret labyrinth. We walk along a small corridor with containers on each side and doors behind which I assume there are offices. On my right I can see wreckage from military vehicles hung up on the walls.

We turn several corners and I quickly lose my sense of direction.

Suddenly we step into something that most of all resembles an English pub under an open sky. There are benches and cushions of red velvet, posters on the walls and an upright supporting a pent roof that could just as easily be from a bar in Hawaii.

'Evening, ladies,' a voice says.

'AC, this Gary. Gary, AC,' Rebecca says formally.

Gary is a muscular little Brit with longish fair hair and a big red beard. To call him good-looking would be an exaggeration, but he exudes something along the lines of the Rolling Stones and is kindness itself.

He takes my hand, looks me in the eye and says: 'So you're the girl everyone's talking about. I've been looking forward to meeting you.'

Gary introduces me to the two other guests in his establishment, a couple of lads who both work for him, or so it seems.

One of them fishes a can of beer—strictly against regulations—out of an inflatable paddling pool, which I seem to have overlooked in sheer astonishment at discovering an outdoor pub in a corner of Brigade HQ.

'Are you the one who beat up an interpreter?' the lad with the cans asks. 'No, I didn't beat up anyone! He was a cleaner and I never touched him!' 'What happened?'

'He said something inappropriate and I gave him a bollocking.' 'He said "Hello, sexy" and she tore him apart in front of Charlie

Company's building. The whole company was there and the fella died of shame or from his injuries. Fancy a beer, AC?' Gary hands me a can.

I decline and grab a Fanta instead. We're not allowed to drink. The Brits aren't either. I listen to Rebecca and Gary talking about some people I don't know. An officer who's a pain and another who's incompetent. Gary asks if she wants to go out and blow something up the next day. She's welcome to bring a friend. I know Lars would be mad if I just disappeared off on strange missions. Rebecca excels at vanishing from the office and coming back hours later with gunpowder in her hair. I lean back against the soft cushions and relax. It's like being at home in someone's living room, away from the camp and its internal pecking order.

I gradually realize why the place is so well hidden and surrounded by metres of sand. Gary is Weapons Intelligence Warrant Officer, abbreviated—in the manner of just about every other British military designation—to WISWO. Or simply 'The Wizard'.

Gary disarms bombs. He doesn't talk much about it, but I think to myself that it's one heck of a job to do. It's one thing to disarm old Soviet mines, in itself dangerous enough: because of the harsh climate here, explosives become unstable and can go off at the drop of a hat. It's quite another to disarm one of the Taliban's home-made bombs, constructed according to the principle of whatever happens to be at hand. It's the equivalent of trying to solve a potentially lethal crossword puzzle in a foreign language in which rules of orthography keep changing by the minute.

It's said of soldiers who go into the field of ammunition and bomb disposal that the day they choose their living is the day they choose how they're going to die. Perhaps it's the ever-present nature of death that makes Gary so calm, so intense, so much here in the now.

I sit watching the little bushman chatting away with Rebecca as though they've known each other forever. He pulls her leg and self-mockingly explains to her that she is madly in love with him and that it's quite normal because there's not a woman on this earth who can resist him. The thought makes me smile. He may be a lovely bloke, but the idea is outrageous.

'What did I tell you?' he says, and points at me. 'Look, AC's obviously a lot brighter than you are, Rebecca. She's realized that you're doomed to fall on your knees for me.'

I hear myself laughing for the first time in ages.

'In fact, she's probably starting to warm to me herself. Look, she's laughing at me,' he adds solemnly.

'Oh, yeah, right.' Rebecca giggles.

I fall quiet and start thinking about my ex. I'm still not over him. But Rebecca and Gary soon take my mind off him. We watch a film whose only ambition is to entertain.

When eventually Rebecca and I make our way home later that evening, my stomach's hurting from laughing and my head feels light as air. I decide to come here again. This mad cave would seem to be one of the only places in the camp where I feel normal.

12

IN THE DOGHOUSE

Waging war and promoting development at the same time require planning and decision-making. The main authority in Helmand is a civilian body made up of British officials planning according to an overall reconstruction strategy for Afghanistan. The members of this Provincial Reconstruction Team are politically responsible for the success or otherwise of reconstruction efforts. It's their job to ensure that the Afghan people begin to believe in development.

The PRT views the war and development activities in holistic terms. The military machine is just one of a number of means. Some of the others are development funding, national reform programmes and diplomatic pressure. The British government, which has taken on responsibility for Helmand, may say to the Afghan government that the UK will not contribute financially unless visible improvements take place. As a last resort, the politicians can threaten to pull troops out.

The British brigade and its subordinate Danish Battle Group operate according to the plans laid down by the PRT and its civilian members. Naturally, the brigade decides how it will wage war, but if advisers discover any political opening by which to gain control of a new town, the brigade will do its utmost to ensure security and make sure that the conditions are right for development.

The civilian advisers hold a lot of meetings in which brigade representatives often take part.

One day in early October I'm given the chance to participate in a so-called steering committee meeting focusing on development initiatives in a number of specific towns. Here, advisers seek to establish monthly targets and to encourage those responsible for areas such as policing and public security to come up with estimates of how much can be done. It's all over my head, but all of a sudden there's a chance to go along as an observer.

I settle down at the back of a small conference room in which men in ties are gathered around a table along with a few high-ranking officers. One of them is Colonel Richards, the senior British Army officer with overall responsibility for CIMIC, the engineering troops and Hazel's bomb-disposal team. He's Lars's boss and Hazel's too.

At the back sit the rest of us who are here to observe, to learn something about the overall picture and to take notes. All in all, we number about thirty-five. The room is packed and I'm excited. This is where the plans are made and where the future begins.

The meeting is headed up by Sakander, a British official hailing from Kashmir, a slight, raven-haired man with eyes so dark he seems always to be staring, his pupils being wholly invisible. Sakander has a strangely deep, hoarse voice and speaks in an unchanging, monotonous tone. Nothing in his face, his eyes or his voice reveals anything about what he might be thinking. Sakander ranks next highest in the civilian structure.

To begin with I enjoy myself: the civilians are highly educated and the preciseness of their language presents a challenge. As the meeting progresses, however, it becomes apparent that a number of the experts present are able to speak for a very long time indeed without saying anything at all.

One of them in particular prompts me to prick up my ears and scribble down his words as quickly as I can. He possesses a remarkable ability to utter sentences only a few people would have the syntactic ability to construct even with the aid of pen and paper. Behind the fine words, however, is only resounding emptiness. No action, and no intention of any.

Out of sheer boredom, a number of the attendant military observers have long since begun to fill their notepads with elaborate doodles. Next to me is Lishman, a British warrant officer of the engineering troops. Lishman clearly has a well-developed sense of humour and scribbles a couple of sarcastic comments on my copy of the agenda. The warrant officer is not impressed, but seems to be having a whale of a time anyway.

I look down at the latest civilian outpouring to have found its way on to my notepad: 'We should like to hope that in future we may look forward to the Afghan government aspiring within legal and judicial— and here I refer particularly to locally constitutionalized instances—to bring forth some measure of heightened responsibility, although …'

Five minutes later still nothing has been said of any immediate relevance at all. It's a vanishing act performed by way of language. Linguistically, I'm impressed. As a human, I'm offended. How can he sit here and explain everything away, while my colleagues are out there dying in a war.

Lishman leans towards me and scribbles yet another incisive comment about the wonderful concept of 'civilian leadership' on my agenda. I can only shake my head.

Suddenly, Sakander looks at me and says: 'AC, if you have anything to say, I should very much like to hear it.'

Everyone at the table turns to look at me. I can feel my cheeks going red.

I'm a schoolgirl who's been caught passing notes around class.

'No, Sir, no comments for the moment,' I say, managing, I think, to stay calm.

Sakander's monotone, however, is insistent: 'AC, I believe you have something to say. It may be relevant for the rest of us too.'

'No, Sir, no comments for the moment.' 'AC, I think you ought to speak up.'

It's the third time he's asked me to say something. I'm being pushed into the role of the little boy in *The Emperor's New Clothes*. As I open my mouth to speak, I am painfully aware that the Danish captain, who is here merely as an observer, must now undress a civilian adviser right down to his undies, as a consequence of which she most likely will be hung, drawn and quartered at daybreak.

As politely as possible, I try my best to say something diplomatic that nevertheless still bears some resemblance to reality.

'Sir, it may simply be a question of different cultures being at odds, whether Danish against British, or civilian against military, but it does seem to me to be rather difficult to see the relationship between the item on the agenda—item seven, i.e. aims for next month—and the actual issue at hand as it is being worded at present. However, I'm sure it is just me. No further comment, Sir.'

Thirty-five people hold their breath. An embarrassed silence fills the room.

Sakander stares blankly at me for a long time. Eventually, he clears his throat and says casually that he's sure my nationality has nothing to do with it. Calmly, he turns towards the representatives around the table. His gaze falls on the next person due to speak.

'John, I believe it's your turn. How do things look in your area?'

My heart is racing. I'm both relieved and scared witless. I can sense that Sakander is letting me off the hook. I think through what I've just said. I did the best I could. But I hit out at someone far, far higher up the ladder than me. This is going to cost me dearly.

The meeting changes character. The remaining speakers are briefer and more to the point. One even says that prospects are dim in his area. After two more items, the meeting reaches a close.

Lishman can hardly contain his merriment and whispers: 'Nice one! You certainly barked up a few trees there—and way outside your own territory too, if I may say.'

My stomach's hurting. On my way out of the conference room I literally run into Andrea, who's been sitting at the other end of the room as press officer and who presumably is now faced with the task of putting some journalistic slant on proceedings. She shows the whites of her eyes.

I cast one last glance back into the room. Sakander is standing engaged in discussion with Colonel Richards. Suddenly, he looks me straight in the eye while the colonel goes on talking. Somehow I know it's not going to be the last time I run into Sakander.

I leave the building and cross over the crunching gravel to the office. No sooner do I get through the door than Colonel Richards comes dashing after me with a big smile on his freckled face. The beam goes all the way up to his eyes. He puts out his hand. I've no idea if he wants to congratulate me on putting my foot in it big time, or whether he is genuinely pleased. He looks sincere enough, but then I don't know the man at all. I have him pigeonholed as someone who has been in the army for so long that the system has taken over his soul.

'Well, I must say you certainly know how to speak your mind. You really got things moving in there!'

Richards shakes my hand, laughs heartily and marches out again.

Lars looks at me in amazement and asks what all that was about. Half pleased, half embarrassed, I mutter something about diplomatically having put someone in his place.

'Sorry, run that by me again, will you?' he says.

There were a lot of people at that meeting. Quite a few of them mention my involuntary contribution to Lars. A few days later, he calls me in and makes it clear to me in no uncertain terms that I'm way out of line and if anything like it happens again I'll be on the first chopper home. We're a unit and we pull together. Working off our own bat isn't an option.

I'm shaken. My comments have reflected badly on Lars in the British hierarchy, making it seem that he hasn't got a grip. Quite some time passes before I have a chance to tell my own side of the story.

I'm absolutely devastated at the thought of being sent home in disgrace. I want to stay. I feel I have a job to do. It may be a job the military doesn't find important, but it's important to me. What's more, I think it's important for the people I work with too. But what am I supposed to do? I go around like a little mouse hugging the skirting boards, waiting for something to happen that can take away some of the attention on me. A week later, the Taliban unexpectedly lend a hand.

Andrea was the first to declare that I was the only one who actually said anything useful at the infamous meeting of the steering group. I'm truly grateful for her support. I know Andrea has a temper and is a thousand times more impetuous than the average Brit. She was on the brink of blowing a fuse too. Sarah and Hazel think I needn't take it all so badly. There's no way they'd send me home, they say. I'm not at all convinced, though, and the girls have their work cut out trying to cheer me up.

Late one evening, Hazel, Sarah, Andrea and I manage to sneak away from the office to see a film. The last couple of times we've watched *Pride and Prejudice*, the six-part BBC series based on Jane Austen's novel. Sarah is the last of us to arrive.

'Oh, thank God I made it,' she says, trying to catch her breath and closing the door behind her. 'Have you been waiting? You needn't have.'

'Is it bad?' I ask.

Sarah has the longest days of all of us and is moreover embroiled in a war of attrition with certain elements of the staff. My bad days are nothing compared to hers.

She shakes her head: 'Don't even ask. It's been sheer bedlam today.' Sarah lets her fine blonde hair down and slumps on to Hazel's bed. 'Right, are we all set, girls?' Hazel asks.

We nod. Hazel's laptop is ready in front of us on the cable drum that pretends to be our coffee table. It's episode five of *Pride and Prejudice*. As it starts I glance at the three girls who have become my family. I feel so fortunate to have ended up with them. It's so empty to come into the room when they're not here, and so lovely and warm whenever we get the rare chance to be here together, all four of us.

With sweets and chocolate positioned within arm's reach, we slide back into a strange universe of old-fashioned honour and decorous language, handsome noblemen and brocaded gowns, scheming ladies and pure and impoverished young girls. The war can't get us here, I think to myself, not for an hour, at least. But of course I'm mistaken.

In the middle of the climax, with the heroine involved in a crucial exchange with the female baddie, the place is shaken by a huge explosion. The walls tremble and something falls on to the floor. My immediate thought is this: 107mm.

Hazel screws up her eyes: 'A 107mm Chinese, I do believe,' she says, putting on her poshest Queen Elizabeth accent.

The film goes on. I note that I'm actually quite proud of having guessed what sort of shell it was. Sarah clears her throat. We look at each other enquiringly and especially at Hazel. She's the expert.

'Seriously, Hazel, is there something we should do? Helmet, body armour?' Sarah asks.

None of us needs to say much. What we've just heard is one of the Taliban's favourite weapons. The rockets are designed to be launched from a Katyusha launcher, better known under the sobriquet Stalin's Organ, but the Taliban lay them on the ground and calculate an angle before launching and hoping they'll hit the target. Often, they'll launch four or five just to have something to go by.

Hazel glances calmly around the room.

'No, honestly, I think we'll be all right here. There's nothing we can do about it anyway. The building's made of concrete. There's no need to go into the shelters. Charlie Company will send some lads to check it out, maybe tonight, maybe in the morning, but we're not going to know anything before lunchtime tomorrow at any rate.'

I admire the calm way in which she deals with the situation. This isn't an exercise. It's proper war.

'Rewind a little, then. I want to see that bit again,' says Andrea, drumming eagerly on the floor with her feet.

The next day we learn that it was a 107mm that landed north of the base, though no significant damage was done. Everyone is talking about the attack, the CIMIC unit included, and I sense the pressure ease somewhat from my shoulders.

In the weeks that follow we're on heightened alert, expecting more attacks, perhaps better coordinated. People lug body armour and helmets back and forth between offices and billets, but soon everything dies down and life returns to normal. In our area, the biggest threat continues to be outside the camp in the shape of suicide attackers.

13

THE SECOND WOMEN'S *SHURA*

It's early morning. In the shower room I spend ten minutes chasing frogs and toads out of the cubicle, where they've spent the night sheltered from the cold. I dress quickly and step out into the cool air. The sky is clear and blue. In a few hours, temperatures with soar to more than thirty degrees, dropping again by twenty degrees during the space of the afternoon.

Physically it's taxing, the body heating up and cooling down like that in such a short space of time. I roll down my sleeves as I pass through the camp.

In the little church tent, I sit on one of the six benches. To my right hang laminated sheets of photographs and words of remembrance about the soldiers who have been killed. I find Reese and Sørensen. Next to them now hangs Major Anders Storrud, commander of the Danish armoured infantry company, killed only a few days ago in a battle with the Taliban north of Gereshk.

I look up at Father MacPherson. The camp's towering British chaplain is kneeling before the altar.

Sarah sits down next to me. She and I are two of the most faithful churchgoers, along with two lads from Special Forces and a colonel of the parachute regiment.

Father MacPherson turns and begins the prayer. In my first six weeks of war, I have attended ramp ceremonies for more than twenty fallen colleagues. I know the Lord's Prayer better in English than in my native tongue.

Anders Storrud's coffin is being flown home today. Having met men like him, one only wishes there were more of his kind. Men who lead by example, with enthusiasm, determination and courage. His death is a major blow to the battalion that provides the power of the Danish Battle Group.

The British are concerned the Danes may never recover.

We pray for Anders's family and friends. We pray that God may give them strength to come through the grief. Losing colleagues is so hard. We honour them every time we think: What would Thorbjørn, Mikkel or Anders want us to do?

As I get to my feet, that is exactly what I do. I continue my work. I go and pack my gear for yet another outing into the town. The town, where anything can happen. Today, for the second time in the history of Helmand, we're gathering together all the women who wish and are able to meet with representatives of the international forces.

Coincidence has allied me with a British language officer who speaks Pashto. She's so good at what she does that she's constantly on the go between Lashkar Gah and Kandahar. Ann is a tall redhead in worn jeans and a shirt. She works with the British and American Special Forces and with civilian advisers. I've talked her into coming to Lashkar Gah for the *shura*. She's found an excuse and is really excited about seeing the women in action, and I've need of an observer. Rebecca and I have booked the big conference room at the Bost Hotel.

The women are thronging outside, all excited and eager to say hello to us and each other. Many are quick to exchange phone numbers, which makes me extra happy. The more who know each other, the greater the support I imagine they can lend each other. About twenty turn up, and for that we can thank Fowzia.

Fowzia begins the meeting. Like so many women, she is a true anti-leader, almost apologetic and low-voiced in this large gathering. Everyone must be in agreement; no one must feel they've been stepped on.

I glance at Rebecca, who looks stern and is obviously trying to encourage Fowzia to take the initiative. Fowzia hands the floor to Gulaley, who, full of energy and enthusiasm, tells the meeting about the projects that have been funded. She highlights the hens as one particularly suited to elderly women, widows who have difficulty getting by, and also to small girls in poorly situated families.

The sewing project is what she and Fatima enthuse most about. By turn they relate how they have been given the chance to help women of poor families to learn a skill to boost family income rather than merely becoming resigned to life as a servant in their own homes. When they're finished, the room is silent. The assembled women seem to be angry.

'Why did they get the chance and not us?' one of them asks, looking directly at me.

Another points at Fatima and Gulaley: 'Why do you each have two projects?' she asks accusingly.

'The projects should be divided equally between all the women.' 'Giving hens to a hundred women in Gereshk is unfair to those in Lashkar Gah,' another shouts.

Others chip in and are quite as angry. I find myself gawping in astonishment, utterly gobsmacked. I glance at Rebecca, but she has no intention of stepping in.

'It's up to Fowzia now,' she mutters.

It's all more than I can handle. I ask for the floor and end up giving the women a right rollicking. Most of them I've never seen before. I had no idea they even existed.

'What angers me most has nothing to do with the projects at all,' I say, getting to my feet. 'I've never before been in a country where women have so many enemies as here. It saddens me that as soon as you get the chance, you start squabbling among yourselves. What's got into you? You're acting like bedraggled little birds pecking at each other to steal a grain or two from your neighbour. You're just not thinking big enough. There's plenty of money in Helmand, believe me. We put a lot of funds into projects and rebuilding. Why don't you go for the sack of corn rather than just stealing grains from one other? I'd love to start off more projects, but I'm not going to stand by and watch you fighting among yourselves. You've enemies enough outside without having to turn on one another!'

I sit down again. I've only let off a modicum of steam, but the effect is obvious. The women are at once astonished and ashamed of themselves.

I should have realized why they reacted in the way they did. That much I've learned, at least, about life in an Afghan family. The women come from a society of scarcity in which there is rarely ever enough of anything, food included. There's a reason why most of them are so sinewy and tough-looking. They're used to giving the best cuts to their husbands and children and making do with what's left themselves. The poorest among them must look at their children and decide which of them can do without today. The women just can't imagine there being money for projects elsewhere. They think Gulaley and Fatima have taken all there is.

The women are still indignant as the meeting breaks up. I seek guidance from Ann.

'You have to step in and take charge, lead a meeting for them so they can get an idea of how it should be done. Fowzia's afraid of losing support, so all she's doing is treading water,' says Ann.

I'm still shocked. I'd been so looking forward to being able to help these women, yet they are consumed by jealousy, suspicion and fear.

It's late evening by the time I finish the day's reports and walk back through the camp. I follow a stony path that winds its way alongside an area dotted with satellite dishes and aerials. It's cordoned off with yellow tape and signs warning of nuclear radiation. I've always taken it as a joke to stop people nosing. There's no more radiation here than in the desert.

I turn down the corridor of North Block, passing a couple of offices before stopping outside Room 7. A few days ago someone pinned a laminated A4 sheet to our door showing a lovely young witch in silhouette on a broomstick. Underneath it says: 'Witches' boudoir—keep out!'

We've been laughing about it, taking it to be a declaration of affection, perhaps from some of the guests who regularly come to visit us in our cosy little room. Or maybe from one of the lads who have subjected themselves to watching a film with us on the condition of first having a mud mask applied. Another of Hazel's madcap ideas. As she says, it's hard to take yourself too seriously when you have mud all over your face.

Behind the door I can hear Hazel laughing. Andrea seems to be back too.

It'll be so nice to just hang out and relax.

'Oh, AC, there you are. Tell me, do you think he's really suicidal? I mean psychogically?' Hazel's sitting on her bed and looks up as I walk in. Her glasses are balanced on the tip of her nose and her voice is thick with the irony she's so good at.

'Who?'

'The suicide attacker. You know, the bloke lurking about out there.'

'What bloke?'

'Woops, I don't think she knows. I suppose we'd better tell her,' says Andrea from her own bed on the other side of the room.

Andrea can smile as cheekily as a little mouse, as though finding constant amusement in all the tiny peculiarities of the world and in all the news stories that can be angled in just the right way.

'You mean to say you really don't know? There's a lockdown,' Hazel says.

'A lockdown? I was in the town this morning,' I say.

'Yeah, you just got back in time. They've closed the base. There's a suicide bomber out there,' Hazel says matter-of-factly.

'There are *always* suicide bombers out there!'

'True, but this one's different.' Hazel peers over the rim of her glasses. 'Intelligence are 100 per cent certain. They've got him nailed, name, photo, the lot. They know he's been issued with a bomb vest. And they know he's intent on blowing himself up.'

'So that's why my patrol's been cancelled tomorrow,' I say pensively, and wonder why they didn't just say so over at Charlie Company. I'd felt like we were just being given low priority for no apparent reason.

'They've got sharpshooters on duty outside, and we're all of us locked in!' Andrea pummels her duvet theatrically.

I sit down on my bed. I've been in a lockdown once before. It's something they resort to only when the risk of attack is imminent. I don't like being confined indefinitely. For those of us used to driving about town every day or every other day, it feels like being forced to stop breathing.

Nonetheless, I can't help being impressed by the work Sarah and her team are doing.

They have their sources outside, of course, but they still have to tread cautiously. Sources need to be protected, trust maintained. In a constant fight against time and without exerting too much pressure, they are faced with the task of finding a man who intends to commit a crime and identifying him before he manages to act on that intention.

I suddenly remember I've a meeting with Fowzia tomorrow. Damn. It'll have to be postponed. Indefinitely, so it seems. All we can do is wait for the sharpshooters to find and eliminate him, or for the police or the Afghan soldiers to do the same. Either that or wait for a bloody great bang.

'Andrea and I were just talking about whether he's really suicidal—you know, depressed. What do you reckon, AC?' Hazel enquires enthusiastically.

'Of course he's not depressed,' I reply, annoyed.

'Are you sure about that? I once worked on a helpline for people thinking of killing themselves,' Hazel goes on. 'I mean, it's serious business. You have to go through all these tests to see if you're suited to talking to these depressed people without getting depressed yourself. But I was wondering if I should try to give him a bit of counselling.'

Hazel lets her glasses slide even further down her nose. I can hear from her tone of voice that she's messing about. Queen Elizabeth with a twist of irony.

'I mean, I could ask him if he feels badly about himself, his childhood and stuff. Perhaps he really is depressed. Maybe it would help if he had someone to share his problems with. I could ask him if there's anyone in particular he's pissed off with, or if it's just the world and life in general. We could start a helpline for suicide bombers.'

Hazel looks as though she's weighing up the pros and cons. She nudges her glasses back into place. The thought of a depressive suicide attacker is absurd. The thought of Hazel trying to get a desperate man wearing a bomb vest to talk about his childhood in poverty-stricken Afghanistan is even more absurd. I feel a smile coming on, even if I am still annoyed about the *shura*.

Over in her own corner, Andrea's already committed to the idea. 'That'd be so cool. I can just imagine it. Hazel can coach them and I can sell the story: "Suicide bomber saved by woman major, 36! Abdul Hammad gives up mission of death following therapy! Suicide attacks plummet! Army to take up new methods in fight against suicide attacks!"'

We fall about laughing. Andrea's voice hits just the right note of tabloid sensation.

'What would you ask him about, Hazel?' Andrea asks more seriously. 'Well, the important thing is to listen. That's what people really want.

Someone to listen to their strange thoughts that usually aren't that strange at all. I'd ask him if he'd spoken to his family about it. That's always a good place to start.'

Hazel leans her head back against the wall and begins to talk calmly: 'Have you told your family about how you feel? What would your mother say if she knew you wanted to commit suicide? Have you got a girlfriend? What does she ... or he ...think about it? Or rather, what do she and your wife and the other one you're cheating on think about it?'

As Hazel lists her questions, they become more and more lifelike and for some reason we find ourselves dissolving into laughter.

'You'd be surprised by how often people have problems with their partners or at work, and eventually they've completely lost the plot and can't cope anymore,' Hazel protests, trying to find a serious note.

'I don't think this one's got problems at work,' Andrea splutters. 'This *is* his work!'

'True, but it may be rather short-term. You know, career opportunities and all,' Hazel says, keeping a straight face.

'Seventy-two virgins?' I suggest.

'Quite honestly, hasn't anyone ever told them how hard it is?' asks suburban housewife Hazel, peering over her glasses again.

We can't stop laughing, and we're still smiling by the time we go to bed, giggles twitching at the corners of our mouths, a suppressed snort threatening now and again to set us all off once more long after we've decided to turn off the light. Eventually, I fall asleep thinking of a video I just saw on YouTube. An American ventriloquist and stand-up, Jeff Dunham, and his incompetent suicide bomber, Achmed the Dead Terrorist. There's probably not a soldier who hasn't seen it yet. The clip's hilarious in a ghastly sort of way, and you can't help feeling for poor Achmed, who died because of premature detonation.

For those of us who live with the reality, it's doubly pertinent, since many suicide bombers actually become so nervous they detonate their explosives too early.

After four days, our suicide bomber approaches a police checkpoint early one morning on one of Lashkar Gah's wider thoroughfares. He's challenged by an Afghan policeman who immediately senses something's amiss. The suicide bomber hesitates. When asked to remove his jacket, he runs away.

Police fire shots but miss.

Half an hour later he tries again at another checkpoint. Police fire warning shots. He makes off between piles of rubble. Two Afghan soldiers take up pursuit, chasing him on foot through streets and alleys. Fifty metres from the base he's shot down by the Afghans and one of our own sharpshooters.

Hazel sends two of her lads out to pick up the vest and bring it in for examination. Its twelve kilos of explosives land on Gary's desk, the vest intact apart from a couple of bullet holes and a smearing of blood.

14

GLASS BEADS AND ARMS FROM IRAN

During September and October, Gereshk is hit by a number of suicide bombers. One of the worst attacks occurs when a man blows himself up in the bazaar, taking forty-two lives with him. Even more are injured.

A few days later one of the women, whose name I can't reveal, calls and asks to meet with her. It is a meeting whose purpose is simple: to provide me with information. Over four hundred women are involved in our CIMIC projects. Some of those women in our network are married to men who in some way sympathize with the Taliban. Their wives are forced to keep quiet and to live with the knowledge. Until now. The women are fully aware that I will ask questions and that their information will be put to use.

The suicide bomber stayed in Gereshk for three days before blowing himself up and killing people the women knew. The woman who has called me is incensed. Many people in Gereshk are angry about the brutal ways of the Taliban, she tells me.

She takes a deep breath. 'AC, I'm going to tell you what I know and what I have heard. Then it will be up to you to decide what is to be done about it,' she says.

'He came from Iran and had journeyed for many days. He had an interpreter with him. He was young and was married a year ago. His wife was pregnant and soon due to give birth. The last evening he was alive, his mother called him and begged him not to blow himself up. She told him that she had been with his wife to the hospital and had paid for a scan of their unborn child. She told him he was to be the father of a son.'

The woman sends me a triumphant look. She is clearing up a murder. 'I have heard of those examinations myself,' she says. 'But I think perhaps it was something his mother just said to make him proud and to persuade him to return home and become the father of a son.'

I ask her to elucidate here and there.

In terms of our need for exact information, the woman demonstrates an unfailing ability to think sideways in anecdotal leaps. People who can neither read nor write are good at remembering. They tell things in a way that makes sense to them and which lends cohesion to all the other stuff they cling on to and remember.

She gives me the names of the man who delivered the vest and the man who is believed to have made it. I know from talking to Gary that bomb vests can be made in a variety of ways, but that only a few are used in this area. Intelligence already has the names and fingerprints of a couple of local 'manufacturers'.

The suicide bomber had a mobile phone on him. That was how his mother was able to call him. He had also told his family that he was going to become a martyr. I'm given a description of the place he stayed. Much of this information is from the woman of the house. She is not involved in any women's group herself, though some of her friends are.

I look down at my notes, a scribble of jottings, names and arrows connecting observations. None of it can bring forty-two people back to life. But perhaps we may be able to add another piece to a jigsaw of a man putting together a vest of explosives. Perhaps the picture will show a woman in the background, ill at ease with her husband's work.

Having escorted the woman to the main gate, I stride directly towards HQ. I've a standing order from Lars that all information of value to intelligence is to be handed on immediately to Sarah's unit. I assume it's still valid, despite my being in disgrace.

HQ is a densely populated open office landscape set up in a cube of white containers. The intelligence unit is situated at the far end. It would be underplaying things to call it a section, comprising as it does hordes of specialists and experts as well as a lot of other people stuffed away in places I've never even heard of.

Only five or six are at the computers when I come by and all of them seem to be pretty busy. Neither Sarah nor her second-in command, Julia, is present. A bald, round-headed sergeant looks up from his screen. He's got a yellow pencil sticking out from behind his ear.

'Can I help you, Ma'am?' he asks.

'Yeah,' I say hesitantly. I wonder how this is going to be taken.

'I've just come from a meeting with a woman from Gereshk who has given me information about that suicide bomber. I'm going to be writing my own report, but I thought maybe you should have some of it now.'

'Fire away,' he says, pulling the pencil from behind his ear.

I run through my notes with him. Gradually, the other computers in the little section begin to fall silent. The sergeant is scribbling away as quickly as he can. A first lieutenant comes over to listen.

'I'm sorry, could I just have that name again?' he asks.

I state the name of the man who housed the suicide bomber and provide a description of the place. There are no street names in Gereshk, but there's a description of a shrine nearby. He writes it down and hands it on to an office assistant.

'Give it to Madison,' he mutters.

The office assistant goes out through a door into a corner of HQ closed off to us mortals.

By now there are four people gathered around me, asking questions and taking notes.

'These women, do you meet with them on a regular basis?' one of them asks. 'And are there reports?'

'Yes, we send them on to you after every meeting. Do you want me to find them?'

'No, I'm sure we've got copies. I'll find them myself. Can I ask you for a printout of the report you'll be writing on this? As you know, it takes a while before the electronic distribution channels get things out to all of us.'

I promise to come by with a copy as soon as I'm ready.

A few days later, I meet with Nargiss. Fatima has called me and asked for a meeting. All of a sudden they're standing there inside the container by security. I chuckle gleefully at the sight of Nargiss's big, round, pregnant stomach. She sends me a coy smile, only then to cover her mouth with her hand.

I serve tea and cake. Nargiss wolfs down the cake and puts the leftovers in her pocket. We exchange a few introductory pleasantries, after which I allow her to sit and watch me while I speak to Fatima. Nothing of what has been said so far could not have been said a lot easier over the phone. Yet the two women have driven more than thirty kilometres to get here, passing through an area plagued by robbers. It's clear to me that this is about something else entirely. Fatima has brought Nargiss with her so that she can look me over.

A week later, Nargiss calls me herself and requests a meeting. I follow the exact same procedures with her as she has seen with Fatima. I pick her up at the main gate and we retreat to the same room. It's the same interpreter, the same tea, the same cake.

Nargiss has married into Fatima's family. The two women's husbands are cousins. Nargiss's husband must be fairly wealthy, having a house with his first wife in Gereshk's bazaar and another with Nargiss in a village on the eastern side of the Helmand River. The two wives are not the best of friends.

A few months ago, Nargiss managed to gather together the women of her village. Together they make jewellery out of colourful glass beads. She hands me a lovely twisted armband.

I ask how the village reacted to the women's decision to make jewellery and earn money.

'I knew you would ask,' she says, and pushes a crumpled piece of paper towards me over the table.

It's a declaration of the village council. Surprisingly enough, the men of the village support Nargiss and her project. Nargiss would like us to help with the project, but that's not why she's here, she says. She has information about the Taliban.

I'm startled. The identity of the woman who told me about the suicide bomber has been known to me for some time. Nargiss is a completely new acquaintance. Nonetheless, she wants to help us. The jewellery project comes second.

Other things strike me too. Nargiss is relatively well dressed. Her mobile phone is one of the newest models. I assume it's a gift from her husband.

Nevertheless, she spins her own yarn to be used in her jewellery production. This is a woman who insists on her independence, no matter what the cost.

I explain to Nargiss that I would be grateful for any information she might have that could help my colleagues in fighting the Taliban. However, I can't promise that a patrol will be there in the morning. In fact, I can't promise her anything at all, only that in time her information will be put to use. I tell her that we will take care of what she divulges to us, but that she must take care of herself. She must not do or say anything that might arouse the suspicions of the Taliban.

Clearly relieved, Nargiss nods and begins to speak. Arms have recently been delivered to the village on trucks. Nargiss doesn't know what sort, but she calls them missiles. They are long, longer than a man, perhaps as long as two, and there's Iranian writing on the sides. Her husband conducts business and knows what Iranian letters look like. It is he who has seen what's been going on. He is afraid and believes that the Taliban presence and the trafficking of arms, which he thinks are now being stored in a depot in the village, are putting the area at risk.

Nargiss doesn't know where the arms are being kept and she is too afraid to ask her husband. I nod. This is a difficult one. Her information is vague. Rumours of major weaponry, often old Russian anti-aircraft guns, coming into Helmand have often circulated without anything ever being turned up. On the other hand, we are obliged to take the information seriously. Once again I make my way over to HQ. The bald sergeant with the yellow pencil behind his ear gets to his feet straight away.

'Nice to see you again, Ma'am. I'm sorry, I didn't actually get round to introducing myself. My name's John.' He puts out his hand. 'What have you got for us today, then?'

'Well, I'm afraid it's a bit vague, but apparently Iranian arms are coming into a village called Noorzai, east of the Helmand River and north of Highway 1.'

'OK, let's have a look, then,' says John, and pulls the yellow pencil from behind his ear.

The days pass. Nargiss appears several times, each time with new information and from various sources. I draw up an application to the development fund and the Helmand Executive Group as regards securing support for Nargiss's jewellery project. She is reluctant to ask her husband for help to buy yarn and small fasteners for the items the women make. All the jewellery is closed by safety pins or press studs. The yarn is uneven and snaps easily. The women tie knots in it and carry on the intricate work with the tiny glass bead. But the knots are blemishes on the final result. I give Nargiss a roll of nylon cord I've brought with me from home. It's like a thin fishing line and very strong. Unfortunately, I've no fasteners.

The development fund turns down the application. Her village lies in an area considered unsafe and the powers that be apparently don't seem to think the place is ready for trailblazing female liberation. I'm angry and disappointed. Nargiss shrugs. She is determined to carry on, help or no. And she continues to tell me about the Taliban trafficking routes and anything else she knows.

Twice, John tells me that the information the women have contributed has been essential to the broader picture, adding crucially to existing intelligence. In both instances, the information is considered so compelling, the brigade sends in Special Forces against a specific house and a specific building.

One evening when I've gone out to find Hazel, I'm stopped by a tall and rather charming officer. He tells me that Special Forces are going to strike that night against an arms depot about which Nargiss has provided me with information.

'You can come over and watch if you like. They're your contacts,' he says.

'How do you mean watch?' I ask.

'Surveillance camera. We monitor the operation with a little drone. It's not normally as exciting as it sounds. No big bangs, no dramatic soundtracks,' he chuckles.

I watch a series of shimmering green night images of a building being stormed, an arms depot. Or rather, what used to be. The Taliban have moved most of their hardware out. Nevertheless, there seems to be satisfaction all round. Five roadside incendiaries are confiscated. Five Hazel won't have to send people out to remove, five Gary won't have to dismantle and itemize for future reference. A few handguns, some money and some passports were also found.

I deliver my knowledge and someone else acts on it. It's exactly what the women expect. Often they are impatient after having revealed that, this or the other person is involved in this, that or the other. How come we still haven't done anything? But all information has to be confirmed by other sources. Often it's best to observe the little fish to find out where the big ones are.

After meeting with Nargiss and other women I sometimes need to go out into the garden behind the CIMIC unit and think about what I'm doing. The intention behind our work was never to turn the women we help into informers. The idea was to help them create a better life.

But there's no holding them. No one has more to lose if the Taliban come to power than the women and children. No one will pay a higher price. The children will lose the right to go to school. The women will lose the right to go to work and to have a presence in public.

The *shura*s and the various projects initiated combine to get women talking to each other. At one meeting with Fowzia, I realize she now has contact with eighteen women's groups meeting in Lashkar Gah and in Gereshk. When we began only three months ago there were four.

At first, the women do little more than meet and complain about their circumstances. Gradually, increasing numbers decide to try something new. Some apply for funding for projects they devise. Some are helped by us, some by Fowzia and the ministry in Kabul. Sometimes all they get is moral support, but even that makes a difference. And still there are women who choose to approach us because they possess information they think may help us get rid of the Taliban. The international soldiers are the only ones the women can see who are prepared to fight the Taliban on their behalf.

I talk to Sarah about it.

'Do you know what?' she says. 'To tell you the truth, we've actually considered taking some of them away from you and using them solely as informers. But you're doing a great job. They know you and they trust you. It would take us at least six months to establish the kind of trust you've got going with them. And remember, intelligence isn't your responsibility, it's mine. All your women have to do is make sure they look after themselves. If they want to help us, then fine. But they must never put their lives in danger.'

I nod. I'm glad Sarah's the one in charge of the intelligence section. Her morals are robust and she's as sharp as a knife. God have mercy on the poor soul who decides to do something daft and put themselves and others at risk when she's in charge.

Because the women's groups have become so numerous, and because we still lack insight into how Afghan families really work and the role women play in the home, I devise a questionnaire along with a female British officer. We go through it with Fowzia, who then passes it out among the women. Most are unable to read, but if the leader of each group reads the questions out loud, they're more than willing to provide answers.

We learn heaps about their income, levels of education and the frequency of violence in the home. The UN organization UNIFEM has conducted surveys showing that 87 per cent of women in Afghanistan suffer violence in the home. Our figures are lower, perhaps because women who take part in *shuras* are women who already enjoy a certain amount of freedom.

Nevertheless, 65 per cent of our women say they experience domestic violence. Two more things become apparent. Most of the women are financially independent of their husbands or male family members. Their greatest wish is for a better future for their children and an education from which they can benefit themselves. They want to learn. And they want to earn their own money.

Finding the right projects isn't always easy. The women need to be committed to the extent that they're willing to dig in their heels when meeting resistance from male members of the family. The project has to be something that can provide income, yet be feminine enough to keep the men from stealing the idea. Moreover, the business must be able to be run from home and not take up too much space. No woman would ever have a stall in the bazaar, even though legislation allows it. A female shop owner would be so much in breach of the Taliban religious view that they would make a point of killing her.

One woman I support in Lashkar Gah opened a beauty parlour in her home. She is a very shy and reticent woman who had pondered the matter for a very long time. Her husband was against the idea, only to capitulate completely on seeing the results. Now he can't resist his beautified wife. I bump into him now and again when I'm out on other projects. Whereas before he would say that women were unfit to run a business, he now enthuses about the divine nature of the organization whereby Allah has made women beautiful so men can derive pleasure from them.

It's a small-scale project: six women meeting in the home of the woman to receive training. They buy cosmetics, mirrors, exfoliants and artificial flowers they hire out to weddings. It doesn't look like much on paper. But it snowballs. Girlfriends make appointments and ask their husbands for money on all sorts of pretexts. One man after another bows down when his woman comes home with gorgeous eyes, red lips and smelling sweetly of perfume. In a very short time I learn from the shy woman's husband that sending your wife to the beauty salon has become a status symbol. It's a shift, however slight, in the balance of power.

Encouraged by the results, I apply for funding for a similar project in Gereshk, this time for twenty women. The application is successful and I'm given the money. The beauty revolution is on its way.

Fowzia is now running a course in English for eighty women. To the astonishment of their teacher, many of the women secretly listen to the BBC when their husbands are at work, so some of them are actually quite good at it. He divides them into four classes of twenty, each receiving an hour's teaching a day, four days a week. The teacher is a former interpreter for the international forces, but now has his own carpentry business as well as teaching English on the side. It's a fairly well-paid job, though nothing like what he could earn doing carpentry. On the basis of the contracts he's entered into with us for providing school furniture alone, he earns three times as much as if he had bought a field for his savings and grown opium.

He charges two dollars more per piece than other carpenters we know, but his work is long-lasting. Forty-five dollars for a bench and desk for two children. He has six people working for him and he delivers on time. Even so, he considers his four hours of teaching each day to be time well spent.

Through meeting with him to discuss furniture orders I'm able to keep abreast of how things are going with the English course. When we start a second course, women turn up who can't even read or write Pashto or Dari. They don't care. They want to learn something. We start a reading course, and I discover that only half the women tell their husbands they receive instruction. The other half don't believe they'd be allowed, so they come without bothering to ask.

The results of our questionnaire and of the women's projects initiated by the CIMIC team are to be put forward in a symposium to take place at military regional headquarters in Kandahar. The theme of the symposium is so-called psychological operations, i.e. efforts to gain influence over the Taliban and local populations by means of anything from flyers to radio programmes, from propaganda to teaching.

My British colleague who helped with the questionnaires takes part on our behalf. Her briefing receives a standing ovation.

She tells excitedly of the reactions as soon as she gets back, but none of it sinks in. I could really do with the kind of appreciation and acknowledgement she found in Kandahar. In this unforgiving war, I am beginning to flag, and many of the battles I fight seem increasingly to be uphill struggles.

15

WOMEN AND THE LAW

'A little civilian chap's been asking for you,' says Torben as I enter the office. 'George, I think he said.'

'Oh? Who is he?'

'No idea.'

'What did he want?' I ask.

'Didn't say. Only that he'd come back another day. What are you up to?'
'Nothing. I've really no idea who he might be,' I insist.

I leave the office shaking my head. I've been out on patrol and it's not my fault if civilian advisers sidestep the normal channels and speak to me directly instead of going to Lars first. But I can sense Lars and Torben are increasingly annoyed by it. It worries me.

George turns up again a couple of days later, again while I'm on patrol. I try to find him so as to get an edge, but he finds me first.

He's in his mid-forties, a head shorter than me and regular-looking. His work consists of advising local authorities how to go about setting up a decent legal system. My first thought is how huge a challenge it must be in a country in which the Taliban want sharia law and members of the incumbent government and most of the police are corrupt.

I ask him straight out what he wants.

'What do I want?' George hesitates. 'Well, I've been holding *shura*s for men around the province to get an idea of how they look at the legal system, how it works in practice, what kinds of problem they encounter and so on. But there are never any women there.'

'So you'd like to invite women to a *shura*?'

'If at all possible, yes. If that was something they would be interested in. It would be fantastic.'

He sends me a glance and holds back, as though things might be moving too quickly now. But then adds: 'I'd like to get an impression of the consequences for women, find out how they see things, whether they find it credible at all.'

'I think we should do it. We'll hold a *shura*. No problem,' I say.

'Really? You make it sound so easy.' He laughs. 'They told me you were the one to speak to.'

I feel a sudden warmth inside. The recognition contained in those words is just what I needed.

'Do you know any women in Gereshk? Would they be interested in a meeting, do you think?'

'Loads. And they'll definitely come.' 'Interesting,' he says, nodding pensively.

I ask him why he's interested in Gereshk in particular.

The tone of his voice when he replies is as flat as a pancake: 'The problems we have in Gereshk are fully comparable to those I've witnessed in other countries in South America and Africa. Meaning, we've got judges there who are so corrupt and incompetent that the law has no validity. We know who they are. But the consequences are that offenders can pay their way out of murder, violence and all sorts of other crimes. The upside is that we know what's going on. We want to put pressure on the government to get rid of these people.'

'Is it really that bad?' I ask.

'Worse. There's one in particular I'm hoping we can get shot of as soon as possible, if I can put it like that.'

'Will you be able to?'

'Well, it's by no means an easy task. What we need is tangible evidence, otherwise we can remove neither police nor members of the judiciary, that being an internal matter for Afghanistan alone. But of course there's nothing to stop us pointing to certain deficiencies and breaches of practice. That way, through the advisory system, and through political and diplomatic channels, we may conceivably be able to exert pressure on government to eradicate corrupt and badly functioning elements.'

I'm at once fascinated and slightly annoyed by this man, who talks like a government bill. He reminds me of my Latin textbook at school, and brings back memories of sitting hunched over exquisite sentences in Latin and trying vainly to bring them forward into the modern age.

Yet there's also something fascinating about a man who can speak of murder, rape and corruption without being in the slightest bit affected by it. It's the order of the day. It goes on, here and now and again tomorrow.

George seems like the type who keeps on going without ever yielding or giving up. The sort who could never get depressed or angry. He's like a little lawnmower in a big field. The task may be daunting, but you've got to start somewhere.

'Do you want to find a date?' I ask.

His eyebrows pop up over the top of his glasses, as though this is just too easy.

'Can we do that now?' he asks, incredulous.

'Of course. The women might not see the point entirely, but they'll definitely come. The question is what can you deliver in return? If they turn up with evidence, what will you be able to do?'

I'm given a long diatribe about not being able to promise anything. George is, however, willing to say that he's 95 per cent certain that the judge in question will be relieved of his duties within two months following pressure from various channels. I think how amazing it would be for the women to meet in council, deliver evidence and then witness such a tangible result of their coming together as the removal of a corrupt judge.

That would surely fire an interest in engaging in politics.

George and I decide on a date, agreeing on a Thursday, which is the day the women usually prefer. If they don't feel like telling their husbands where they're going, they can always say they're off to the baths or to visit family before the Friday. That kind of double bookkeeping is a common way of avoiding reprimand or physical punishment.

George nods appreciatively as I tell him about it. He looks like a man who wouldn't knock a fly off course without having first consulted animal rights legislation. We must seem a pretty odd couple: a tall woman with a pistol strapped to her thigh and this little man clinging to his briefcase.

A couple of days later I approach one of our interpreters and explain to him that I need to call some women and invite them to take part in a meeting.

'OK, Miss AC,' he says, most likely thinking it's business as usual. Both of us, however, are in for a surprise.

We call Fowzia first. As official women's contact, she's the right place to start. She answers straight away and after a few pleasantries I get to the point.

'Fowzia, I'd like to invite the women to a big *shura* at the Bost Hotel next Thursday.'

'That sounds like a good idea,' Fowzia says.

'It's a rather special *shura* this time. I'd like to invite a lawyer who is very interested in hearing your views on the legal system.'

The interpreter turns to me in astonishment. Is that correctly understood, that I want to know what the women think about the law? I nod. He translates.

Fowzia falls silent. Then hesitantly she says: 'I don't know if that would be a good idea.'

'I'm not sure she understands what you mean,' says the interpreter, then adds: 'I'm not sure I do myself.'

I explain that we're aware of some problems with certain members of the judiciary. We know the views of the men on the law, but not what the women think, and we don't know what kinds of problem they encounter in that respect.

Fowzia sidesteps, but eventually agrees, albeit reluctantly, to send out the invitation. There's a proviso, though: she wants to consult the provincial governor first and hear his views on the matter. My thoughts are that something is very wrong. Normally, Fowzia is very subdued, not the kind who goes charging off, but still. I can't see why the governor should be dragged into this at all.

I call Gulaley. She doesn't answer.

Then I call Fatima and invite her to our *shura* on the law.

'Why on earth do you want to talk about that?' she asks angrily. 'There's nothing we can do about it!'

'But Fatima, if we don't talk about it, if we don't find out how it affects you and what experiences you have of it, we're never going to get anywhere.'

'You can forget all about it. They're corrupt, the whole lot of them.

Scoundrels and villains, they are. That's how it is, how it's always been, and nothing can be done about it. It will never change!'

'She's very angry. And I think she's angry with you,' the interpreter says. 'This is no easy subject,' he mutters, shaking his head.

'Fatima! You don't have to come if you don't want to, but I'm asking you to come for my sake,' I say as firmly as I'm able.

'I think you should find something else to talk about,' she says. 'Something we can do something about.'

After another fifteen minutes of remonstrating, I manage to talk Fatima into coming, though, as she says, she's only doing it because she knows me and because I'm asking her to. After this battle of wills, my interpreter and I are both exhausted.

I've got the mobile numbers of around twenty women and with each call I make, my mood darkens. Only half even answer and those who do are pretty worked up. I've never known them to be so negative before. It's like going down into the cellar of the house I've got to know so well: now we're approaching the foundations of what is truly wrong with Afghanistan. But the women won't go into the basement. It's dark and damp and filled with unpleasant memories.

Time and again, I explain that I can't promise tangible solutions here and now, but that at the very least the issues must be discussed so that we can gain an understanding of the kinds of problem that exist. But I've got hold of an issue here they are astonished I even dare to mention. It seems to be implicit that speaking the truth about the judge in Gereshk may involve fatal consequences. I think to myself that the very act of putting into words the injustices that are occurring renders them irrevocably real and past recall.

The last of the women I call have already had word. The only positive thing to be said is that they all say they will come for my sake alone. I feel I've laid every ounce of my credibility with these women on the line.

In the little garden behind the CIMIC office I wonder about whether I'm doing the right thing. Will they accuse me of trying to impose Western models on Afghan society over the heads of the Afghans themselves? Will they accuse me of trying to start a women's liberation movement in Helmand? My head feels like a beehive, but the gut feeling is good. I can't explain why, but I know it's a step in the right direction. Even if I am scared to death.

After a couple of days I get in touch with Gulaley.

'I'm sure you've heard I've been trying to get the women together to discuss problems with the legal system.'

'Yes, so I heard,' she says in a quiet voice. I explain to her what I'm trying to do.

'It won't be easy,' she says. 'But I'll do what I can.' That's all she says. Then she puts the phone down. The same day, Fatima calls me.

'AC, some of the women are too afraid to come and meet your lawyer.

They are frightened someone will recognize them.'

'I understand. But I'd be grateful if you would pass on anything they have to say. We need to get to the bottom of this.'

My words echo hollowly and I think to myself I'll be lucky if we just scratch the surface.

'I still don't understand why you're doing this. But I'll be there. I promised you that,' says Fatima.

We agree that if any of the women are in possession of documents from court cases current or past, they should bring them along or send them with those women who are not afraid to turn up themselves.

A couple of days later, Fatima and Gulaley meet with me in the camp when I'm paying out wages for those in the sewing project, as well as the first instalment for equipment for the new beauty salons.

Talk gets round to the coming *shura*, and Gulaley calmly and convincingly explains to Fatima that issues must be confronted if anything is ever to change.

I try not to think of the disaster that potentially lies ahead and cling instead to frail hope. If Gulaley has grasped what is at stake, then other women too will surely understand in time.

16

UNFINISHED BUSINESS

Amid the tumult of planning the third women's *shura* I'm sent off on a three-day patrol with Babaji as the main focus. During September and October I've held meetings with school leaders and others in Babaji. A number of people have turned up at the gate with ideas, suggestions and plans. Security call CIMIC, and all from Babaji are directed to me.

One comes to complain about a gravel road we're laying. It leads to the wrong place and isn't being done properly, the man claims. After a lengthy chat, I realize he wanted the contract himself, but our engineers gave it to someone else. The man is a schoolteacher. He has no experience building roads, but believes nonetheless he could do things a whole lot better.

Out on patrol, I get a chance to take a look for myself. The road is being built in four sections. It's the best gravel road I've seen in my life. It's watered and rolled according to the book and concrete drainage channels are put in underneath. Everyone I speak to along the way is thrilled. It's the most progress they've seen in the area since the irrigation channels were dug over fifty years ago.

The last night on patrol before going back to Lashkar Gah, we spend the night outside Gereshk. We have to drive through the town, going on into the desert east of the river. The Brits have respect for Gereshk. Since coming to Helmand in 2006, the town has suffered more suicide attacks than any other. The Brits are scared out of their wits driving through.

The Danish Battle Group has just assumed responsibility for Gereshk and suicide attacks are frequent. I think of my friend Charlotte sitting in Camp Price. But Gereshk is also the town in which Fatima, Gulaley and many of the other women I know live.

It's three in the morning as we drive into the town along a dark road. The town is windswept and empty. A dog almost frightens the life out of us as it runs into the road and is hit by one of the cars. A few minutes later we rumble over the first bridge that leads us across a canal in the middle of the town. Less than a minute later, we cross the long, flat bridge that stretches across the Helmand River. We turn right and soon afterwards we're out in the desert.

Was that it? I think to myself. Was that the town we're so frightened of?

We bed down in the sand. There are mines in the area, but having open desert around us makes us feel safer.

Next morning at six, the Brits set up a firing range so we can test our weapons and make sure they're still targeting correctly. We've no firing range for carbines at Lashkar Gah, so a cardboard box up against a sandbank makes a target. On our way back, we CIMIC officers begin to smile. We've planned a surprise for the Brits and now, so close to home, we can start to let off steam.

All of a sudden, heavy metal blasts out into the desert from our CIMIC vehicle. 'Thunderstruck' by AC/DC has the British lads out of their cars and leaping around madly in the sand. Others stand gawping until they realize we've got a pair of hefty external speakers on the car and a microphone picking up the music from a laptop. It feels so good to just freak out once in a while.

The Monday morning before Thursday's *shura*, I present my observations and conclusions about the Babaji area to a group of civilian advisers and military bosses.

I'm feeling pressure. The women's *shura* this week is going to be a lot more difficult than I'd imagined when so confidently giving it the go-ahead. The brigade is now well aware of how much information the women provide, and I must balance the needs of the brigade, those of the women and those of my male colleagues who are really pissed off about people sidestepping command structures in order to speak to me. Sometimes people just want to talk because I'm a girl, a fact I can no more change than my male colleagues can help being men. We're halfway into our mission now and people are beginning to get irritable.

I scan the gathering of civilians and soldiers crammed into the little briefing room. The overall civilian boss, David, is here. Sakander is here. Assorted majors and lieutenant colonels are here. I take a deep breath.

I run through where roadside incendiaries have hit and where people in Babaji want schools and other development projects. I recommend that we hold back on investing military resources in the area while the locals seem to have a fairly decent grip and military resources are stretched to the limit. I see a chance of winning wide support in Babaji if only we get started as soon as possible on a number of rebuilding projects, with particular focus on schools. We have the money. The downside is that we haven't got the soldiers.

It seems obvious to me that those areas that keep the peace should be rewarded and that advantages are to be gained by letting less peaceful areas see the green grass on the other side of the hill. I feel convinced people will soon stop opposing the government in Kabul if it shows itself capable of raising quality of life and opening up prospects for the future. I urge the advisers to consider the opportunity of experimenting in this reasonably controllable area with development models that may later prove fruitful in other rural districts further up the Green Zone.

PRT boss David asks a few questions about roadside incendiaries and security in the area. Unfortunately, civilian advisers have limited access to information on attacks, and on the personal level it doesn't interest them much since they don't have to be out there. The military, of course, maps incendiary attacks in minute detail.

Talk of mines and roadside incendiaries impacts negatively on the civilian advisers' conceptions of what can be done in Babaji, though most attacks occur outside the area.

Sakander questions me for ten minutes. I still have no idea where I stand with the man; for all I know, he may very well hate my guts because of my disastrous comments at the meeting of the steering group. Rumour has it that he can be a very serious opponent. I answer his questions as best I can and am glad when it's over.

The next day, Sakander calls me to a meeting behind closed doors. It is impressed upon me that what is being discussed is to be treated in the strictest confidence. Sakander is taken by my proposal to make Babaji a pilot area. It is the first rural district in which we have seen relative stability and a local population that quite remarkably has managed to stave off the Taliban following the Anglo-Afghan operation of March 2007.

Sakander asks a number of intelligent, albeit rather odd questions about possible scenarios in Babaji. It is clear to me that he has plans; that there are certain things he wants me to recommend, but which he is unable or unwilling to divulge. I become increasingly certain of the man's intellectual capacity, though I am no clearer about whether he is actually leading me into a trap or not. My biggest concern is that he bears malice.

After an hour or so, Sakander brings the meeting to a close and sends his secretary out with a pad full of notes. He leans back in his chair and crosses his legs casually while holding me in his gaze.

'You are very reserved. I could even get the impression that you do not like me. Why is that?'

Without doubt, Sakander has by far the greatest analytical capacity I have met. But what's he playing at? I shift uncomfortably in my chair.

Hesitatingly, I mention what happened at the meeting of the steering group. I explain that his little game almost cost me my tour of duty in Helmand and has seriously damaged my superior's confidence in me.

Sakander is genuinely shocked. He apologizes politely and offers to speak to Lars personally. I decline, fearing Lars will take Sakander's approach as a sign of my going behind his back.

Sakander nods pensively. His secretary has mentioned that he is already late for another scheduled meeting. Still, he takes his time. Then he says: 'That steering group has been driving me mad for months. Nothing was getting done. I am glad you spoke out and said what I could see you were thinking. Sometimes it works better when other people say what is on my mind than if I do so myself. I apologize for having landed you in trouble. If you change your mind about allowing me to speak with your superior, please let me know.'

I nod. Sakander gets to his feet and puts out his hand.

'Promise me you will let me know if there should be any sign that you are to be sent home. Your unit may consider itself better served without you. My own opinion is that you are indispensable. Should you encounter difficulties, I would be happy to step in.'

I shake his hand. It's a farewell and an agreement at the same time.

That afternoon, George the legal adviser suddenly appears in the office. He's white as a sheet. I know straight away that he's come to say goodbye. He puts out his hand. His wife is in intensive care in England and a chopper is picking him up in twenty minutes.

He gives me the name of a female adviser who can deputize in his absence and stresses how important the women's *shura* is to him. He wants it to go through. Reading between the lines, he's not expecting to be back.

I pay a couple of visits to the civilian advisers. Women's projects aren't generally accorded priority in war, but this time I'm given everything I ask for. Maybe someone put in a good word for me.

I book the big conference room at the Bost Hotel and make sure tea and cakes are ordered—not by me, but by a cultural adviser who seems to have more clout than a mere army captain. He sees to it that our women's meeting is accorded top priority; this means that a men's meeting in which the mayor and seven other high-ranking officials are to take part is moved to another room. My immediate thought is that moving the men is bound to cause antagonism on the day, and that the mayor and his men are going to end up in the big room anyway, leaving us women to cram into the small conference room.

The evening before the *shura* I'm excited and exhausted at the same time.

The risk is that the women will fight and the council will take a nosedive. Maybe they won't even turn up. Maybe the mayor will put his foot down and throw us out.

Whatever. I've done my best. The die is cast and only Allah knows the outcome.

17
THE THIRD *SHURA*

It's Thursday morning and I'm striding expectantly through the camp, wearing my helmet, combat vest and body armour. I've got my pistol, my carbine and magazines of ammunition, and my pockets are stuffed with the usual standard-issue stuff, as well as the essential notepad and ballpoint pen. In the corner of my eye, I see an Afghan general halt in his tracks and gawp at me, but I'm too busy to pay him any heed.

The patrol leader is poring over his orders, even though we're already late. He has laid a world-record route of zigzags through the town to the governor's compound, where the Bost Hotel is situated. It's going to take us three-quarters of an hours to get there that way, which means we'll be half an hour late. Not the best of starts. The route home, of course, is the most direct.

I clench my teeth and try to keep a cool head. The guy's past it and always miserable, yet he heads up half our patrols. I know he can cancel my future patrols at the drop of a hat with all sorts of excuses if I step on his toes.

Eventually, one of the soldiers suggests we turn the route around and go straight to the hotel. His proposal is accepted. I smile to myself. He'd never have agreed if I'd asked him myself.

My driver, Winther, is full of banter and pulls my leg for being in such a good mood all of a sudden.

'Off to cackle with the other hens, eh? Suppose you'll be talking about hens too, come to think of it.' He laughs.

I just smile. Today, nothing else matters. This is the start of something big! I load my weapon. Winther chain-smokes and tugs on my ponytail.

Next to us we've got ArmorGroup, the civilian security firm that drive the advisers around and act as their bodyguards. They make ready, then roll off in their Land Cruisers with two female civilian advisers who are also taking part in the meeting. One of them I'm not sure about; the other seems OK.

I climb into our car. My interpreter, Javeed, is in the back smiling. I don't think I've ever seen him as happy as these past couple of weeks after his father died. He's the man of the house now and no longer needs to put up with being bossed around by his grumpy old man. Javeed's the jovial type, not always the most industrious, but generally fastidious with his translations; what's more, he doesn't care what the women decide they want to talk about. Other interpreters get embarrassed when a woman tells us her husband slaps her about; a sheepish interpreter just makes things more difficult all round.

After zigzagging our way between donkey carts and the usual white Toyota Corollas that may or may not be bombs on wheels, we turn into the governor's compound and pull up outside the hotel. ArmorGroup have just arrived and the soldiers park so we're facing the gate and can get out again in a hurry.

I give Winther a pat on the back. He finds the book he's reading and yawns ostentatiously. I know he won't be left in peace with it: he and the young Brits are going to be cracking so many jokes he'll have a sore stomach for hours from laughing. One of them said the other day that Winther was the spitting image of his dad. He's now taken the role upon himself, not least in respect of any dad's right to tell his son what to do and how to do it. They're now known by all as Daddy and Sonny and turn themselves into a latter-day Laurel and Hardy at every opportunity.

ArmorGroup's pumped-up minder accompanies the two civilians from the car. He bears an astonishing resemblance to the bodyguards you see on telly: big as chest freezer and mute.

I've brought two women soldiers along with me, Brits both of them.

They're curious to meet the Afghan women, and my thought is that it'll do the women good to see other female soldiers besides me.

Although we're fifteen minutes late, none of the women have turned up. The thought occurs to me that maybe they were here and went away again. But I realize it's not a plausible explanation. They would have called to ask where we were. To make sure, I call Fowzia. She assures me they're on their way, but they wanted to meet at her office first and not everyone is there yet.

We chuck our gear into a corner. The room is big and high-ceilinged. The walls have pictures of Afghan landscapes and there are vases dotted about the place with artificial flowers in them. Some of the plasterwork has crumbled away here and there. Sofas with brown and yellow patterned covers of velvet have been arranged strategically around the room, together with coffee tables of dark wood and blue glass. It must have all been very swish in the 1970s. We push the sofas together to make a big square with room for all of us.

My eyes are on the clock all the time and I call Fowzia three times before I finally see signs of activity on the other side of the glass doors. An elderly gentleman shows the ladies in. I see the shadow of the man from ArmorGroup lurking behind the door. He steps aside for the trail of chirping women and his square head smiles. Hopefully, they all feel well protected by his presence.

I greet Fowzia and am introduced to three women from the provincial council. Running for election and having your face on placards all over town demands great courage for a woman. I have only met one of them before, but all three offer hearty greetings.

Shortly afterwards, Gulaley and Fatima arrive with a small contingent from Gereshk. Fatima sweeps into the room, nodding proudly to those already assembled. She's the biggest prima donna I've ever met. She can be annoying and manipulative, yet she is courageous and her need for attention ensures that she will speak her mind when others are afraid. All in all, twenty-one women attend the *shura*.

Since I called the meeting, it's only natural that I head it up. Originally, the idea was for the Afghan women to steer the *shura*s and decide for themselves how they should proceed. The fact is, though, that they have been ill at ease with their role and in doubt as to what is expected of them. They want to observe first and see how things are done, so they can do the same and be secure in the knowledge that the way they're doing it is right.

I start by telling them what the meeting is for and explain to them that our legal adviser, George, has had to go home because his wife has fallen seriously ill, but that one of his female colleagues is here in his place.

Sakeena, one of the two female civilian advisers, the one I find most amiable, takes over. She's a junior adviser and I sense she's not always at ease among the old male elephants of her legal herd. In that way we resemble each other. I've bumped into her a couple of times when she's been wearing dark glasses and each time I've had the feeling she was hiding tears. She sweeps her short, dark hair behind her ear. No sunglasses today: her brown eyes look out attentively on the assembly.

'As I'm sure you appreciate, we're interested in hearing about the kinds of problem you encounter with judges and the legal system in general. We can't promise that particular things will be done, but we do need to gain a broader understanding of how you find the system in practice. So what kinds of problem do you find yourselves running into?'

The room falls silent for a moment. I feel as though I'm sitting on top of a dam that could collapse at any moment or otherwise remain intact for hundreds of years. I start wondering if we've been too direct.

Fowzia encourages the women to speak freely, to share their views and experiences. Eventually, a large woman from Lashkar Gah plucks up courage.

'It's a big problem for us women that we earn no money, because it means we have no chance of bribing our way to a fair decision in the courts!'

Several others nod their agreement. I catch Sakeena's eye. What a start. Wouldn't the issue here be corruption, rather than lacking the means to pay out backhanders? The main thing is, though, that we're under way: the dam is teetering. A pattern quickly emerges: the women have three main problems with the law.

First, they have no money with which to bribe the judiciary; therefore they lose.

Second, there are no women in the court registries. That alone keeps women well away. They find it unnatural to approach a man, since doing so under normal circumstances is forbidden. Even when they're out shopping they need to be accompanied by a male member of family.

Third, women have no authority. If they do get through to a judge, they will not be taken seriously, regardless of whether they have the law on their side or not. It means that women are faced with the extra burden of having to argue for rights already accorded to them by the Afghan constitution and other legislation. The judges simply fail to uphold the rules of the constitution that accord women the same legal rights as men.

Having been given specific examples, Sakeena asks if the women can imagine a future in which judges are not corrupt and instead are totally attentive to and fastidious about their work. They fall quiet.

'Do you mean like under the Taliban?' one asks.

'No, that's not what we mean. Where we come from, the judiciary works to uphold the law. They receive a decent salary, and if they are corrupt they will be punished and lose their jobs.'

The women nod appreciatively. That would be a good idea. However, as the women of the provincial council explain, it is a state of affairs they hope will come about, but which at present would seem to be a long way off.

'Could you explain a bit more about the judges not being corrupt under the Taliban?' Sakeena asks.

'That was much better. They actually punished the criminals then. And punished them hard. There were no thieves then.'

I think back to when I was fifteen and lived in the countryside in southern Spain, where people still had pictures of Franco on their walls. They said exactly the same thing: there were no thieves then. In the eyes of a law-abiding rural community, military dictatorship solved a lot of problems.

'Would you rather have the Taliban back?' Sakeena asks.

It's a reasonable question. She is calm and composed and it sounds as though she'll have the whole British army pack away their tents and go home with her tomorrow if that's what the women would prefer.

The women are silent, their eyes darting around the room enquiringly.

What do we do if they say yes? I think to myself. But surely not? They hate the Taliban with all their hearts. They hate not being allowed to do anything.

A provincial councillor takes the floor and says: 'No, of course we don't want the Taliban back. What we mean is that we could trust the judiciary then. But innocent people were also punished, especially those who crossed the Taliban. People were hanged in trees and from lamp posts. But ordinary people who looked after themselves and did as the Taliban said still had a fair chance. Now the criminals can bribe their way out of anything. Today many judges are like a shop and those who are right are those who have the most money.'

The women nod.

One woman tells us how her uncle had her husband killed only for the court to rule that the uncle, rather than she, should inherit the man's land. The ruling came after the uncle had paid the judge. Justice is a commodity.

She has lost not only her husband and provider, but also the land that is rightfully hers and which is her sole source of income. In the space of only a few months she has been forced out of her home and has had to send her children to live with relatives able to give them food. She throws her arms into the air in despair, then hides her face in her hands.

The judge George has targeted is mentioned several times, and quite spontaneously. Everyone has heard of him. Instances of murder, bribery, glaring miscarriages of justice and forgery are cited.

'What kinds of case would you bring to the courts ideally?' Sakeena asks.

Razagul from the provincial council takes the floor: 'A good Afghan should endeavour to resolve her problems without recourse to the courts, but in certain cases mediation, whether by the intervention of family, elders or clan councils, fails.'

'What sorts of problem would find their way to the courts?'

The women glance around at one another enquiringly. Many look down at the floor. There's something they are unable to say. They are afraid of bringing shame on themselves and their families. Whoever speaks up now is saying that the things she mentions go on in her own family or in a family with which she enjoys close relations.

Fatima breaks the deadlock: 'Some men beat their wives, and not just in small measures either. You all know that I have been beaten by my own husband and you know that I have had to seek help from the doctor.'

The collective gaze shifts at once from Fatima to Gulaley. All of us know that Gulaley is the one the women go to in cases of domestic violence.

Gulaley's gaze remains fixed to the floor.

Another woman now in tears speaks out: 'My sister is beaten. Her name is Aisha. She is my youngest sister and she has always been like a daughter to me. I always looked after her especially. She was married last year. Her husband is not good to her at all. He is old. We thought he would be gentle and mild, but he is a tyrant. She is so unhappy. But what are we to do? My husband will not interfere.'

Many of the other women nod their understanding. Perhaps they know who she is talking about. I find myself wondering how old the girl is and picture a slender young waif in bed beside a snoring old man. I think of hands moving across her skin, filling her with feelings of duty and terror.

Gulaley clears her throat and the women are at once keenly attentive. 'Honoured sisters ...' Gulaley lifts her gaze to the assembly. 'In my work as a doctor and midwife I see many things I would rather be spared, but which my duty demands I must confront. One of the major problems in our country is that many girls are married off at a time when they are still too young.'

The women nod. Some glance up to see our reactions. I'm aware that now is the time to listen and to keep an open mind. This is delicate enough on its own; Western contempt now would be to bite an outstretched hand.

Gulaley continues, calm and measured: 'Some girls are married as early as eight years old. It destroys them for life. We all know some of these girls. They live in misery. Many die in childbirth.'

It is as though the women have swallowed themselves up. Not a breath is heard. They are filled with shame.

'What are your feelings on what Gulaley says?' Sakeena asks gently. 'What are we to do? We can't stop it,' one woman says.

'Our husbands find it natural,' says another. 'This is the way it has always been.'

'But do you feel it is right or wrong to allow a child to be married when she is only eight or nine years old?' Sakeena asks.

Her pointed use of the pronoun *you* urges them to speak up, to tell us their thought and feelings.

The women are silent. Some lean towards their neighbour and begin to whisper. One stares at her feet. Another weeps.

I can see how difficult it is for them to put this into words. It's an issue that has remained unspoken. Some are in doubt as to whether they even have the right to consider the giving of children in marriage as being reprehensible while all the time men accept it. More examples follow.

Suddenly, the large woman from Lashkar Gah takes the floor.

'I find it wrong to marry off girls so young. It is a bad custom! As women we must fight to do something about it. It is not right that the foreign soldiers should come here and put their lives at risk without us doing our own share to make this land a proper country with respect for people.'

I should be used to it by now, but it always surprises me to hear how much support and respect we enjoy in the eyes of the Afghans. Another source of constant amazement is how suddenly the decision-making process often gathers momentum. When long-suppressed emotions or opinions become conscious thoughts and are uttered in public, the women are like a shoal of fish suddenly changing direction as one collective organism.

They still feel shame. But now it's been said.

Child marriages are outlawed by new legislation but mothers still have a hard time preventing them. I can tell from their faces that all the women here are familiar with the problem, but the fact that the law says girls must be eighteen before being married is completely new to them.

Domestic violence is another serious problem, the women agree. Razagul points out that radio programmes providing information for women—and indeed men—about Islam's views on the issue could be an advantage.

Verses of the Qur'an giving men the right to beat their wives are widely known. Yet women are generally unaware that the Qur'an also states that a man must treat his wife with respect.

It takes less than a minute for the women to reach the conclusion that education and information are the way forward. They expect no immediate change. But if the future is to be any different, change must begin now.

Helmand has no university and the culture precludes the idea of girls studying away from home. At the same time, the province is faced with the problem that when suitable young women are put forward for foreign scholarships, the Ministry of Education in Kabul routinely selects a young man or woman from another province.

The women are of the opinion that Kabul sees the people of Helmand as Taliban supporters. If you're from Helmand, then by definition you're also a peasant, a traditionalist, someone who hinders growth, involved in crime and a religious fanatic.

It's a national prejudice that continues to flourish.

I lean back on the sofa and gaze around the assembly. An hour and half has passed and we've come a lot further than I'd dared to hope.

Compared to the problems faced by the child brides, the fact that six of the women present have received death threats from the Taliban is accorded little attention. Fowzia's driver was killed in an assassination attempt two years before.

We've long since run out of time. The big muscleman sticks his head round the door and gives me a nod. Time to go. I look around at the women; they've all sussed that the big guy wants us to get going.

'Your views are extremely valuable to us in our continued advisory work in the judicial area. I realize how difficult it has been for you to talk openly about the things we've discussed today, but you have taken a huge and important step towards creating a better Afghanistan. We would like to be able to go on, but unfortunately time dictates that we must return to base,' I say by way of conclusion.

The women seemed sad and mutter quietly among themselves. Fowzia shushes them.

'Thank you for coming, and thank you for being here in our country, far from your families. You are a source of great inspiration to us,' she says, and smiles.

I pull on my body armour and my combat vest, and grab my carbine; get my earpiece and microphone in place so I'm in radio contact again. As the two Brits and I make the transformation from girls in desert khakis to Amazons in armour, the women gather round and watch us admiringly.

'You are our woman warrior!' one of them laughs.

'Aren't you afraid? The Taliban can see who you are, and your hair sticks out from under your helmet.'

'You are so very brave. If only we were like you,' they say.

Inside I'm brimming with respect for these women, whose lives are so hard, yet who are clearly so fond of me.

'You're the ones who are brave. I'm giving you six months of my life, but you must live here. You didn't flee to Pakistan. You stayed. And you're brave because you speak out and say what you think.'

The women thank me and proudly draw themselves up.

Just as I'm about to leave, one of the women from the provincial council pulls me aside and asks if I can teach her to shoot.

'All of us who are voted on to the council are issued with a pistol for self-defence, but we're given no instruction in how to use it,' she says, and opens her bag slightly for me to see. Inside I can just make out a Russian Makarov snuggling next to a lipstick and a little mirror.

'I always carry it with me. It makes me feel better, but I must confess I have no idea what to do with it.'

She shrugs dejectedly.

I'm surprised, but shouldn't be: why shouldn't dishing out arms to politicians be just as natural as giving five-year-old boys guns for their birthday? Not that the boys are allowed to use them, but later their fathers will teach them to shoot. No equivalent tradition exists for five-year-old girls, so the female members of the council are at a disadvantage.

I don't think it'll make that much difference in the long run, but I'm sure it would improve the self-confidence of the women considerably if they were actually able to use the kilogram of iron that weighs down their handbags. I promise to ask the PRT if they could organize a course.

One of the women gingerly touches my carbine.

'Is it a real gun? Can you really shoot?'

I laugh and nod. Beside me, the two British girls are involved in similar discussions. We're their heroes.

Outside on the step, the women gather to have their picture taken. They're wearing their burkas but lift up the veils to show their faces. This is how they leave the *shura*: in high spirits. As they come by our vehicles, I wonder to myself if they will pull down their veils, but they do not.

The British soldiers don't know where to look. Many of them have never before seen the face of an Afghan woman. They know they're not supposed to look, but what can you do when the women pass by only a few feet away?

Winther takes it in his stride. He's the one who's been around the most, and he revels quietly in the warm gazes he receives from some of the women when they notice his vivid blue eyes. Most of the lads, however, fall silent and try to look as though they're busy at the vehicles all of a sudden. Some remain standing and take in the sight: a bunch of women old enough to be their mothers, striding out into a society in which a woman must be covered and risks being killed for voicing her opinion.

The moment the women reach the gate it's burkas down.

18

CALLED HOME

Andrea's ragging me after the third women's *shura*. Not because of the *shura* itself, more because of the Afghan general who saw me dashing through the camp with a pistol and carbine on my way to my women. Andrea has it from the escort officer that General Mhajadin's sunglasses slid all the way down his nose as he stood gaping. Whereupon he apparently declared: 'I want some of those in my army!'

Andrea is convinced I'm well on my way to being married off to General Mhajadin for a considerable number of dromedaries. My own thoughts are that regrettably it's going to be a long time before we see women in the Afghan army, despite there being a woman general in Kabul, a parachutist and one of only a few hundred women who enlisted in the 1980s.

I've only a couple of weeks to go before I'm due home on leave and I can't wait. I miss my younger brother especially. He's a UN observer in the Lebanon. The welfare phones can only be used for calls home to Denmark, so I haven't heard his voice since I left. Every few weeks or so he descends from his patrol base on some mountainside and goes into one of the bigger towns where he can buy things and use the Internet. We keep in touch on Messenger. I'm completely off guard and thrilled when all of a sudden he's online one evening.

'Hey, Sis, how's it going?'

'Hey, great to hear from you! Things are OK here. Doing reports. You?' 'Dead busy. Spoken to the folks?'

'No. Will call them later.' 'OK. Any news?' he asks.

'Going to have a big glass of juice,' I write. Juice is our code for patrol.
'How big?'

'Long delivery time for juice. This lot has to be flown in. I'll have half a litre or so pretty soon,' I write. Now he knows the patrol includes helicopter transport and that I'll be away for about five days.

Later that evening I step into the little cubicle where the welfare phone is.

Afghanistan is two and a half hours ahead in the summertime, so I'm sapped by the time I manage to get hold of my mum. She's well, she says, and my dad's doing fine with his dialysis. They're both looking forward to me coming home. I say hello from my brother before saying goodnight.

This is not a regular patrol. There's a party of journalists visiting the Danish Battle Group at Camp Price and the press officer wants a CIMIC officer along. I get chosen. More than likely it has to do with being a girl. Torben makes no bones about it.

'All politics,' he says, and shakes his head. 'Have a nice time.'

Lars is home on leave and Torben's in charge. Maybe I can get on to a patrol in the Green Zone. Whatever, five days away from camp is an offer most would jump at.

Next morning, Torben's finally managed to get me a helicopter ride. The office is full of people checking emails and making plans for the patrols coming up. I'm on my knees in front of the computer our internal mail system runs off. I write to the Danes at Gereshk and tell them I'll be landing the next morning.

I'm getting too old to be kneeling down on concrete floors. I look round for a chair, but they're all taken. Somewhere beyond the faint hum of computers I pick out a ringtone. It's one of our phones, the satellite from Denmark. Usually it'll be HOK, Army Operational Command, kicking up a fuss or wanting information about something or other, preferably yesterday. I just happen to be around, so I take the call.

'CIMIC, AC.'

A pause. Then the guy introduces himself. I catch something about the communications centre back home in Vordingborg.

'Is this Anne-Cathrine?' The guy in Vordingborg sounds unsure of himself, ill at ease with the situation.

A thousand thoughts run through my mind. Vordingborg is the place next of kin get in touch with in emergencies, when they need to get hold of family stationed abroad. I think back to the night I left, the night my mum, my brother and I made an agreement. Message as quickly as possible, whatever the circumstances, however unpleasant.

'Has something happened to my brother?' I ask.

'No, your brother's fine, but he was worried as to whether you'd still be there. You're due off on patrol soon, yeah?'

It's not that. That much I know. Something's up. Is my dad in a bad way?

Has my mum been in an accident?

'You're to call your brother. He wants to speak to you.' 'What number can I reach him on?'

'He's on his own mobile. I've got it here—just a sec.'

Torben looks up. There's the faint sound of a voice on the welfare phone in the cubicle next door. Torben points in the direction and sends me a quizzical look. I shake my head. No need to chase whoever it is out. A single stride and I'm at the chief's desk, grabbing the phone, punching the number.

'Sis, that was quick. Have you heard?' 'Heard what?'

'Dad died last night.'

I'm sitting with the notepad with my brother's number on it. My hand writes: DAD DIED LAST NIGHT. The words look all wrong. Tears fall on to the paper. Small, hard drips.

It's a long time since my dad stopped being violent. Not that he didn't still terrorize his family. He was an old man. Tired and intractable. But he was my dad. I weep out of shock and sorrow. I wish I could have said goodbye. That's what gets me the most: I never said goodbye.

After the call I just stand there, punctured, in the middle of the office. My cheeks are wet. I don't know what to do with myself. Torben puts his arms around me.

'I'm sending you home,' he says.

I hand on my contacts, all my meetings, all my projects to two British girls. I pack a bag and leave a note for the girls in the room saying I've gone home. It's still unreal to write: 'My dad died last night.'

Around midnight I'm standing at the head of a long line of thick-set Nepalese Gurkhas off home on leave. It's gusty and the choppers are late. I lean into the wind. I'm at the front, priority because serious illness or death takes precedence over ordinary leave. The soldiers behind me have been in battle. They want to go home too. I think about some of them maybe having seen their mates get killed. My dad's dead. But he died of natural causes at a good age. I hope the Gurkhas get home all right.

Inside an empty Coke bottle lashed to an iron stirrup in the concrete at my feet, a small green snap light shines in the night. There's one at each corner of the little landing area. I turn round and gaze back at the waiting area, noticing a similar Coke bottle attached to a radio mast on high. That one's red. In the left pocket of my combat vest I have a number of snap lights just like them, as well as a couple of infrared lights. Light is a whole language of its own. In battle, lights can tell a helicopter where to pick up casualties. But no light can tell anyone about my dad.

We hear the choppers before we see them. They come in low over the town like two overgrown insects, blacker than the night. I pull on my goggles. The thrust of a Black Hawk can't be imagined. Then they come, thundering over the container town, blades beating a thick wall of dust and dirt from the earth in front of them. Noses to the ground, they seek us out. Small stones fly into the air towards me. A guy from the ground crew waves us forward, indicating for us to run.

'Drop your bags!' The co-pilot is out of the cockpit now. His round helmet, the dark visor where his eyes should be, makes him look like another insect.

I've no idea why we're supposed to dump our packs, but I do as I'm told, let the pack fall to the ground and clamber inside on to one of two primitive benches. My hands find the seat belt and click the four straps into place in the round buckle at my waist.

We're four on each bench, facing each other. The heads of the Gurkhas reach to my shoulders. Then comes our luggage, flying into the cabin.

Backpacks and holdalls thrown on to our laps, piled up to the roof. The whirring of the engine's suddenly different and then we've left the ground.

We sweep fast over the short strip of concrete, over the gravel, then rise sharply upwards, almost on our side, as though it were a show. This is my first time in a Black Hawk and its maneuverability surprises me. We zigzag into the desert.

I lose track of time. An hour passes, maybe two. There's so much luggage I can't see my watch. All I know is we're flying tactically. The pilot follows the contours of the landscape, hugging the ground. We swerve from side to side, but I don't care. I'm tall enough to be able to see out of the window beyond our packs. Endless desert, blue night. Sandbanks and narrow riverbeds. Now and then I catch sight of the other chopper or its shadow.

Always in pairs, ready to defend or to attack. The noise is excruciating. I'm wearing my moulded earplugs, but I can still hear that this is a machine with flying hours. There's a sharp, piercing sound like an electric drill on metal. I scan the impassive faces of the Gurkhas around me. They're exhausted. We stare blindly into the night. Lost in our own thoughts.

We reach Kandahar at two in the morning. A Danish staff sergeant picks me up and will drive me to quarters where there's a vacant bunk. On the way he tells me he can't get me out of the country until the following evening.

There's a British TriStar leaving for the UK, from where I go on to Copenhagen by SAS.

He takes me to an accommodation container, shows me the bathroom and the room in which I'm to sleep. I'm thinking about my dad. I haven't spoken to my mum yet. My brother says she sat up at the hospital all night.

Next morning I finally get hold of her. She's calm. I call a couple of friends in Denmark. On and off I cry, often at the most inconvenient times. But after a while I settle down.

At lunch I run into Sarah. As chief intelligence officer for Helmand, she's in Kandahar to meet with colleagues from the four provinces covered by Regional Command South. They're planning a strike against Musa Qaléh, the last of the bigger towns in Helmand still under Taliban control. Sarah knows what I'm doing in Kandahar. She's spoken to Andrea and Hazel. It's nice to see her and say goodbye.

Later on, I bump into Sakander. We sit down and drink coffee together.

He's immaculately dressed in a dark suit and white shirt. I find myself wondering how he manages to keep up appearances in the middle of a desert. For him, being posted to Helmand perhaps isn't that much different from his next diplomatic job, though here security is another story, transport is by helicopter and there isn't a cocktail party in sight.

'So it finally happened,' he says.

I'm not sure if he's talking about my dad or the strike against Musa Qaléh that's just been given the go-ahead.

'How do you feel about it?' he asks.

I've come to regard Sakander as a friend this past month. I sip my iced coffee and try to address the emotions that are flapping around inside me. We've spoken about my dad before, and about Sakander's father, who is also dead and who played a similarly dominant role in his own family.

A few hours later I check in my luggage. We're in a big hangar filled with exhausted British servicemen going home on leave. Someone puts a cup of tea in my hand and I smile. No Brits without tea, not even when they're at war.

Then there's an enormous explosion.

Mortar, I think to myself. But not as close as the night we sat watching a movie, and nowhere near as close as another day when all the buildings shook and Charlie Company claimed it was an F-16 flyover.

The Danish staff sergeant comes hurtling in: 'Helmets and body armour! Mortar attack!'

He takes it a good deal more seriously than the rest of us. On average there's a rocket or mortar attack on Kandahar once a week. Calm, I put on my helmet and vest. It strikes me how we are all used to it. We carry on drinking our tea and reading our newspapers, waiting to hear if there are casualties, whether the attack's going to put back our flight.

The crew have elected to leave the plane and have taken cover on the ground, but no damage has been sustained. The strike has been localized and we get off pretty much on time. The crew don't want to hang around Kandahar airport any longer than is absolutely necessary.

'British Rail could learn a thing or two here,' a British officer comments. 'Yeah, mortar attacks do bring out the best in folk,' another Brit replies drily, then downs the contents of his mug.

I'm picked up in Copenhagen by my brother. Together we drive to Fyn. I'm tired, but glad to see the family.

In the hospital chapel we each lay our right hand on my dad's frozen chest. Some people say they don't like to see their loved ones when they're dead. They want to remember them as being alive. I remember my dad being alive. But if I hadn't seen his body, I'd have found it difficult to understand he was dead.

We lay him to rest on 29 November 2007. The same day, two privates of the Reconnaissance Squadron's 2nd Platoon are killed while on patrol in the Upper Gereshk Valley. They were under fire for an hour. Home in Jutland, a motorist is killed by a ghost driver on the E45. Osama bin Laden urges the European countries to pull out of Afghanistan.

I think about death, but nothing can change my basic position. I'm in Afghanistan because I can do something that needs to be done. There's a risk I might die doing it. In Denmark four hundred people die each year in traffic accidents and no one raises an eyebrow. Four hundred. Dying in a traffic accident is trivial and meaningless. Dying to help Fatima, Gulaley, Nargiss and all the others find a better life is something else altogether.

Two days after the funeral, *Weekendavisen* carries an article I've written about my efforts with the Afghan women. For me the war is about a whole lot more than bullets and bombs. The war has a purpose and some of our intermediate aims have already been reached. People back home need to know about the results if they are to bear the burden of dead soldiers.

But I find myself appalled by the debate about our mission in Afghanistan. I'd no idea how misleading it was, how much attention there is on coffins.

The dead deserve attention for the choice they made. The families deserve care. But media coverage of the war draws a picture of a pitiful effort without progress. I get the impression that the Danes have dug themselves into trenches and are being picked off one by one. It sounds as though the Taliban attack us at will.

I feel I should write ten articles instead of two. But I know I haven't the strength to play correspondent alongside my quiet little job in the middle of the war.

During the autumn of 2007, the Danish Battle Group carries out a series of offensive operations. The Danes seek out the Taliban warriors to force them back or eliminate them. They flush the enemy out of the area surrounding Gereshk, pushing them back out of the valley and giving them all they've got.

The Danes are intent on asserting themselves and establishing peace enough for the civilian population to begin to flourish. Soldiers die fighting to make things better for people.

We get killed doing a job of work.

19

HERCULES 210 TO BASTION

The Metro glides to halt at one of the stops just before Copenhagen airport. Snow flurries in through the doors. The group of Danes and Americans next to me gaze in fascination at the big white flakes as they settle on the floor and turn to water. One of the Americans, a black guy, turns to face me.

'Where you going, soldier?' 'Helmand, Afghanistan,' I tell him.

The doors close. It's 2 January 2008. Five weeks have passed since my father's death and I'm on my way back to war.

'Isn't that where people are getting killed?' a pretty Danish girl asks. 'It's where the Taliban are getting their backsides kicked!' I reply. 'Aren't you scared?'

'Not really, no.'

'Did you know anyone who got killed?' 'Three. One I knew quite well.'

I don't feel like talking about the coffins. I'd rather talk about all the good things we're doing. I want away from the isolationist paralysis that says five dead soldiers in five months of battle is an unacceptable price to pay for the freedom of others.

'I work on rebuilding projects, mostly with Afghan women.' 'Does the army really do that? I had no idea.'

'We certainly do, yeah.'

I start telling them about it. They ask questions and add little exclamations.

'Wow, why don't we ever hear about this at home?' 'I suppose bad news sells better than good,' I say.

They wish me luck and say they hope I get through my final stint unharmed.

My two best girlfriends are waiting for me at the airport. One of them passed the gruelling third term of her medical studies just a few hours ago. We're thrilled for her and in high spirits.

I drop my bags on to the conveyor belt and catch sight of one of the wounded Danes, a staff sergeant called Asferg, resting his mutilated leg on a crutch. I give him a friendly pat on the behind and a big hug. He's been home in Denmark for a while. He looks as though he might be on the mend. Asferg injured his leg for the first time in Kosovo. He died, was revived and refused to let them amputate. In Afghanistan he drove over a mine: again, the doctors wanted to amputate, and again he refused. This time, too, he's convinced he'll walk again. Asferg must be the most indomitable person I've ever met.

A lot of soldiers are here to say goodbye. Some are from previous tours. Some are our own. Some had to go back home because their wives couldn't cope with their husbands being in combat. They want to go back and finish the job. But their families have given up.

I stay the night at a military base in Kabul before going on to Bastion by Hercules transporter. The snow is thick and the room I'm sleeping in is bitterly cold. It's only just over a month since I left the warmth of Kandahar. Winter has turned Afghanistan into a different place.

As I stomp up the ramp into the Hercules the next day, I'm buttonholed by one of the crew.

'Hey, there's our air freshener! Come with me!'

I follow the man in the pilot's suit without any idea what he's up to. He points to a narrow set of steps leading up into the cockpit. I give him a quizzical look.

'Come on, keep us company,' he pleads. 'We sleep, fly, fight and shit together. We're desperate to talk to someone else, hear some new stories. Plus you're a girl, if you don't mind me saying ...'

I smile. Fair enough. At least he's honest.

I go up the steps and the moment I stick my head inside the cockpit the words just fly out of me: 'Right, lads. Is this a treat for me or for you?'

The pilot with his back to me quips back: 'I'll let you know once I've had a look at you.'

'Same here,' I tell him.

He laughs and turns his head to greet me, revealing a gorgeously cheeky face and sparkling blue eyes. Definitely a treat for me I think to myself.

The pilot's name is Mike. He introduces me to the others on the flight deck: co-pilot Tom, navigator Luke, and Allen, the loadmaster who shanghaied me. All four crew members have glued Santa hats to the back of their helmets, and the windscreen of the plane is decorated with fairy lights in a variety of colours. It's the kind of insistence on laughter in the face of madness that is so typical of all soldiers. Some of the lads on patrol in the Green Zone gathered together shovels, hoes and other tools and put up a sign saying DIY. No one would be able to stick it without humour.

I'm given a pair of headphones so I can listen in while they make ready. They ask about me, where I'm from, what I do, where I'm based. Mike interrupts. Ready for take-off. I listen in on communication with the tower. We're given the go-ahead and the plane lunges forward.

'Hey, mate, you forgot to put the hydraulics on,' says Mike. 'Shit, yeah. Thanks. I couldn't figure out why the brakes weren't working,' Tom replies.

I catch myself thinking I'd most likely be better off not being in on all this. Perhaps it would be better just to sit out back, oblivious.

We roll out on to the runway and go through the procedure for take-off. I'm standing up, gripping an iron stirrup by the window with my left hand, my right holding on to a strap behind Mike's seat. And then we're off.

Kabul is surrounded by high mountains from where, in theory at least, anyone with a rocket-propelled grenade could hit a plane if he had anything to aim at. For that reason the cockpit is almost totally dark. I gaze out at the city lights glittering in the valley below and gradually thinning out up the slopes. The mountains are blue-black against the dark blue sky.

As we ascend over the city, small clouds vanish beneath us and stars appear. In the depths of the darkness below, the lights of Kabul are a distant galaxy. My hand, still at the window, becomes icy cold as we ascend. The cockpit is silent but for the necessary communication with the tower.

Suddenly a female voice comes over the airwaves. The lads exchange knowing looks. Luke whispers: 'Wow, she's there …'

'Eagle 4 to Tower. I'm hot, please advise.'

At first I smile. Besides its more libidinous meaning, 'hot' means 'ready to bomb' in military aviation terms. I gaze down at the lights of Kabul.

From the continued exchange I gradually realize the woman pilot is on her way back from a bombing mission and has run into problems with the weaponry beneath one of her wings. Her voice is crystal clear. It's an advantage women have in war: their voices come through a lot clearer on the radio.

'Five hundred pounds, malfunction,' Eagle 4 replies to the question of the extent of the problem.

'Did it let go of the wing?' the tower enquires.

I imagine her looking out of the window as she answers coolly: 'No, not yet anyway.'

'What about the others?' the tower asks.

'This was the last. The others hit target,' the pilot says. 'Fuel?'

'Low. Very low.'

She has to land in Kabul. She also has problems with the instruments that are to guide her in the dark. We listen to the exchange as we continue our ascent. We see the flashing lights of her wings pass by at breakneck speed as she steers her fighter down between the mountains. Far below, Kabul sends its fire engines to the runway.

We leave Kabul airspace and click on to a different frequency, flying on in silence for a few minutes.

'Is she going to be all right?' I ask. Not knowing the fate of Eagle 4 feels uncomfortable.

Luke replies: 'If anyone can do it, she can. She's one of the best we've got. I don't think I know a single guy here who isn't in love with her. I mean, she's just so cool. Hell of a looker too.'

'Good thing we've got you girls to keep us on our toes,' Mike says, smiling.

Luke hands me a mug of coffee.

'Fancy a doughnut?' he asks, offering a box big enough for four or five six-packs. 'Just got them in Kabul. Yank connections.'

I burst out laughing. It's the small things that count. Dunking doughnuts in fresh coffee is total luxury when you're on your way to war.

For a long time, we've got the sky to ourselves: no other planes, no control tower, just ourselves en route. We fly in over Helmand. I gaze down into the darkness below. Once in a while I see flashes of light.

'That's Sangin.'

Luke hands me a pair of binoculars. The others have pulled down visors. 'There's always fighting there,' I mutter to myself.

It takes a moment to adjust to seeing the world from above, a shimmering green haze, a bit like looking into an aquarium at night. Mike flies in over the Sangin Valley. The base is under attack. It looks like hard combat; a lot of planes have been called in. A huge flash has us all blinded for a moment. I can see tracers and shells exploding. I think of the soldiers running around down there in the dark. Radio messages: aerial support requested.

Hazel's brother is in Sangin. He was there when they took Musa Qaléh.

The others wrote to me and said Hazel was sitting at HQ trying to concentrate on her job all the while her brother was in combat. Many of them kept a constant eye out to see if his number came up among the wounded or dead. All of a sudden I miss Hazel. I hope her brother gets through all right.

We're approaching Camp Bastion in the middle of a ferocious thunderstorm. The atmosphere in the cockpit is tense, the crew concentrating intently.

'You can take her a little bit more to the right, but not much,' says Luke. 'Stop! Steady as you go!'

I see lightning flash just left of the windscreen. Radar shows it up as a yellow and red field extending towards Bastion.

Luke points at it: 'We'll stay well clear of that unless it's a matter of life and death.'

We zigzag our way down to land as the rain lashes against the windscreen. I keep a tight grip on my stirrup and my strap. The wheels touch the ground and the Hercules is allowed to run far down the wet, sandy runway.

'Well, that turned out all right,' says Mike.

'I've never actually tried landing in the rain before,' Tom mumbles.

Yet another piece of information I could have done without. I shake my head and thank them for the lift.

I'm soon on my way again by chopper to Lashkar Gah and before long I'm striding through the camp. Most of those I meet are people I know. They greet me cheerily and say: 'Good to see you again!' I feel welcomed.

In the gloom I can see light round the door of Room 7 and can't help but smile. Naturally, the girls have got the fairy lights on.

I open the door and burst out laughing. I keep on until the tears begin to roll down my cheeks. The place is an indescribable jungle of fairy lights, paper chains and tinsel. The girls have gone ape. It's like living in Santa's grotto.

I chuck my bags on to the bed, unravel myself from various decorations and go off to HQ to find the girls and tell them I'm home.

That evening we get together. The girls ask about the funeral and about Christmas. I thank them for the flowers they sent to my mum. They ask if I had time to see my ex. I nod. But it's definitely over. The girls look sad.

Both Hazel and Andrea are happily married. Soon Sarah too will be off to the altar. I know the girls would really like me to find someone.

'How did your Christmas go?' I ask, changing the subject. They crack up laughing.

'Well, you just wouldn't believe it! It's awful, really,' says Sarah. 'We were on the front page of this dreadful tabloid wearing these ...'

She holds up a plastic hairband with reindeer antlers of brown felt. 'I've never seen anything as stupid in my entire life—and in a national newspaper too. It's all her fault!' Sarah points at Andrea, who is sitting triumphant on her bed.

'You're forgetting you had red noses on too!'

'My reputation as a serious, hard-working officer of the British Army is forever tarnished ...' Sarah can only shake her head.

'I'm sure you must have looked lovely,' I say, laughing. 'Spreading the joy of Christmas!'

'We've had half the camp in here, including the brigadier himself. We've had a good laugh, but we haven't half missed you,' says Hazel.

'Yeah, we're glad you're back,' says Andrea, more seriously than usual.

I've really missed Hazel, Sarah and Andrea. Unfortunately, our time together is limited. While I've been away in Denmark, a decision has been taken to pull all Danish CIMIC personnel up to Camp Price in order to get development going in Gereshk. I don't want to leave Lashkar Gah and my friends at all. I spend a couple of days sorting out six months of accumulated stuff to go in the chopper to Gereshk.

In the evenings Hazel and I gaze up at the stars as usual. Every time we see a shooting star, Hazel takes my hand and says: 'Make a wish, love. Make a wish!' Together we've seen many. But my wish has yet to come true.

The last couple of evenings before I go, Andrea, Hazel, Sarah and I make plans to meet up in Europe once we're all home. Sarah devises an ambitious scheme to invent an operation in Babaji demanding my presence. But there's nothing to be done. We're being split up.

On the morning of 9 January 2008, the Black Hawk settles gently in the sand of the landing area at Forward Operation Base Price, one kilometre outside Gereshk. The co-pilot slides open the door and six months tumble out into the sand in duffel bags and backpacks.

Price is my new home for the last month and a half of my tour. I'm assigned a camp bed in a women's tent that's home for six Danish girls, myself included. It's cold, it's raining and it's snowing. Even the elderly Afghans can't recall it being so cold and there are rumours of infants freezing to death. CIMIC has been busy sending out blankets. Intelligence says the Taliban are freezing and talk about poor jihad weather.

In the morning there's frost on the ground. The tent's sopping wet. I try to find my place among soldiers who are tired and want to go home.

The next day I receive a message from brigade that has the cold stabbing at my heart.

20

GOODBYE, NARGISS

There's a telephone message for me in the office from Sarah's unit at Lashkar Gah.

I call the number and recognize the voice at the other end. It's John, the guy with the pencil behind his ear. He says he's sorry to hear about my dad and that he's glad to see me back. More cautiously he gets to the point.

'AC, I'm calling because I need your help. We've got a report in about a woman maybe having been killed. I think she's one of yours, so I'm calling just to check.'

'I haven't heard anything. Have you got a name?' 'Nargiss.'

Images of Nargiss flash through my mind. Nargiss filling her pockets with leftover cake. Nargiss self-consciously telling me about Iranian arms.

'Do you know her?' John asks.

'Yeah, I'm afraid I do. Listen, I don't know anything myself, but I'll check it out and call you back.'

'OK. Let's hope it's just rumour,' says John.

I find my most entrusted interpreter.

Fatima and Nargiss are close family, but Fatima's not answering her phone.

I hesitate. Gulaley will always be the most reliable. The interpreter calls her up. I listen in on the initial pleasantries. I can tell from his face it's true.

After a couple of sentences he turns and look me in the eye: 'Miss Nargiss is no longer with us.'

Gulaley is weeping. She's just come from the family's home, where Nargiss's body is being made ready for the funeral. Relatives and many of the women have gathered to mourn.

Two hours before, Nargiss was leaving the building where the women meet to work on their jewellery. Her husband was meeting her as usual on his moped. On the street they were stopped. Nargiss was killed. Three shots to the head.

Nargiss's husband was injured and is being treated at the field hospital at Camp Bastion. The women are convinced the Taliban are behind it. Fear spreads like a plague.

Gulaley breaks down, sobbing uncontrollably. Between the tears, she gasps out one of the few phrases she knows in English: 'I am so sorry. I am so sorry.'

I go back to the office to call the brigade. The sound of Gulaley's sobbing won't let go.

'John, she's dead,' I say almost inaudibly.

'OK. I'm sorry to hear of it. How much do you know?'

I tell him what Gulaley told me. For each word I sense the grief welling up inside. I give him the main outline about the family and what information Nargiss has given us since that first time she came to the gate with Fatima. I promise to follow up with whatever information comes my way during the next few days. I hang up. I want to cry, but I'm standing in an office surrounded by male colleagues who have been listening closely to what I've been saying.

'Are we sure it's her?' one asks.

'Is it anything to do with us? How did it happen? Was it the Taliban?'

I answer some of the most immediate questions, but quickly sense I'm about falling apart. I turn round and leave.

Standing by the flags in the parade area the whole thing hits me like a hammer. This is where the ramp ceremonies are held every time a coffin with an allied soldier inside is sent home. My stomach knots. I'm on the verge of throwing up. Nargiss, with her crooked teeth and her gold fillings. Nargiss, who gave us more information than anyone else. Nargiss, who chuckled sheepishly every time I body-searched her and stroked her big, pregnant tummy. The baby was due in a month.

Am I to blame? Could I have done anything different? Why did she have to die? Beautiful Nargiss, with her strong, steadfast gaze. Nargiss, who spun her own yarn, because the Helmand Executive Group wouldn't approve and finance her jewellery production.

The last time we met I bought ten of her longest necklaces in bright colours. I bought them to give as presents back home. Now I don't know if I can give them away.

I feel completely alone with my grief. We cry when our comrades die. But the local people aren't comrades. I realize how much these women mean to me.

I eat in the tent as usual. My colleagues pat me on the shoulder, try to cheer me up with a joke, utter empty sentences. I withdraw to the girls' tent and write my diary. I'll never see Nargiss again, and the sadness is beyond belief.

Perhaps it's true, after all. Perhaps the Taliban can strike out so hard at the women that all hope of a better future dies.

It's ten o'clock by the time I go out to brush my teeth. I run into my friend Charlotte, who works in intelligence. She asks how I'm feeling and tells me the brigade are in doubt as to whether it's Nargiss or her husband's first wife. I can only shake my head. I should have realized they'd ask, there being two wives. First or second wife? How do we know? Questions posed from afar.

Charlotte tries to comfort me: 'Perhaps it isn't Nargiss at all.'

But I know what Gulaley said. For me there is no doubt. Nargiss is dead.

I stand motionless in the shower tent for a long time, empty inside.

The next day, the women arrive. A couple of Americans have asked to take part in our meeting. I'm sitting there in my uniform with tears rolling down my cheeks. Fatima is so grief-stricken that no one can understand what she says. She holds out a camera, one of those lent by CIMIC so the women could take pictures of their work on the projects. I take the camera, turn it on and know instinctively that I am about to be confronted by something awful.

Nargiss is lying on her back on a table. Her face is bloodied and scratched. There is a bandage around her head. She has two bullet holes in her forehead and one to the right of her nose. I realize the bandage is a white cloth tied so as to keep her jaws closed. My father's mouth was allowed to be slightly open. Nargiss will stiffen so no one will ever again see her crooked teeth.

There are more than thirty photographs. I look at them all, out of respect for Fatima, who took them. She weeps and points. Nargiss's stomach has collapsed. The child is dead.

The last image I see is Nargiss's face in the half-light as the coffin is closed.

The women are more than willing to let the Americans investigate the case. Nargiss's husband's wounds are only superficial. A bullet has been removed from his arm. They now know that Nargiss was shot at close range with a 9mm Makarov, a Russian pistol that's easy to get hold of.

The women say there were only holes in the back of the burka. Her face was uncovered when she was hit. The street was empty and there are no witnesses. Someone told them to disappear.

The Americans have the husband's mobile phone and are tracing the calls he made leading up to the murder. They ask detailed questions and show photographs of possible suspects. They're particularly interested in relatives and whoever took the husband to Camp Bastion. I sense it's only a matter of time before sufficient evidence has been gathered. But how will a murder case be handled in a country whose legal system is so frail and corrupt?

I leave the meeting, bid the women farewell and try to find my feet again in this new situation. The murder is on a lot of minds, including soldiers'.

Rumours are rife, even far up the valley. Was it a mistake to work so closely with the women? Were the Taliban more interested in Nargiss's husband?

Was it a family feud?

I listen to the questions and the conjecture. It all passes through me like water through a sieve. No one else has the same perspective as me. They don't know what I know about the women.

The question I pose is not about who killed Nargiss. For me, it makes no difference if she was killed by the family or by the Taliban. It's murder. It isn't a mitigating circumstance if the murderer isn't a member of the Taliban. Nor is it an aggravating circumstance if he is. What plays on my mind is whether the women will be able to go on after this murder. And what if it happens again? Will they be able to go on then? What if it keeps on happening? This is going to stick with us for a long time indeed.

A few days later I receive a call from John at Lashkar Gah. A source has given word of a highly unusual and completely improbable demonstration going on in Gereshk.

'It seems the women have decided to protest. Does that make sense to you?' John asks incredulously.

'If it's true, John, then it's … one of the best days of my life,' I answer quietly.

I've no more reason to believe the story than John has. But HQ has decided to send an unmanned drone to fly over the town with a camera.

When John calls back, I close my eyes and try to imagine what he has just seen.

Two hundred bright blue burkas marching slowly through the streets of Gereshk. The women say nothing. They carry no placards or banners. No one knows who they are. No one attacks them. No one stands in their way or tries to stop them. The blue procession is a veiled threat. The women are anonymous in their burkas. They move as one through the community, silent and accusing, and all who see them stand incredulous and watch as they pass.

I find a corner in which to hide as the tears well up inside me. I know I'll never need to ask whose idea it was. The answer's obvious: Gulaley and Fatima and some of the others have put their heads together and come up with this.

News of the silent demonstration spreads to Kandahar and Kabul. Though none of the women step forward to explain, the procession is widely taken to be a protest against the killing of Nargiss, against the subjugation of women, and as a sign that the women of Helmand can no longer be kept down.

21

THE LAST PATROL

I knock on the little blue door in the wall of the Girls' High School in the centre of Gereshk. It's my final patrol in the town and I've arranged to take part in a *shura* that has not yet been attended by any soldiers. An old man opens the door and nods amiably.

I turn to face the soldiers outside. On the other side of the street I can see Georg on his way in to his first meeting with the district governor. Georg is the Danish Foreign Office's first civilian adviser in Gereshk. The district centre and the girls' school are almost opposite each other, and to minimize risk, we've set the meetings up to take place at the same time.

One of the soldiers peers into the compound of the girls' school.

'You sure you're all right, AC? I don't like the idea of you going in there on your own.'

'I'm fine. I'm taking two of the other girls with me.'

He gives me a doubtful look. The schoolyard is surrounded by an intricate labyrinth of buildings and rooms; no one knows what they may contain. A soldier can see any number of risks of ambush.

Nonetheless, I'm taking it easy. The meeting's been set up with the help of Gulaley and Hadja, one of the school's teachers. I know the women are fond of me and will look after me. They would have called if there was any danger.

The two women medical orderlies who are part of the escort provide my back-up. Neither of them is particularly muscular, and both crack jokes about me most likely having to drag them out if anything happens. It's a calculated risk. With all the gear on, I weigh over a hundred kilos, so they're right to think they'd be hard pushed to pull me out if anything untoward should happen. But that's not why they're with me.

The schoolyard is empty and I give the old man an enquiring look. He points towards the far corner.

I open a door and can just make out some figures in the darkness. Happy voices and greetings in Pashto and English gush towards us. Gulaley smiles and gets to her feet. It's only a few days since I visited her at the women's centre along with my two medical orderlies. Hadja is here too. She's about thirty, mild and rather shy, yet every inch the teacher. Now and then she raises her voice slightly to address the whole room. There are nods and laughs in return. To my surprise, Fatima is here as well. I didn't think they could stand each other.

As my eyes adjust to the gloom, I discover several more women I know. But most I've never seen before. They're sitting lining the walls all the way around the expansive room. About fifty women in all. Only a few are elderly. Some look to be pupils of the school. It occurs to me that this *shura* is different, because most are teachers with plenty of resources on which to draw.

I introduce my two minders. The reaction is just as I'd hoped. The leading women step forward to greet them and sit them down with glasses of steaming-hot tea, gazing at them in approval, laughing and touching them. Not only is there me, there are others like me. I smile and think to myself that the Afghans will soon need to invent a word for woman soldier.

We pack ourselves around the two stoves, warming our fingers on our glasses of sweet-smelling mint tea. The sugar dissolves gradually at the bottom. Every time I've drunk half, the women pour me more.

Everyone agrees it's been unusually cold this year. We talk for a while about the weather. I chuckle to myself: the weather is probably the one thing I can't do anything about.

Gulaley and I have a long chat about the sewing courses, which are progressing extremely well. Many of the women are earning money now. The religious festivals have been a good time, the honour of the Afghan family being tied to the women, who should be not only virtuous and well mannered but also well dressed. Afghan families spend more money on women's clothes than on men's. Many of our almost fully trained seamstresses and beauty experts have had their work cut out following Ramadan.

For a while now I've had the women sewing rag dolls for the women soldiers to sell in the camps at Lashkar Gah and Kandahar. We've been ordering batches of between two hundred and five hundred dolls at a time and selling them to the soldiers at five or ten dollars a piece. It's great business for the women and nice for the soldiers to be able to buy local handicraft for their daughters back home.

The hen project, however, has met with rather mixed fortunes. The first few months were a success. The women were using some of the eggs in their own households, selling the rest and saving up. The cold of winter, though, has taken its toll. With temperatures down to minus twelve degrees Celsius at night, many of the hens have perished and the women have slaughtered a good proportion of those that survived to provide more meat for the children, who have been ailing too.

Gulaley never complains, but I sense she's found it hard to first give hens away and then lend an ear to grumbling about them dying in the cold.

Hopes and dreams dissolve even with the best of intentions.

I'm due home in less than two weeks and it feels strange to finally take part in a *shura* with women who aren't fighting for survival. Many are well educated and enjoy a surplus of resources. I'm introduced to a woman who is almost fluent in English. For years she has kept her skills and knowledge secret so as not to be hanged by the Taliban, like so many other educated women. Many of the women present teach at the school.

'Teaching needs to be done,' they say. 'And who else is there to do it?'

I get a strong sense that they see teaching as a calling in much the same way as the medical profession: they are teachers first and women second. They conduct themselves with the dignity that comes with doing good for others. Most can read and write and do arithmetic. All have an opinion about where the country should be headed and what needs to be done. For me, it's a fascinating experience to listen to these women discuss the issues at hand. It's clear that no one is giving up.

At the back of the room I notice an elderly man with a long white beard. He speaks English well and tells me he is the school's computer teacher. He and Hadja want to show me round the school. We get to our feet and a stream of women follow on behind.

In a corner facing the street, the old man unlocks the door of a room containing ten computers. This is the only school in Gereshk with such facilities. By our standards, the hardware's outdated. Nevertheless, I'm impressed.

Although Gereshk has a hard reputation and suicide bombings are frequent, I get the sense that there are opportunities here. If we focus our efforts here, this town could be just as good as Lashkar Gah.

After an hour I have to say goodbye to the women, who would clearly prefer us to stay all day. Unfortunately, we've a schedule to keep. Our soldiers are outside on the street waiting.

Georg hasn't finished his meeting with the mayor and the district governor yet. While we wait, I chat with an elderly gentleman who stops to thank us for having sent more soldiers to Gereshk.

I accept his praise. As he's talking I notice an irregular movement out of the corner of my eye. A man is slowly approaching. At first, I don't realize what has made me jumpy. Then I see he's walking in an odd way. He's wrapped up in a black cape and it's impossible to see what's beneath it.

He's inside the ring of soldiers now and making a beeline for me.

This isn't happening, I think to myself as my index finger slides into position around the trigger of my carbine. I see he's got dark hair under his grey turban. He's sweating and his gaze is empty. He's walking like he's on drugs. I know almost all suicide bombers are high on dope. I tense. The patrol leader's briefing from this morning echoes inside my head: 'The moment you see triggers in the hands, or visible wires, then shoot, and shoot to kill!'

I raise the carbine, staring at the man's hands. He's six or seven metres away and coming straight at me. My gut feeling is there's nothing amiss and that I'm not to shoot. But reason says there's something wrong. My gaze is fixed on his hands, the emptiness of his eyes, the sweat of his brow.

This has got suicide bomber written all over it. I'm ready and in no doubt: the first hint of a wire and I'll shoot.

Then, in one nerve-rackingly slow movement, the man spreads out his arms. His eyes loll in their sockets. And there he remains, perfectly still. No triggers in his hands, no wires.

Angered, I demand to know who he is and what he's doing. I don't catch what the interpreter says in detail. All I know is I've just been told the man is blind from cataracts. He has come to ask for money for an eye operation, has followed the sound of my voice, having heard talk of a female officer who helps people.

All I can think of is that I almost shot him. I feel like ice inside. The thought occurs to me that no one would have blamed me. He could have killed maybe ten soldiers all at once. All I had was a split second. And all he is, is blind.

I've no alternative but to turn down his request for money. We're not a charity organization. No matter how much I'd like to pay for his operation, I can't. He accepts my rejection without grumbling and disappears again with the same unsteady gait. Being blind can't be easy on an unmade road full of potholes.

I report to my comrades: the man's blind, harmless.

One of the lads walks up to me laughing. He's met the man before and knew he was blind. That's why he sent him on to me. He thought that CIMIC might know someone who could help.

I clench my teeth. I could punch him, or wipe the smile off his face with the butt of my gun. Why the hell didn't he say anything?

The tarmac of the main road sounds hard and frosty beneath my feet. We walk back to the building where we left the vehicles. I think about the blind man all the way home.

There are numerous reports of soldiers saving the lives of comrades after acting on a sudden impulse. It's so common that patrol leaders routinely tell their lads to speak up if they sense anything out of the ordinary. Our senses pick up on signals and details not always instantly obvious to conscious thought. Paying heed to intuition meant I didn't kill someone today.

In the evening, one of the two medical orderlies treats us to freshly baked buns. Her mother sent out butter and jam, and she's borrowed the oven in the kitchen to bake for us. We're only a few: a handful of girls and a couple of lads from the reconnaissance squadron who were on patrol with us today.

The day of my father's funeral, two of their comrades were killed in an hour-long exchange with the Taliban. It's clearly left its mark on them. One of the lads tell us about the day it all went wrong; about how scared he was, and about how he still managed to do the right thing and got away without a scratch.

I feel in awe sitting watching him. He's in his early twenties. I can see that he's still shaken by the experience, but that he's acknowledged his team pulled through because they did what they were trained to do in the situation.

It's not the first time I've heard soldiers talk about combat, about ferocious exchanges with the Taliban under all sorts of impossible conditions: close combat in fields of maize; house-to-house fighting; soldiers trapped in irrigation channels with badly wounded comrades.

Those who have the worst time of it afterwards are those who lack the courage to admit it when they make mistakes along the way.

Those who tell it like it is, who grieve over comrades no longer among us, possess unusual strength. I always look upon them as much more deserving heroes than those whose stories boost their own part in events instead of saying what all of us are able to understand: 'I was scared. I thought I was going to die. If my mate hadn't yelled to tell me which way to run, I'd be dead.'

It occurs to me that few of us are able to do everything right the first time we try something new. This is even truer when you're being shot at. I respect the soldiers who make it possible for me to carry out my work. I've been lucky. I've been on countless patrols and have spoken to many Afghan people. And yet I have not been in combat once. Not once has someone fired a shot at me. Today, though, I almost killed someone.

22

THANK THE MOTHERS

Gulaley calls me and asks for one last meeting. She and Fatima and Khanumgul, one of their most skilled seamstresses, want to say goodbye. Though it's dangerous for them to visit me at Camp Price, they come anyway.

Inside the main gate the women climb out of the car and allow themselves to be searched behind makeshift screening in a corner of the camp. They have brought a little girl with them whom I've never seen before. She looks about eight or nine years old and greets me politely.

Thinking all will be revealed, I decline to ask questions.

The conference room is being used, so I've borrowed one of the Americans' tents. It's a fair distance, tucked away at the far end of the camp, which means going past the shooting range. I bring Gulaley's car in along with her son, Hamid, who as usual is doing her driving. I explain to them that we'll be going past the shooting range, that some of the soldiers will be training. They may hear shots, but there's no need to be afraid. They nod. I catch myself thinking they're more used to it than the journalists and politicians who visit us here.

Inside the tent, the women take off their burkas and glance around inquisitively. They sit down on the sofas while I apologize beforehand for the tea I pour them. It's a standing joke that we Europeans have no idea how to make tea.

It's odd to watch Gulaley's son in the women's company. He's in his mid-twenties, polite and reticent, yet ventures now and again to tell a joke or a good story. There's a lovely balance between him and his mother, and the other women are clearly at ease with him.

Gulaley introduces the young girl: 'AC, this is my daughter, Osia. She heard us talking about coming in to say goodbye, and she wanted so much to meet you. I didn't want her to come, her being so young. There is a danger in our being here. But she was insistent. She wanted to meet you.'

'Osia hasn't slept a wink all night, she's been so excited about seeing you,' Fatima says, laughing.

I realize this is a big moment for the little girl. For six months I have been the subject of so much talk in her home, and I know how difficult it must be for a little girl to imagine a woman soldier.

I ask her how old she is and if she would repeat her name for me, her language being hard for me to understand. She is shy, yet she answers politely and is very attentive to what's going on. Osia is ten years old. She goes to school and likes it very much. I look her in the eye.

'Osia, now I know a little bit about you. Is there anything you would like to ask me?'

She casts a shy glance at her mother. Gulaley nods and says something that sounds like an encouragement.

Osia has three questions: 'What did you do before you became a soldier?', 'How long did you go to school?' and 'What did your mother say about you leaving home and going to Helmand?'

I answer her questions carefully. The adults listen attentively to our conversation. It strikes me as a pleasant, innocent moment that perhaps heralds brighter times for the young girls of Helmand.

Hamid speaks a little English. All of a sudden he looks up at me, points at Osia and says: 'You understand, she wanted to meet the strange woman who is a soldier! Thank you for talking to her!'

'You must thank your mother for bringing her with her,' I say, and smile. 'I will. My mother is a very intelligent lady.' Hamid smiles too.

We return to adult conversation. It feels odd there being no other point on the agenda than saying goodbye. Normally, we have loads of information to exchange and projects to discuss.

I've bought perfume for Fatima, Gulaley and Khanumgul, and I even give them a little speech. The women have presents too. They have sewn a beautiful black velvet bag with gold embroidery and little mirrors for my mother. For me they've bought a green sequined bag that glitters like a Turkish wedding.

After much laughter and shared recollections of some of the things we have been through together, Gulaley has something to say. There is something she wants to ask of me. She looks me straight in the eye and utters long and sombre words. Tears well in her eyes. I wait for the translation.

'Yes, Miss AC,' the interpreter begins. 'Miss Gulaley says that when you get back to Denmark you must thank all the soldiers for what they have done here. Miss Gulaley and the women know that you have lost five men of whom you were all very fond. Miss Gulaley and the women want you to know that they are grateful to you for leaving your own country to come here.

'Miss Gulaley and the women would moreover ask you on their behalf to thank all the mothers of the soldiers for allowing their sons to come here to help the women of Helmand. It is not an easy thing for a mother to do without her children. But if they could see us, perhaps they might better understand why it is so important. We would like to thank every mother who has sent us a soldier from the bottom of our hearts.'

Gulaley falls silent. The other women nod.

Tears come to my eyes. Images pass before me. For a split second I find myself thinking that Gulaley and the other women must think I hold regular *shura*s with women in Denmark. Or that I know the mothers of all the soldiers, the way people know each other in Helmand and know that the son of so-and-so has joined the police and that someone else has started trading carpets in Kabul.

There is no doubt that the women are sincere; they mean what they say and expect me to do them this favour. I promise unconditionally. How it's to be done is something I'll have to think about later.

It's time to say goodbye. We drive back up to the main gate again. The women get out; we kiss in farewell and hug. There are lots of wishes for peace and prosperity. Fatima is the first to get back into the car with Osia.

I've sent the interpreter back to his tent, so Gulaley's son translates for the final parting.

Khanumgul hesitates a moment: 'Nargiss ...'

'Miss AC,' Hamid says quietly. 'It may not have been the Taliban. Not as far as we know.'

Khanumgul looks at me with big, sad eyes. Her slight frame seems burdened by secrets.

She mumbles a few words. Hamid translates, his gaze fixed to the ground.

I can guess more from Khanumgul's eyes than from Hamid's words. 'The family?' I venture.

Khanumgul nods.

I can't handle any more. Fatima must have known, or had an idea at least.

Why didn't she let on? Why all that anger? Because the Taliban are the excuse for everything?

They get into the car. Hamid beeps the horn and raises his hand in farewell. The women look out at me through the peepholes of their burkas. A pair of hands wave. Hamid's car disappears slowly, enveloped by dust.

The last thing I see is Osia's little face, white against the grime of the rear window. She is smiling and waving to me.

I'm looking forward to going home. I'm tired, but also relieved. Soon I can hand on the responsibility. But for the women nothing changes. For them it's an ongoing struggle.

I'm saddened by Nargiss's death. I'm upset I couldn't do more, even though these past six months have demanded more of me than any other time in my life. I can't handle anything else now.

I shall miss the women. I wish I had the energy to keep up the struggle with them: the struggle to learn to read and write, to be allowed to work, to shake off an oppressive and violent regime. But I'm tired now. I've reached the end.

Yet there's a hope that was not there before. The women want our help to get on and are more than capable themselves. Even if I'm tired, I'm still proud. I can see Osia's face in front of me. Little Osia whom I only just met and who is now smiling and waving to me.

PART

2

23

THROUGH THE GLASS DOORS

It's summer in Denmark. I'm driving with the window down and a warm breeze in my face. Once again, I'm on my way back from the military base at Varde. In an auditorium a few hundred metres from the dental clinic where they gave me the works last year, I've just given a talk to a group of cadets from the Officers' Academy about my work in Helmand—work that came to an end four months ago.

The holiday traffic is dense. The Lillebælt Bridge joining the Jutland peninsula and the island of Fyn rises into the sky ahead, but I'm unable to take in the moment. My thoughts are on the messages I found on my phone after winding up my talk. Two were from the Foreign Office. The second went something like: 'We'd like to hear from you, preferably before the end of the day.' Said in that friendly yet insistent tone cultivated by certain ladies in certain government offices.

I imagine someone opening a filing cabinet and my name falling out by accident. A few years ago I worked at the Danish embassy in Moscow because of my training as a Russian language officer. After coming back from Helmand I was called in for a couple of meetings at the Afghanistan section to pinpoint areas of future civilian efforts in the province.

Recollections of the convoluted pathways of diplomacy in a country such as Russia suddenly cause me to shudder. Russia makes everyone paranoid to a certain extent—either inconsequentially or all-out destructively. In the same way, the Foreign Office hits everyone with a certain sort of political cynicism.

The messages on my phone make no sense to me. Instinctively, however, I know I'm being brought into play again, a tiny pawn on the chessboard of world politics.

I turn off the motorway and drive a few kilometres out into the country.

Eventually, I stop and call the Foreign Office and am connected to the friendly and insistent lady. She urges me to apply for an advisory position in Gereshk that will be posted soon. The ministry would like to discuss perspectives with me over lunch tomorrow. As I hang up, I know I'll say yes.

The next day, I step through the glass doors of Denmark's Ministry of Foreign Affairs into a world populated by humanists, many of them women. I have forgotten what it's like to work somewhere like this, a place where men and women are equally represented, men in suits and ties, women in the equivalent. Everyone speaks nicely to each another. No one could ever dream of saying: 'Get your arses into gear!'

The contrast to the world I left behind in Helmand could not be more pronounced. Soldiers are, with very few exceptions, men. They are practically oriented and geared to act. The Ministry of Defence is very much influenced by the culture of the armed forces: wordings are precise and without ornamentation. What's important is action, not words.

By contrast, the Foreign Office is diplomacy. Often, the important thing is not what is done, but what is not. With few exceptions, everyone here has a university background in the humanities, law or politics. It is a place populated by intellectuals thinking, considering and diplomatically wording. They are the masters of suggestion.

In terms of culture and ways of communicating, there is a gulf between the two ministries.

The section head I'm meeting with is a woman. She has come directly from a hearing in parliament and is handed the relevant papers by a smiling and highly professional secretary who sits down to take notes. Also present is the friendly, albeit insistent lady who left the messages on my phone. I'm probably the only one of us to whom it occurs that we are all women. Their words are as gentle as those of my girlfriends. But their boss sends the soldiers to war.

What has prompted the Afghanistan section to call me is a combination of the articles I have written, a recommendation from Georg, the knowledge and insight the ministry believes me to have on the basis of a couple of meetings we've held, and possibly a few kind words about my work from our British allies.

During the course of our lunch meeting, in between salads and Anglo-Danish foreign policy, they send me off to war again.

I cycle home through the city to Nørrebro. Yet another demo in support of the Youth House is on its way along the main thoroughfare. I can't get past and have to walk with my bike. At one point I pass one of the activists, a bloke my own age. He's withdrawing money at the cashpoint, but still effing and blinding about the fascist society in which he lives. My only thought is: Shut the fuck up! You've got money coming out of a wall, what's the problem?

I've not got round to acclimatizing to the problems of little Denmark and already I'm on my way back to Afghanistan. In fact, I find myself wondering if I'll ever become a normal citizen again. If I even want to be. A run-of-the-mill bellyacher with a nine to five, a roof over her head, a car with no dents in it, two healthy children and a lively interest in prime-time TV.

I gather my desert kit together in the attic: helmet, body armour, boots, desert scarf and the rest of it. And all the while, I'm putting off calling my mum to tell her about my new job as a stabilization adviser in Helmand.

24

DON'T ROCK THE BOAT

The yellow, powdery clay dust yields under my boot. I know the smell and the dust of Camp Bastion so well it feels like home. I know where tent J2 is even before the warrant officer has told me that's where I'm sleeping the night. Only my civilian clothes are out of place.

I've dyed a pair of khaki trousers black in my mum's washing machine and bought a couple of nice shirts. In my thigh pocket is a red diplomatic passport the Taliban probably won't give a damn about if things come to that. But apart from the lack of a weapon and the incongruity of being issued with a nice jacket and pair of trousers with creases in the right places in a war zone, everything is much the same as last time I was here.

Along with the others who have come in with the Hercules, I stand by the flagpole and wait for my name to be called out.

'Høeg, Jacobsen, Jensen ...' Somewhere down the list, the cheery warrant officer stumbles over the foreign-sounding name: 'Ribinsky?'

I raise my hand.

'Oh, it's you, AC. What are you doing here?'

Denmark's involvement in Helmand has entered its third year and we're now as far as ISAF 6. As the new troops are on their way in, the others of ISAF 5 are on their way home. I was one of the old lot when they arrived six months ago. They shake their heads and wonder what I'm doing back, convinced I must be mad.

ISAF 5 are tired and marked by a long, hard summer and the accident that will forever be its legacy. A soldier shot one of his own comrades by mistake. No matter how competent a unit is, headlines like that are always going to brand them in the minds of others. The same way as I'm always going to be the girl who beat up an interpreter, even if it's untrue.

Georg has got me on a chopper going to Camp Price outside Gereshk the next morning. I stand in the sun's first rays with a cup of coffee in my hand as my favourite bus dips towards the landing area in a tight downward spiral. The Chinook kicks up a cloud of dust that surges forward like the sea towards the shore. Tiny stones and sharp grains of sand rain down. I duck and put my hand over my coffee.

The chopper lowers its ramp and we run inside. We're airborne before I've even got my seat belt on. The ramp is raised and the rear gunner once again kneels at his gun. My coffee is still warm and my smile couldn't be wider. The pilot takes us up at top speed and we sweep over the desert at three hundred kilometres an hour.

I gaze out at the landscape below. Soon, the two-lane Highway 1 appears: Afghanistan's ring road. Clockwise, it runs from Kabul in the east, through Kandahar in the south, dissecting Gereshk in the Danish area of responsibility, to the old cultural capital Herat in the west, then by way of a number of northerly towns back to Kabul in the east.

It occurs to me that more fields and houses have appeared along the road since I was last here. It would be by no means unlikely. Because of a shortage of helicopters, ISAF 4 set up a logistics convoy running according to requirement between Camp Bastion, Camp Price and the forward bases of the Green Zone north of Gereshk. It still runs and demands increased patrolling of the area.

Outside Camp Bastion, a whole Afghan village has flourished, people having moved there for safety. Suspicious vehicles and individuals carrying weapons are kept away. Maybe the same thing has been happening along the highway.

I try to cast my mind back to that cold day in February six months ago when I drove away from Camp Price. Have all these houses and fields really appeared in the short time I've been away? I'm not sure how, but it certainly looks that way.

I'm in no doubt, however, as we make our way in to land at Price that the camp has grown considerably in size. The chopper comes down on one of three concrete platforms where before there was only bumpy ground.

Of all Afghanistan's ingenious modes of transport, Georg picks me up in a black Toyota Corolla with Afghan plates. He's more than pleased to see me: being the only civilian adviser among changing teams of soldiers has been a tough and lonely business.

Georg is a major in the reserves and did eight years in the Balkans as war and ethnic purges scarred more than just souls. He's in his late thirties now, has lively, brown eyes and laughs a lot. His hands are fine and slender, not like other hands here. He wears a signet ring on his little finger, a mark of Danish nobility along with his cultivated speech. His academic background is supplemented by training as a boat builder. The wind in the desert makes him think of being at sea.

During the summer Georg was called home twice when his pregnant wife fell and gave birth prematurely. The PRT at Lashkar Gah sent a civilian colleague from the British defence ministry to take over as adviser to the Danish Battle Group. He's been kept on; Georg is back, and with my arrival advisory efforts are now further reinforced.

'He's a bit of an oddball. His name's Geoff, pronounced Jeff if you're in any doubt. He fits in well, though. A wizard with a computer, and of course he knows the British ministerial lingo. Do you want to say hello?'

Georg parks the Corolla casually in front of the familiar old concrete buildings that once housed American troops but have been HQ for the Danish Battle Group since ISAF 4. The two buildings are enclosed by Hesco bastion. This is where the CIMIC office was when we moved from Lashkar Gah to Camp Price.

We go in through a wooden gate and step inside. The two buildings are separated by a gravelled area, three or four metres wide, used for smoking, chatting and drinking coffee. Someone has dragged CIMIC's battered old sofa outside along with a couple of velour armchairs. They've rigged up a coffee table out of old plywood and put up a camouflage net to provide shade. The sight if it all makes me smile. February, when I was here last, wasn't the time for it, but now the sun is beating down again. People want to be outside without being in the sun.

A sheet of A4 with the letters PRT—Provincial Reconstruction Team—is fastened to a door with a single drawing pin. Georg knocks. This is where the civilians work. A cheery voice tells us to come in and Georg opens the door.

'So you're AC?'

Geoff gets to his feet and puts his hand out. He's a tall guy in his late twenties with dark hair, glasses and a slight paunch.

'You never said she was that gorgeous!' Geoff sends Georg a glance. 'We work together. You're supposed to tell me stuff like that!'

'I'm married,' says Georg. 'Yeah, but I'm not!'

'Aren't you a bit direct for a Brit?' I ask.

'Only because I've been working with you lunatics for so long. But I do \ actually like you Danes,' Geoff says.

'Is it mutual?' I ask. 'Well, it was until now.'

We burst out laughing. I'm relieved. This is going to be all right.

Geoff and Georg take it in turns to give me the low-down, complete with all sorts of animated gestures. The physical environment is pretty easy to take in: our tiny office is dirty, dusty and without a single window.

Neither Geoff nor Georg seem to be genetically disposed to practical work. Everywhere else, space is utilized optimally and clever hands have put up shelves and assembled bookcases wherever they've been needed.

Our office is about four by three metres. Up against each long wall is a small desk flanked by too many office chairs and an overfilled bookcase containing files and office articles. There's no semblance of order any-where. Two maps of Gereshk have been put up on the walls, and in the corner by the door is an ugly little table for Georg's indispensable espresso machine that's accompanied him in the Balkans, in Iraq and now in Afghanistan.

Besides the espresso machine, we're equipped on the technical side with two telephones, a printer and a considerable number of laptop computers hooked up to everything from civilian Internet to classified British and Danish military data systems.

Georg is already feeding his machine with small plastic capsules con-taining the finest espresso coffee ordered off the Internet and delivered by military mail services. I ask for milk in mine. Georg gives me a wide smile and points to the milk frother. He pours long-life UHT milk into the silvery monster, which in seconds turns the disgusting liquid into a milky froth.

'Best coffee in Helmand,' he says, handing me a paper cup of perfect cappuccino.

I'm dubious.

'No, really,' Geoff insists. 'We get people in here we can't get rid of again because of that coffee machine!'

I realize now who Geoff reminds me of: Harry Potter, aged thirty.

Georg introduces me to everyone at HQ. ISAF 6 have moved things about a bit since 4 and 5 were here, but otherwise it all looks much the same as before and I soon begin to feel at home. Both CIMIC and we are involved in rebuilding work and a number of collaborative projects with the local population, though on different scales. We approve such CIMIC projects as are funded by a Danish Foreign Office pool. The rest are financed by what is now a joint Anglo-Danish development fund, an extension of Helmand Executive Group pools.

I've been given half a container in a quiet corner of the camp. There are ten containers in all. The others are home to ArmorGroup, the civilian security firm that also ran patrols for civilian advisers in Lashkar Gah.

Having my own air-conditioned room instead of sharing a tent with six to ten other women is a luxury.

It's equipped with its own toilet and shower cubicle, but neither is hooked up to the sewage system. A number of soldiers offer to sort out the plumbing for us, but we must decline because of rules being negotiated in Lashkar Gah. It's my first encounter with civilian bureaucracy.

Georg, Geoff and I go through the Helmand Plan together, a joint UK-Danish road map for development dividing the region into sectors according to the NATO-supported sector reform of the Afghan state apparatus that Hamid Karzai and his government, with varying degrees of success, are seeking to implement.

A number of countries are involved in the various sectors or elements of them. The United States heads up development of the Afghan armed forces. Germany is responsible for police, supported by the US and the UK. Italy is in charge of the rule of law, which most find rather funny: either the powers that be are aiming at a very gradual transition or else they're banking on lessons learned about the workings of the mafia proving exportable.

Denmark has taken on the leading role in schooling and education.

Estonia has health care. Along with a number of other initiatives, including road development, education and health belong under the banner of 'social and economic development'. There are seven sectors in all, covering the entire state apparatus and impacting potentially on most everything in Afghan society.

Georg, Geoff and I divide responsibility for the overall sectors between us so as best to fit our individual interests and competencies. The real specialists within the sectors are based at Lashkar Gah, from where they fan out as often as possible into the various districts according to need. We advisers are employed in a general capacity as possessors of local knowledge to promote development initiatives at the local level.

Basically, Geoff and Georg take care of politics and governance, rule of law, counter-narcotics and, not least, security, the main players in the Gereshk area being in this latter respect the Danish Battle Group and the Afghan security forces.

Social and economic development and strategic communication are my areas. The latter is about dealing with visiting journalists and, moreover, the setting up of a local radio station for which three older staff officers along the corridor have developed a particular fondness. The idea behind the radio station is to offer an alternative news source for local people in the Gereshk area. Social and economic development takes in the nine schools now functioning—and functioning well—in Gereshk, as well as efforts towards reopening some of the twenty-seven schools in the Green Zone north of the town. Besides that, there's also infrastructure, electricity and a whole lot more to be getting on with.

All in all, the three of us have plenty on our hands, as well as having to cover for one another as the need arises. Dealing with all these different areas is akin to that circus act with spinning plates on poles. Experience shows that as soon as you leave one area unattended it soon begins to stagnate or even degenerate.

The Helmand Plan is the collective development plan that military operations and civilian development efforts seek to fulfil. If it is to succeed, an integrated approach on the part of our little advisory team and the Danish Battle Group is imperative.

We meet with battle group commanders once a week to plan ahead. A number of the soldiers play crucial roles in the various sectors. A whole platoon of Brits are involved in training Afghan police. But military efforts aren't just confined to the area of security. ISAF 5's military legal adviser has done sterling work in the legal field and military nurses have played a part in evaluating standards at the town's hospital.

Georg and Geoff run me through the system of regular weekly meetings they've established along with the battle group. Internal meetings ensure that knowledge is handed on so as to push forward continued development efforts. We meet too with the mayor of Gereshk and with the district governor, who at present is unknown to us, having been appointed only some three weeks ago. Our hope of course is that he proves to be a good man. His predecessor, Manaf, was corrupt and uncooperative. The new man has been handpicked by Gulab Mangal, the visionary provincial governor who took up office in April.

Further, there is a weekly security meeting in Gereshk with the participation of the chief of police, the commander of the Afghan troops, the mayor, the district governor, civilian advisers and representatives of the Danish Battle Group and its attached British units.

Physical security is a prerequisite of social and economic development.

The seven sectors are interacting cogwheels. On the whole, there's an atmosphere of optimism: things have been steadily moving forward since the Danes took over Gereshk a year ago with three times as many troops as the Brits before them.

Geoff disappears into town to meet the mayor. Georg and I sit down with a soft drink outside the camp's little kiosk. It's nice to be able to speak our own language and for me to get Georg's personal angle on how things are going.

Georg says I can look forward to getting out into the town. The thing he's most proud of is the five kilometres of tarmac road that have been laid around the bazaar during the summer. It's meant a boom in business, and people feel a lot safer because roadside incendiaries have become that much more difficult to place. The massive presence of the Danish troops has also changed the lives of the townspeople for the better. I recall the houses I saw along Highway 1. It looks as though people are moving here now rather than running away, as they did before.

'What are we going to do about your women?' Georg asks all of a sudden. 'In principle, women are the stuff of conflict.'

'How do you mean?'

'What I mean is we need to distinguish between stabilization and development. Stabilization comprises efforts to politically stabilize a geographical area during and immediately after a conflict. Development is a process that can take place once the geographical area has been politically stabilized.'

I nod, and Georg continues: 'Stabilization is about reinforcing political power and re-establishing a sense of peace and security. Basically it has to do with making progress visible to people, sometimes at the cost of other equally important but less visible projects. Development, on the other hand, is a process by which we try to change the order and priorities of the society, and that generally tends to spark new conflicts. Working with women is a classic example of something one would hold off on in so far as it automatically generates conflicts in respect of male powers. Giving women better rights and enhanced opportunities is like putting a question mark against the prevailing societal order. You can do that in a society that's stable. But Helmand's not stable yet. It's a bit like a rowing boat. How much can you rock it before it turns over?'

Georg must be able to tell by looking at me that I'm not intending to give up on my women.

'I'm not saying we should stop the women's projects. What I'm saying is that we need to argue that your work with the women can have a stabilizing effect.'

I present my own arguments. The women have shown they can work and generate income, thereby creating momentum. The women rear the children and they bring them up to be against the Taliban. They support everything that can bring the Taliban down.

Georg nods appreciatively.

'But we need to tread carefully. There may be people in Lashkar Gah who think it's too early to focus on women. If women are to be empowered, the men are going to have to relinquish power. And they're not going to do that on their own.'

I know Georg is on my side and is merely trying to warn me that I may encounter intransigence within the civilian advisory system of which I now am a part.

I know, too, that I didn't come back to Helmand to ignore half its population.

25

MEN OF THE FUTURE

Next morning a couple of hard-pumped guys from ArmorGroup stand waiting outside my container. The firm employs former soldiers mostly from the UK, South Africa and New Zealand. All are kitted out in neutral civilian togs and bulletproof vests; all carry guns.

'Ready, Ma'am?' one of them asks politely.

It feels strange no longer having to take care of myself and slot into a patrol on an equal footing with men. The world around us is still at war and my bodyguards politely open the car door as though I was getting into a taxi.

The three beefy Toyota Land Cruisers pull out directly on to Highway 1. On our way into the town I notice there's a lot more traffic here now than six months before: heavy trucks, overfilled cars, mopeds and carts pulled by donkeys. Andrew, one of my two bodyguards, points out new buildings that have appeared since I was here last. A police station is being built, along with five water towers and a blue *shura* hall for public meetings.

Strangely enough, it's the road signs that make the biggest impression on me. It's as though they've transformed Gereshk from an outpost into something civilized. In several places along the highway, huge billboards have appeared advertising mobile phones, the preferred status symbol of the Afghan middle classes.

We drive through the town, passing oily garages and workshops and continuing on across the old Russian-built bridge they call Tom, which leads Highway 1 across the Helmand River and on towards Kandahar. The bridge extends its pillars out into the depths and down into the clay of the riverbed. Along the river I can see small groups of men at work making bricks of the same clay, pressing it into wooden frames, patting it out on to the riverbank to be dried in the sun.

This is the exact same route we dared run only at night when I came through here in the autumn of 2007. Today there are people everywhere. Busy people leading normal lives.

On the other side of the bridge is a checkpoint where a couple of police officers keep an eye on traffic and are able to stop suspicious vehicles before they enter the town. My driver forces the Land Cruiser up a steep gravel track. There's a good view of Gereshk from the top.

We drive back and turn along the canal and into the bazaar. Traffic here is dense. The streets are bustling with men in turbans, with beards short and long, and with those who are clean-shaven, those with brown or grey or blue eyes, those who smile and those who appear more ponderous. Camels, goats and braying sheep with bells around their necks are driven through the crowds. From stalls and wooden carts, traders ply their wares: fruit, vegetables and spices. A policeman tries to direct the traffic. Mopeds zoom by.

We pass by a place with rolls of cloth and fabrics outside. They've got women's as well as men's clothing hanging around the doorway. On the opposite corner there's another shop selling the same kinds of things. Big rolls of fabric in bright colours: green with sequins; red and turquoise. A woman stops to feel an orange gossamer between her fingers. My driver curses between his teeth as he realizes we're hemmed in.

I feel an urge to open the heavy armoured door, get out and among the people. Another woman stops by the rolls of fabric as we start to move. I think about the sewing courses and about Gulaley, who had to ask her son, Hamid, to buy fabrics in Pakistan because none could be had here in Helmand. I did more than fifty patrols in Lashkar Gah and never once saw a shop selling fabric.

One stall has slaughtered hens and chunks of meat hanging from hooks. There's an oxtail in there too and the front of a sheep. A boy is posted to wave away flies. An elderly man points to a rear leg and the stallkeeper begins to carve. He laughs and wipes the sweat from his brow with the back of his hand.

'Is it normally this busy?' I ask the guys on the front seat.

'Normally it's a lot busier. Trade dropped away a bit after the suicide bombing in March and there was a period we didn't go out at all. But you know how it is. They're used to it and things soon pick up again.'

I nod without saying anything, taking it all in. The two men killed on 17 March were Danish CIMIC officers. It happened two months after my last patrol in Gereshk. Four and a half months ago now.

We pass three camels and a thin man in traditional garb of blue tunic, loose trousers and a little hat embellished with sequins and embroidery. The hats are characteristic of the young men in the towns. He whacks the camels on the side so we can get past.

The streets in the bazaar have mostly been surfaced just recently. It's won the mayor more support than ever before. This is security in one of its most tangible forms: hard road no one can dig bombs and mines into. Traders park side by side. Carts and mopeds laden with crates full of tomatoes, cucumbers, onions, melons and pomegranates. Here and there a donkey with its front legs tied together. That's how you park a donkey here.

There must be at least twice as many stalls and shops as last time I was here in January. The change can't be down to the summer weather alone. How did all this happen?

Back in the camp I discuss the progress I've seen with Georg. New buildings have been put up, paid for by UK-Danish reconstruction funds. The blue *shura* hall hasn't been inaugurated yet, but building has been going on fine—in contrast to another project, a kindergarten so poorly constructed that official steps have been taken against the engineer responsible. Other building projects are ongoing.

I run through the list. It's long. Colour coding shows how far each project has progressed. Nothing, however, would seem to explain the changed atmosphere in the town. We haven't put up a single building in the bazaar: the Afghans have done it all themselves.

That same afternoon we have our weekly meeting with the mayor and the newly appointed district governor.

Mayor Ali Shar has silvery hair beneath his flat, grey turban. His skin is dark, his beard almost white, brushed soft and shiny. His eyes are brown and his gaze is often contemplative until someone says something to make him laugh. His family has lived in Gereshk for seven generations, but hails originally from Iran. It's a long time ago now, he says. He seems satisfied when speaking of his time in office in Gereshk, though his present concerns are many.

The new district governor, Abdul Ahad Khan, is smaller by comparison, his features more angular. His hair and beard are dyed black, his turban tied elaborately so as to flatten out at the side. As yet, he still seems to be finding his feet in office and consistently holds back to listen to what the mayor has to say first. Nevertheless, there is something about him: he's eloquent and clearly intelligent. His turns a thoughtful gaze towards me and encourages me to tell him about myself and what I would like to do for Afghanistan.

I don't quite know what gets into me, but I end up giving one of the best speeches of my life. I talk about what I learned working here before. I tell him about the women and about my deep respect for the Afghan people. I talk about honesty without at any point making promises I can't keep and eventually I seem to have blown away any existing opposition.

Abdul Ahad Khan livens visibly when I tell him about the women. He informs me with enthusiasm that he had the benefit of working with Gulaley himself in Kabul during the first national assembly after the fall of the Taliban, a time when both were members of the *jirga*.

Georg and I exchange glances. We've been dead lucky here. The new district governor openly supports the place of women in the labour market. If any of the civilian advisers in Lashkar Gah have even the slightest misgivings about my work, they're the conservatives, not the Afghans.

The meeting ends in a truly convivial atmosphere. We accompany Ali Shar and Abdul Ahad Khan to the main gate, where they climb into their cars.

Whereas the mayor has a driver, the district governor prefers to get behind the wheel himself.

'I think he might have fallen in love with you.' Geoff grins, nodding in the direction of the district governor.

'Yeah, I'm sure we could get a camel or two on that account,' Georg pitches in. 'What do you reckon, Geoff? I suppose camel meat tastes all right.'

'Can't stand it myself. They probably start better than the Corolla, though.'

The banter goes on.

I ignore them and watch as the mayor's white car drives slowly off up the road. I have a message for him from a man in Denmark, a message I'm as yet unable to deliver. No one's to know yet that I've found a boyfriend.

26

REUNION

My Afghan mobile rings and I gaze dumbfounded at the display: Fatima! Where on earth did she get this number? Have the interpreters tipped her off?

I've coded all the numbers in that I could find in my old reports, but I haven't called anyone, so they shouldn't know I'm back yet. It's still ringing and I take the call.

Fatima's brimming over with greetings: '*Salaam aleikum … Tse tsenga yeh?*'

I answer as best I'm able, but there's no interpreter around, so she soon hangs up.

After a while, the phone rings again. This time it's Gulaley. She sounds surprised and happy.

'You Helmand?'

'Yes, I'm in Helmand.' I laugh. 'You Lashkar Gah?'

'No. Camp Price. Gereshk.'

'*Po Girishke*. You come see me?' 'Yes, soon,' I say, beaming.

Georg comes by and jingles the keys of the Corolla. We've got two advisers coming in from Lashkar Gah for a meeting with the district governor and the mayor. I'm supposed to be going with Georg to pick them up at the chopper, but my phone just keeps ringing. This time it's Khanumgul.

'See you by the containers when you've finished yacking,' Georg says, laughing.

In the next half-hour, Hadja, Fowzia and a host of others call me on the phone. When eventually it stops ringing I stand for a moment looking out across the camp landscape of sand-coloured tents and dusty roads. Now the peace is over.

I wanted to give myself a chance to find my feet in my new job, to familiarize myself with my new role so the women wouldn't be able to just pull me back into being a CIMIC officer and boss of sewing projects. I'm looking forward to seeing them all again, but some of them can be quite demanding.

A lot of the civilian advisers are new since I was here last. Before long, Georg and I will make a trip to Lashkar Gah to meet the advisers there, receive our official instructions and pick up a computer.

The two here today are the new legal adviser and the governance adviser.

They are to assist Georg and Geoff in a series of meetings with the new district governor and a number of elders from the outlying villages. I'm especially looking forward to meeting legal adviser Fraser. Apparently, he's really clever and enthusiastic and looks like a hippie.

Gereshk is without a judge and has been for some time, a fact that makes upholding the law rather difficult. The previous legal adviser, George, at whose request I gathered the women for the *shura*, never managed to press for the removal of the judge in Gereshk, who was shot and killed by his own son in what is rumoured to have been a feud about drugs.

The legal area is a powder keg. Honest and impartial judges are few and far between in these parts, and the minute they oppose the Taliban they're risking threats and in some cases their lives.

For want of a better solution, Fraser and Derek, the other adviser here today, are trying to empower traditional village councils so that they can make rulings in minor disputes about land, grazing areas, theft and so on. Parties must wait a long time to see the judge in Lashkar Gah. If lesser disputes could be resolved amicably, citizens would no longer have to wait years to see justice done and rulings could be made closer to home.

Turning into the narrow passage between the housing containers, it's obvious to me which of the two advisers is the hippie. Fraser's hair is gathered in a long, thin ponytail; he's in khaki shorts and a colourful Hawaiian shirt. His eyes are lively and alert, and the man seems to be wholly undisturbed by the nature of some of the cases which undoubtedly play a major part in his working day.

Derek is engrossed in conversation with Georg, so Fraser and I go for a walk around the camp. It's already been rumoured at Lashkar Gah that the new Danish adviser comes from a military background. I seek to soften the blow by telling Fraser about my earlier work, in particular the projects with the women.

'Fascinating. We've actually just helped some women in Lashkar Gah getting a study group started on women's and children's rights,' Fraser tells me.

I find myself moved by the thought and recall snippets of phone conversations with some of the women less than a year ago.

'How many are turning up?' I ask, blinking away the tears that have welled in my eyes.

'Oh, about ten to fifteen, I'd say. It's all very convivial. We've found a woman lawyer, one of those who avoided being hanged by the Taliban, and she's been teaching them. I'm pretty certain there are some women from Gereshk involved too.'

It feels like old wounds healing. I wipe away a tear from my cheek. 'What's the matter, love?'

Fraser gives me a concerned look. I try to explain the situation as it was when I left, and why his little study group has made such an impression on me.

'In October last year I called the women of Helmand to a *shura* about their experiences with the courts. They almost wouldn't come, and I had to draw on all my resources to get them to see the point. In their eyes, it was completely hopeless.'

'Did they come?'

'Yes, they came. It was like opening up a grave. Rape, murder, enforced marriages. It made a very great impression on me. It hadn't been my idea to begin with, but the experience ended up changing something fundamentally for me. Originally it was your predecessor ...'

'George. Yes, I know him well. He did a good job,' Fraser says quietly.

'What happened about his wife?' I ask cautiously.

'She died, unfortunately. Cancer. But he got home in time.'

The thought that our first, laborious meeting on law and order and women's access to the courts has led to a study group in Lashkar Gah is so overwhelming for me that I burst into tears.

Fraser takes it nicely and tells me about things in other countries that have affected him in much the same way. He's worked on building up legal systems in a number of conflict areas and doesn't see Afghanistan as being quite such a hopeless case as many other places he's been. I'm not really listening to what he's saying, though. A study group on its own isn't going to stop a single one of the violations that occur every day. But it's a step in the right direction. Just to think that the women are learning about the Afghan constitution; that they now know the law says they have the same rights as men. I have no doubt that they will put that knowledge to good use, whether it's sooner or later.

After a few days I see Fatima, Gulaley and Khanumgul for the first time since leaving. They've decided to come to the camp to meet me. It's exactly the same as when they came to say goodbye six months ago. I borrow the Americans' old conference room. All three women look well, and little things about their dress and their handbags indicate they're prospering. I've been worried about Khanumgul in particular, because she's a widow with six children to feed. Now she seems self-assured and certainly not in need.

Fatima looks wealthier, even prouder, but also unhappier. Gulaley is so happy to see me, it's as though I were a long-lost daughter. I ask them how they are, and to begin with they're full of beans. Khanumgul laughs. Fatima says straight out that Khanumgul has found a friend who takes care of her. A lover, someone she likes. When I ask Fatima about her own life, the rage surges inside her and the tears appear in her eyes.

'My husband has married again. I was so angry when I heard about it. I was livid. I never thought he would do a thing like that. I tore three dresses apart in a fit. Like this—' she puts her hands to her collar.

I think of Fatima's powerful arms that carried a big crate of pomegranates over to me one day in Lashkar Gah. She's as strong as an ox, the other women say.

Fatima weeps. I think how strange such a marriage must be. On several occasions he has beaten her. Yet still she is jealous. This is her husband's third wife and it must seem to Fatima as though she has been discarded.

Fatima is thirty-seven and has six children. Had she lived in the West, she would almost certainly have left him.

Fatima's laments can go on for some time, so I try to change the subject. 'Have you heard about the study group in Lashkar Gah on women's and children's rights?'

Fatima looks up in astonishment, then retreats again into her grief. 'Yes. With the man, the Englishman ...' Gulaley says, a snigger twitching at the corner of her mouth.

'Fraser, the one with the ponytail,' I say.

Gulaley nods and tries to hide her mirth behind her hand. Even Fatima has to smile. I can tell that men with ponytails are just about the most ridiculous thing they can imagine. I can't help but admire Fraser a bit for sticking to such an unconventional hairstyle and still being able to get the Afghans to cooperate and respect his ideas.

'We haven't missed a meeting,' says Fatima emphatically. 'What do you think?'

'We have learned a great deal. And we're ready to pass on our knowledge,' says Fatima, clearly determined.

Her eyes are still ablaze with jealousy. She is angry too that, unlike others, I'm not swooping down on to the cadaver of her domestic bliss to feed on the meat of the personal drama she has laid out before me. She's not getting the sympathy she expects and now she glares defiantly.

'Of those I know who's been taking part?' I ask, unperturbed. Gulaley mentions a few names. I note three from Gereshk: Fatima,

Gulaley and the teacher, Hadja. I find Hadja's participation interesting.

She's a widow, though only in her early thirties, and highly intelligent. 'You must come and visit us soon,' says Gulaley.

'I'd like that. When would it suit you?' I ask.

I'm looking forward to seeing the centre and all the women again.

Gulaley is going to Kabul for a few days and I'm due to go to Lashkar Gah to meet with the other advisers. We agree to call each other when we both get back. The women make ready to leave. Before we say goodbye, I ask Fatima how she knew I was in Afghanistan.

'You sent me a message,' she says, and looks at me in astonishment. 'Not me,' I say. 'I didn't send any message.'

'Yes, you did,' Fatima retorts angrily.

I let it drop. The main thing is they know I'm here now. I patch things up with Fatima. Gulaley smiles.

Afterwards, going through the text messages on my phone, I discover I've accidently texted Fatima. The message is in English and was meant for one of the interpreters. To Fatima it will have made no sense at all. But it was signed AC. Fatima may well have a short fuse, but she certainly wasn't lying.

27

RADIO IN A BOX

Every morning I go down to the welfare phones. It's only just five o'clock back home and somewhere in Denmark a man is stretching as he wakes in his bed. We had only two weeks together before I came out here and it feels wrong to leave him again so soon. He has been responsible for the Danish troops in this same area but is nervous about me being here. It's a whole new thing for him to have a girlfriend on a mission.

I tried my utmost to resist, feeling sure he just wasn't my type. As I slid down the slope towards the inevitable, I was still listing all the things that were wrong with him. Now my heart races every time I call him. At the same time, I'm scared to death he won't love me any more and that I'll lose him.

I lean my head against the thin plywood partition and close my eyes. His voice sounds near and I can feel his presence, five thousand kilometres away, on the other side of the partition. An abundance of hysterically pink Cupids slips through the plywood that separates us and I leave the phone with an aching heart and the kind of vigour that comes only with being in love.

I'm gradually finding my feet in the new job. The radio project is the first thing to occupy me. Radio and television aren't particularly widespread in Helmand, which makes it extremely difficult for the government to get its messages out to the people. There is no national news programme and no credible source of information. Often, the Taliban spread rumours and agitate for their views. Only the most courageous of mullahs dare to speak out against them. Friday prayers are still the most important news media.

The new local radio station plays a significant role in the Helmand Plan, being part of a network that with time is intended to become a nationwide broadcasting system. It's estimated that only 10 per cent of the population of Helmand can read and write. If people are to keep abreast of what's happening, radio is one way of going about it.

I first encountered plans for a radio network back in the autumn of 2007 in Lashkar Gah. I took part in a couple of informal meetings, which at first didn't amount to anything. In the time I've been away, broadcasting stations have been sent out to the military bases in Helmand. They're robust and very easy to operate. With a laptop, a radio box and an aerial we're ready to broadcast news and music on the airwaves. There's nothing more to it, hence the name: Radio in a Box.

Not many Afghans own a radio, so the soldiers give away small transistors when they're out on patrol. A few turns on the crank is enough to provide electricity and to allow people to listen to the stations that will soon be broadcasting.

To begin with, people in Gereshk find the new radio station an annoyance. It's been going for a couple of months now, but with only a limited amount of music, and the Danish operators aren't really familiar with the daily rhythm of Afghan life. At the moment we've got a station that plays the same music over and over again, and when once in a while they put on religious music, the Afghans want to hear pop from Pakistan.

The three greying staff officers responsible for broadcasting are nevertheless determined to fashion a popular and up-to-date radio station. I can't help but be fond of them. One speaks a dialect I've difficulty understanding, another is mild-mannered and down to earth and hails from mid-Denmark like myself, while the third is a stubborn old terrier who occasionally manages to pull off a miracle or two. Some refer to their office as the Funny Farm, yet the Three Stooges end up proving that willpower more than makes up for talent.

I promise them that when Georg and I go down to Lashkar Gah I'll do my best to ask around and suss out how to make a radio station popular.

I'm excited about seeing Lashkar Gah again, not to mention the Provincial Reconstruction Team, which in my time there was marked by internal divisions, power struggles and an extraordinary lack of initiative or the ability to get things done.

As the chopper moves in over my old town, I can see things have changed here too. Whereas before no building was more than two storeys high, a number now seem to have grown.

The number of advisers has also rocketed, and many of the military have now been drawn into the PRT machinery. A whole unit has been set up in which officers take up half the space. I'm pleased about this development, feeling certain that it must promote closer collaboration between civilians and military and at the same time exert steady pressure to deliver development projects of a calibre to match the efforts of troops on the ground.

After the first meetings it's apparent that the main difference between myself and most of the advisers at Lashkar Gah is that I'm personally involved with Afghans as people I'm fond of and want to do everything in my power to help, whereas most of the civilians are here because it happened to be the next step up on a career ladder.

It's taken only a few hours, but all I want to do is swivel them round on their office chairs and get them away from their computers and phones and out through the main gate to the people this whole thing is about.

Rory, an American my own age, has worked for two years in Lashkar Gah for USAID and feels the same way. He and his little team have got their own corner in one of the PRT's offices, and here they endeavour to steer their way through the intricacies of British diplomacy to actually implement projects in which they can work together with the Afghans to make things better.

Rory offers to take us out to visit a farm on the other side of the Bolan Bridge. It's an experimental crop-growing project investigating alternatives to opium as a means of income for the peasant population. Afghan farmers go there to get plants and seeds and to gain new insights into methods of cultivation.

Standing in a field of chilli plants in straight rows, I realize just how much has happened here. Security isn't perfect yet. Lashkar Gah still sees attacks of various kinds. But I'm able to walk about without a helmet, and our own security guys don't seem to be expecting anything in the least untoward.

The farm here is a clear message to the farmers of the area: there are alternatives to maize, wheat and opium. Moreover, some of those alternatives can be very lucrative. Chilli is not indigenous to Afghanistan, but thrives in the arid climate. Grapes too are expected to become a major success. An obvious export market is India, which imports enormous quantities of grapes each year, mostly from South America.

On our way through Lashkar Gah, it's easy to see that the town has grown into a real provincial capital. New schools and other buildings are being erected. The traffic is denser now, and the many shops with their array of wares in front tell me that at least some of the people here are enjoying more prosperous times.

On our way back we stop by a playground. Several of the swings are broken due to adults using them also, and Rory has decided that the playgrounds he funds from now on will be built with adults in mind too. Who says only kids need to play and have fun?

Back at camp, I make my way over to the North Block. When I was living here there was an office on the corridor putting together information campaigns, making flyers and the like. I reckon they must know about radio too, if anyone does. Besides, I'm curious to see the place where I lived back then.

I can see the door of Room 7 from a distance. It feels like I'm home again. The sign with the witch is still there: 'Witches' boudoir—keep out!' I find myself smiling. Five new girls are living there now. I pause at the witch and send her a finger kiss.

The office I'm looking for is still there where it's always been. I'm lucky to come across the officer who has turned the radio station in Musa Qaléh into the most popular and credible news source in the whole area. Musa Qaléh was a bastion of the Taliban until the Afghan army together with British units reclaimed the town in December 2007.

The enormous popularity of the radio station in Musa Qaléh is in part due to a talk show hosted by two interpreters. They chat about music and read out loud poems that people deliver to Afghan or British soldiers on patrol.

Most of the programming is pop music from India and Pakistan, but in the mornings religious music is played. The officer responsible for all this talked the mullah attached to the local Afghan company to record two calls to prayer. They're played in the morning when programming begins and again in the evening when it closes down. It's lent a degree of religious legitimacy to the enterprise that has been highly significant for its success.

The mayor of Musa Qaléh and the town's chief of police give interviews about plans for the future. There's a short piece by the commander of the British forces in the area, who tells listeners about his life back home and his experiences of Afghanistan. In the afternoon there are educational programmes providing adults with some of the schooling they missed because their country was involved in a civil war. News is on the hour.

Should anything out of the ordinary occur in the town, information is broadcast almost as it happens. It's nothing less than revolutionary in a society normally forced to rely on rumour and hearsay.

I take my new-found knowledge back with me to Camp Price. Within a very short space of time our three staff officers have created a whole new style of programming. The terrier among them manages to get hold of a container bound for the scrapyard. Firmly planted in the desert sand at the edge of the camp, it makes a fantastic home for the new station.

We're given permission to use one of the interpreters as a host, and later he's joined by a colleague. The two radio stars quickly make themselves at home in the container and are positively brimming over with good programming ideas. They cover Afghan history and children's fairy tales. From Lashkar Gah we're supplied with educational programmes, programmes on health and medical matters, and programmes aimed at and produced by Afghan women.

What really sends the station's popularity through the roof, though, is an Afghan phone-in programme. The two hosts are inundated with calls from people wanting to hear their own voices on the radio, to say hello to friends and family, or simply request a piece of music.

When one of the hosts goes to Kabul to visit family he comes back laden with Pakistani pop, as well as a few examples of Western music. And so it goes that Michael Jackson and Britney Spears appear on Radio Gereshk.

We meet every Tuesday morning and for me it's often the highlight of the week. I'm completely in love with our three staff officers, who've now become Afghan radio bosses in their old age, and our two Afghan hosts, who are gradually revolutionizing Gereshk and its outlying areas with their blend of music, news, health matters, school poetry competitions and other inspirational ideas.

Radio Gereshk creates a network and a space in which the people of the war are able to listen to each other's voices.

28

A HELPING HAND

A year ago there were nine butchers in Gereshk. Now there are thirty-six, Mayor Ali Shar tells us with his usual solemnity. What are we going to do about it? There's need of a slaughterhouse and a place where the butchers can burn their waste products, he says.

I think of nine as opposed to thirty-six. Meat is expensive. There are a lot more people in Gereshk now than before. Many of them can afford to buy meat. These are the first tangible figures I've seen to demonstrate the progress I've witnessed since my return.

A slaughterhouse would benefit many. It would make it much more appealing to drive cattle to Gereshk if they could be slaughtered and sold here. Most likely it would improve hygiene, increase supply and perhaps bring down prices. It would create jobs. But who should own the slaughterhouse and earn money on what we give away for free? One of the mayor's nephews, maybe? Someone else? How do we decide?

Project Slaughterhouse is an almost impossible task. The problem is that development funds can't be used to support private initiatives. We're simply not allowed to hand out starting capital. It's a huge barrier in a country in which ingenuity thrives. If we support an individual, no matter that his ideas is for the common good, it remains to his advantage, which is always going to be harder to explain than our building schools.

What it means, however, is that many people only have one place to go to borrow money in Helmand: the opium barons. They offer short-term loans to farmers against a share in the opium harvest. If the farmer is unable to fulfil his part of the bargain, they kill him. Unless, that is, he has a daughter who can be given away in marriage to cancel out the debt.

I don't expect any Afghan to risk his life at the hands of loan sharks in order to start a business that probably won't pay the investment back for a couple of years. It's almost certain death.

I try all manner of channels in an effort to find funding for a slaughter-house but draw a blank. Camp Price houses a small American unit, one of whom, a captain called Bob, is responsible for civilian matters. Now and again, Bob and I meet up to discuss projects and exchange ideas. Our two countries and their two funding agencies operate under different rules and sometimes we're able to fund projects Bob can't, and vice versa. The slaughterhouse, however, remains on the drawing board.

A few days later I finally get round to visiting Gulaley at the women's centre. She has gathered more women than I can ever remember having met. Gulaley gives an impromptu speech and the women applaud spontaneously because I have returned. I'm moved and still surprised that the things we've done mean so much to them. Perhaps they're relieved not to be meeting someone new who's going to disappear again in six months' time.

They ask with interest about my mother and how she's doing, whether she's angry with me for going to Afghanistan again. And what about my brother? Is he still in Lebanon? I tell them he is working in Jerusalem, though still for the UN. He's been away for a year now.

They ask if I'm married yet. I blush.

They tease me.

'Do you remember how unlucky I was in love?'

'Yes, you couldn't have the one you wanted,' one recalls.

Some are shy and look at the floor. Others are wide-eyed and absorbed, waiting to hear more.

'Yes, I was sad for a very long time. But then a couple of weeks before I came back here I met someone else.'

'Are you happy?' one woman asks cautiously.

'Yes, I'm very happy.' I laugh. 'I'm very much in love.' 'You deserve it,' they say, beaming with pleasure.

A couple of the women nod, as if to say love will come to them too one day, or perhaps to their daughters.

'But he let you come to us in Afghanistan?' one asks rather gingerly.

'Yes. I decide for myself. But I miss him very much.' Again they nod appreciatively.

'How long will you stay? We hope you will stay for a very long time ...'
'I don't know how long yet. I'll be going home more often than before so I can see my mother and my boyfriend. But at least as long as last time.'

I ask about security and how safe they feel.

The answer is the same as always: 'Bad. The Taliban attacked the town yesterday, but the police chased them away.'

'The police? But aren't they still corrupt? A bunch of fraidy-cats?' I ask. The women giggle.

'Not any more. Now we have a new police force. The old ones have been sent on training courses and the ones we have now are from outside. They are very good,' says Fatima.

I'm amazed. I've never known any of the women have anything positive to say about the police.

'Who are these new policemen? Where do they come from?' I ask.

'We don't know. They're from another province, but they are doing a fine job. They even attack the Taliban.'

I can tell that the women are telling the truth. They're eager to let me know all about it and provide lots of examples. But I've got a nagging feeling this isn't the whole story.

Gulaley and I have a lot to talk about. The women's centre houses a fair number of projects now, some of which CIMIC is responsible for, while Bob's in charge of a couple more.

The first sewing course made sufficient profit to allow the centre to purchase ten sewing machines. A small cooperative has been formed and continues to manufacture clothes. There are four reading and writing courses during the day. Gulaley wants to start an English course.

She invites me over to the small adjoining building. In one of the rooms here, Gulaley teaches basic methods for barefoot midwifes. I peer cautiously inside. A dozen elderly village women are gathered. They exchange experiences from births they've been a part of but are here to learn as well. Through a contact in Kandahar, Gulaley has managed to get hold of picture books from the World Health Organization (WHO). The materials are designed to instruct those unable to read and write in childbirth and delivery methods as well as infant care. An old lady lets me take a photograph of her holding the book. She fixes her gaze on the camera, her beautiful hazel eyes staring directly into the lens.

I'm pleased to see that Gulaley has managed to get the project started.

Last year I tried to secure money from the civilian aid fund but was turned down on the grounds that the government had set up a three-year training programme for midwifes and that we lacked qualifications to evaluate the medical standards of Gulaley's course. I was disappointed about it, but Gulaley just shrugged and found another way.

The course for these elderly women is important in so far as very few women in Helmand would be allowed to leave home to go to college in Kabul for three years. The first statistics from the period following the fall of the Taliban show that Afghanistan held a miserable world record in maternal deaths: one in nine women died giving birth. Figures have improved slightly but remain far too high and way in excess of what has been observed even among primitive peoples.

The three main reasons for this are a lack of qualified midwives and care, the often very young age of the mothers, and the burka. Many women in Afghanistan give birth alone or with help from female family members.

They die from loss of blood or as a result of exhaustion shortly after birth. Some die because diseases such as HIV and malaria are worsened by pregnancy.

Girls who give birth before the age of fifteen have a five times greater risk of dying in labour than women who have reached the age of twenty. The burka is a third, albeit somewhat peculiar factor impacting negatively on maternal death rates. Burkas block out sunlight, causing vitamin-D deficiency and brittle bones. Combined with a number of other deficiency illnesses, this means many women are simply not healthy or strong enough for childbirth.

We move on to a room Gulaley has plans to turn into a fitness room. It's an idea she put forward last year too and which once again failed to convince the civilian aid fund. Now she brings it up again and is firm in her wish. The women are badly in need of getting in shape. It would be good for their circulation and for their state of mind. Some need to lose weight, others simply to strengthen their muscles. My thought is that we need to start somewhere. This time, I can approve the project myself.

Back at camp I solve the mystery of the vastly improved police. Half the Gereshk police have been sent for training in Kabul. In the meantime, the Afghan police elite unit have taken on their duties. I chuckle to myself. The men of Gereshk will have a lot to live up to when they get back.

29

THE CLINIC

I'm really missing Hazel, Sarah and Andrea from my old room at Lashkar Gah. Our little community meant there was always someone to talk to at the end of the day when things got me down. The women soldiers here share a tent, and although they've made it clear I'm welcome, I'm a civilian now, on another level and generally alone with my problems. But then Lone arrives, one of the first women medics to be attached to Camp Price.

Lone is in her mid-thirties, a tall, busty blonde with a good head on her shoulders. She's sensitive and strong all at once and immerses herself with enthusiasm and care into her job at the Danish trauma centre. She's only with us for two months, but in that short time she treats sixty Afghan and Danish trauma patients. It's more that most would be able to treat in four years in the Danish hospital system. We hit it off right away. Lone has the same kind of rage inside her as I do, a devil-may-care attitude that allows us to achieve what would otherwise be impossible. Like me, Lone wants to change the world.

When her work at the trauma centre permits, Lone lends her hand as a volunteer at the American clinic in the middle of the camp. The clinic is financed by Bob and is open for local Afghans on a daily basis. Treatment is free and there are special days for women. Between thirty and a hundred patients seek help there every day.

Critics claim the clinic undermines the local hospital. But the hospital in Gereshk is of such a low standard and lacking in qualified staff that the gap between reality and basic humanitarian need remains huge.

We could deny Afghans access to the treatment our doctors can provide on the grounds that Afghanistan should provide its own health care. But it would mean sharing responsibility for Afghans dying, being maimed or suffering from diseases we quite easily could do something about.

A second objection is that the Americans do not shy away from inviting locals in for a follow-up chat about security. Critics say this makes medical aid contingent upon giving something in return. Yet it doesn't stop local people coming here in droves to be treated.

The greatest challenge is not an American enquiring about problems of security in the local region or whether patients happen to have seen the Taliban recently. Rather, it is the fact that the moment they make their way from Gereshk into the camp, they risk the Taliban finding out where they've been.

The clinic is also manned by a couple of doctors from the local hospital.

They come to learn from their Danish and American colleagues and to share their experiences with diseases that are often rare in the West but are still prevalent here. This collaborative effort is the best example we have of how knowledge can be exchanged and mutual training take place. Here, two cultures meet within the same professional framework.

Once in a while Lone and I go ballistic about problems concerning superiors or some peculiar bureaucracy. When it happens we go for a long walk around the camp. Together we're able to laugh and cry. In a male world such as this, it's a huge release for us to be able to let go of our feelings without the other one thinking tears equal mental collapse. We're not quite as good at kicking things as our male colleagues. Instead, we bellyache and tell each other how right we are.

Now and then, these walks are interrupted by an important phone call or a chopper bringing in a wounded soldier, meaning that Lone runs directly for the trauma centre. Usually, though, we manage to talk things over and we develop a good friendship.

Lone encounters a lot of Afghan women in the American clinic. I tag along with her one day to get an idea of what she does. The clinic has just opened and Lone gets straight to work, ducking behind a curtain with a woman patient.

In a corner, an American doctor is sitting with an Afghan woman. The woman's husband is standing behind her and looks concerned. I can make out from the translation that she has cancer. There's nothing the doctors here can do. Her head is bowed. But then she looks up and is visibly relieved to have been told. She tells the doctor that she has known all along that something serious was wrong.

'You are the first person to have told me what is wrong with me. The others have merely given me ointments and tablets that have no effect. Thank you,' the woman says.

Her husband is clearly saddened, but nods and remains composed. At least they are now able to confront the realities of the matter. I look away. Ten patients in the same room and a whole horde outside. I need to concentrate on my breathing so as not to be overwhelmed.

Lone's next patient is a boy of about fourteen. He's lying on his left side with his right leg bandaged up from ankle to hip in yellowed gauze. Lone lifts the bandage free of the boy's wounds. There is no skin, just a yellow, suppurating wound and stripped flesh with a dry, crackled surface. My stomach turns. The boy makes not a sound.

'Isn't he in pain?' I ask.

'Oh, yes,' Lone says. 'Sometimes we get very small children in with burns like this. They seldom ever cry. This one here has been coming once a week for a month now.'

Burns often arise because Afghan homes are so small. With five or six children around, accidents can easily happen. Some parents punish their children by throwing boiling water at them. Some children come in after having been dipped in boiling water. They are burned from the waist down. The families refuse to provide explanations but are usually deeply affected by what they have done. Some girls refuse to be married and inflict burns upon themselves.

I watch the boy as he lies quietly being treated. As far as staff here know, this was an accident. Piece by piece the gauze is removed and the leg exposed. I stay for half an hour, then leave, unable to take any more. I find it hard to comprehend how Lone can even walk around, smiling and efficient, as she does. I feel as though I'm going to be sick. The smell of infected wounds and unwashed bodies. Wounds, abscesses, burns.

Later, Lone tells me about the more typical health problems. Some come and are in pain because of osteoarthritis and hard physical labour. These are both men and women. Almost all are dehydrated. They don't drink enough because the water is often contaminated. Problems with water supplies give rise to a number of diseases, but also poor hygiene. Particular complications apply to women and children. Women often know little or nothing about sexual hygiene, reproduction, pregnancy and infant care.

Women's lack of knowledge about their own biology is a particular source of astonishment to us. Thirty years of war has taken its toll on handed-down knowledge and much remains taboo because of religion and culture.

Lone meets young women aged by constant pregnancy. Sometimes they come to her and shamefully explain that they think they are dying. They are bleeding from inside. After four or five pregnancies on top of each other, they're suddenly experiencing their first menstruation.

Lone says many of them are made pregnant far too early and far too often. Their bodies simply can't keep up. The culture divides men and women into two domains and insists strongly on women remaining virgins until marriage. This means that some men, in the long period of waiting before being able to afford a wife, have sexual relations with other men and carry their acquired sexual habits on into their marriages.

Lone tells the women straight out that they are to teach their men to wash between anal and vaginal coitus. Because she is a Western doctor she's able to get away with saying what otherwise must remain unsaid.

'Can't we set up a course for them?' Lone asks. 'A little instruction would go a long way.'

Together, Lone and I begin to work out a plan. I know the women and know how far they are prepared to go. Lone knows what the women need to know.

We discuss the idea for a long time, but I'm already convinced. This would impact significantly on the daily lives of the Afghan women, allowing them to take care better care of themselves and their children.

The first ideas for a general health and hygiene course begin to take shape.

I call Gulaley and ask if she would like to meet a Danish woman doctor who might be able to start a course for the women. Gulaley is immediately receptive, but on the condition we use a Danish interpreter.

I smile to myself. The Afghan interpreters at Lashkar Gah were writhing with shame at the mention of wife-beating. Discussing matters of hygiene and sex is out of the question.

Lone and Gulaley discuss the content of the course and how it could best take place. Lone involves the woman officer attached the CIMIC unit, a couple of Danish nurses and two Americans.

Meanwhile we're approaching September and an important visit. The governor of Helmand Province, Gulab Mangal, has announced his impending arrival in Gereshk.

30

GARY AND THE GOVERNOR

It's late morning and I halt abruptly at the gate leading into HQ. In front of me in the gravel, a handful of British soldiers are lying about in the sun between the two buildings. Their uniforms are messed up and their weapons and backpacks are strewn about on the ground.

Where do they think they are? The Costa del Sol?

I realize I'm probably going to have to step over them to get to my office.

I glance around for some sign of rank, someone in charge, someone I can give a bollocking to.

My gaze comes to a halt at a bare chest. The longish hair on the soldier's head is lank and unkempt, the red beard bushy and untamed. His eyes are closed, his face absorbing the sun with all appropriate signs of enjoyment and relaxation. I recognize him. It can't be?

'Gary?'

He opens his blue eyes and smiles in recognition. 'AC! Hello, sexy. Long time no see …'

I decide his reprimand for 'sexy' can wait. Besides, I'm more pleased than anything else, and it's so typically Gary not to care less about ceremony, politeness and what's just not done. I know he'll apologize humbly, say he didn't mean to offend, and then carry on his little flirt—regardless of differences in rank, height and age.

Gary will respect the fact that I don't want to be addressed in that way in front of his men. But once my back's turned he'll tell them exactly what he thinks I'm worth, right down to the details of how many kilos I can bench-press, and he'll amuse them by telling them the story of how I gave an Afghan cleaner a bollocking for the same offence.

'Birds of a feather flock together.' Gary laughs and gives me a hug. It must be days since he's seen a bath.

'What are you doing here?' I ask.

'Living the dream, my darling.'

'Well, how long have you been here?'

I can't be true, I think to myself. Surely he can't be on another tour of duty already? But he is. Barring a couple of weeks' leave here and there, Gary has been out here since we first met in Lashkar Gah in late summer 2007. As he points out, he is a man who is very much in demand.

I don't know if he has family. Most of all he seems like the eternal bachelor type who loves his freedom and the adventure of it all. I know he's extremely good at his job, but that he also does pretty much as he pleases.

His superiors choose to look the other way when it comes to his boozing and his predilection for going around half-naked in his labyrinthine grotto as he pulls apart the Taliban's bombs.

Hazel always preferred to call him on the phone rather than be physically confronted by his liberal interpretation of military dress code and other such details of army life that appeared less than relevant to him. Like everyone else, Hazel was keenly aware of the brigade's dependency on the abilities of its Wizard.

'What about you? What are you doing here?' Gary asks. 'Nice to see you in civvies by the way, though I would have preferred to see you in a dress on our reunion.'

From the corner of my eye I can see his lads trying to suppress their smiles.

I explain to him that I've been sent out by the Danish Foreign Office. 'Oh, so you're the one who's to blame,' he says.

'Blame? For what?'

'For them calling in the best of the best.' He lifts his arm to indicate his lads lounging on the ground beside him.

'You're going to that meeting with the governor, aren't you?' 'I am, yes,' I say. 'Me and a lot of bigwigs from Lashkar Gah.'

'Aye, God bless them.' Gary beams an ironic smile. 'So you're one of them now, eh?' I nod.

Gary shakes his head.

'Is it your lot clearing the road, then?' I ask. 'Sheer hell, but someone's got to do it.' 'How long are you staying?'

'God knows. But if helicopters and the Lord permit, we should be out again in a week. Fancy having dinner? I could use a date.'

'Yeah, let's have dinner together. I'll let you know.' I laugh and head over to the door of the building where my office is.

'Make sure you do, or I'll come and find you!' he shouts after me. 'I will!' I shout back over my shoulder.

I smile and feel a sense of happiness at running into an old friend from before and seeing him still so full of life, at once impossible and indomitable.

In the office I slump down on to my chair and open my bulging mailbox.

If only it were me who could lounge about in the sun. That's one of the fascinating things about Gary. He lives his life wedged up against mortal danger and couldn't care less if any three-star nincompoop should get it into his head to tell him what to do and what not to.

The rest of us are too dull and too protected to realize we're going to die someday. Consequently, we never truly reach the conclusion that life is to be lived to the full each and every day. Gary knows he's going to die and has known it ever since he chose his line of work.

It's two days before the governor comes. Mohamed Gulab Mangal has enjoyed some large measure of success in shaping up obstinate provinces before. The last one didn't want to see him go and people marched in the streets when he was appointed governor of Helmand.

Receiving him is a huge challenge to security. The Taliban would love to get him. Twice they have tried to down his helicopter with rocket-propelled grenades (RPGs). On one of these occasions the chopper suffered a direct hit, but fortunately the grenade failed to explode.

The Danish Battle Group has been planning for a long time. Local police have been involved, but only when intelligence suggested that the risk of anyone leaking information to the Taliban was relatively low. The final date hasn't been announced, and not until the governor has arrived will

Radio Gereshk report on the visit. But his speech will be broadcast many times in the weeks that follow.

To us, the visit is more than real. The people of Gereshk, however, find it unlikely that a provincial governor should ever pay them a visit. It's been more than thirty years since a governor last ventured outside Lashkar Gah, apart from the obligatory trips to Kabul. Most don't believe for a moment that he'll come. Why on earth should he?

Gulab Mangal's reputation is at least in part down to a remarkable *see-for-yourself* strategy. The governor is known to drive around Lashkar Gah in disguise and without protection, and woe betide the poor policeman who happens not to be doing his duty.

Mangal has won widespread support in the provincial capital, and after six months in office he is now on his way around the towns of the province. Despite its relative size, Gereshk was not top of Mangal's list, that honour befalling Musa Qaléh, the troubled town in the north-west. Here it was that the assassination attempts took place.

But now it's our turn. Number three on the list after Musa Qaléh and the little front-line settlement of Garmsir, in the south.

The governor will be arriving by helicopter from Lashkar Gah and landing at Camp Price, where he will meet with the Danish colonel, with advisers and others. From there he will be driven into town under police escort to inaugurate the blue *shura* hall and take part in a *shura* of between two hundred and three hundred clan leaders and official representatives from the town.

Gary's job is to check out the road from the helicopter landing area to the blue *shura* hall and remove any roadside incendiaries. The morning of the visit, technicians with sniffer dogs will go through the *shura* hall with a fine-tooth comb. The rest of the day, the place will be under close guard.

Half an hour before the governor is due to land, Afghan soldiers and police swarm around the camp in their big trucks. Not all the Danes are at ease to see a pickup tearing away with eight soldiers in the back and an unknown number of RPGs and carbines sticking out of the sides. Nevertheless, it is the Afghan army and the Afghan police who are to provide the governor's security. The question is whether they are up to it.

The office is heaving with visiting advisers huddled behind laptops and drinking Georg's famous coffee. I actually like having visitors, but this is more than we can handle.

I reach for the phone and call Buzzard, the man with the updates on helicopter traffic. He takes care of delays, breakdowns and whatever else may ail the flying warships. He reports that the governor is running twenty minutes late. Georg laughs as I pass on the information.

'Everything's as expected, the schedule's down the toilet and all we can do is play things by ear.'

I straighten my clothes for the tenth time. I'm in a white shirt, form-fitting jacket and trousers with creases down the middle. It's hot and I'm glad women don't wear ties.

Nigel, one of the visiting advisers, looks up from his laptop. He's a guy in his mid-forties, mild-mannered, diplomatic and equipped with political nous.

'You look really nice,' he says politely. 'You are going to wear a headscarf, aren't you?'

'Certainly not,' I say.

'I think it would be a good idea.'

'Nigel, there's no way I'm going to put on a headscarf. They know perfectly well who I am. They know I'm not a Muslim and they'd think it highly odd if I started wearing a headscarf all of a sudden. I've been here without a headscarf for more than six months in all and it's never once been an issue.'

'Yeah, but you were a soldier then. Now you're a civilian.'

'Correct, but I meet regularly with the mayor, the district governor, the chief of police, the head of the security forces, the prison director and a whole lot more, and not one of them has ever seen me in a headscarf.'

'Sure. Don't get me wrong. I was just thinking ... I mean, I know a lot of the women advisers in Lashkar Gah wear headscarves in meetings.'

I'm clenching my teeth and trying to choose my words with care.

'I've seen those advisers and I've also heard what the Afghans say about them afterwards. We're not Muslims and pretending to be isn't exactly going to enhance our credibility. I'm not wearing a headscarf. I respect their culture and they respect mine. I would cover my hair if I was going inside a mosque, but I'm not. I'm going to a meeting.'

The governor flies in. With him he has an Afghan TV crew and most of his staff. He doesn't look old, perhaps somewhere in his early forties. His beard is trimmed short, he wears glasses and has grey-green eyes. Like many of the other men, he wears a suit jacket over more traditional Afghan clothing.

We gather in the conference tent for speeches and tea. An hour later, the governor's car drives out of the camp under police escort on its way into Gereshk. We follow on behind.

Outside the blue *shura* hall I make a mistake. The driver parks just ten metres from the hole in the wall. The door hasn't been put in yet. I see the Afghans streaming into the council, none of them, of course, in bulletproof vests, so I take mine off and leave it in the car.

I climb out and go directly inside. The Afghans I know nod politely and those I work with on a daily basis shake my hand vigorously.

The district governor, Abdul Ahad Khan, introduces me to our new judge and whispers in my ear that he is very religious. The judge's handshake is feeble and he consistently avoids looking me in the eye. I explain to him who I am and say that I would like to meet with him in his office.

'That would be good,' says Ahad Khan. 'Unfortunately, the former incumbent took all the furniture with him.'

'But the previous judge was shot,' I say, not with him.

'Yes, by his own son. But he was a bad man. A very bad man indeed.

Then we got another judge, but he ran away with all the furniture. He was only here a couple of days. Not good at all. But this man is good. He has worked in our neighbouring province for quite a number of years.'

I'm sincerely pleased that Ahad Khan has succeeded in bringing a judge to the town, though the new man seems rather concerned about his own safety.

We go further inside and sit down on some of the cushions that have been put out along the walls. As host, Ahad Khan manages to cover a wide range indeed. He strides purposefully around the hall like a whirlwind, shaking hands and saying hello to most people. Some two hundred are gathered in small groups scattered around. No one is offended by my not having covered my hair, the luminaries of the meeting being used to seeing me the way I am and expecting nothing else. On the other hand, I find myself having to put up with a few young men staring. It may be the first time they have seen uncovered hair.

When everyone is ready, a red ribbon is stretched out in the door opening. There is a hum of voices and then everyone falls silent. People get to their feet. The governor cuts the ribbon. The assembly applauds and the governor steps formally into the hall. The Afghans move forward to greet him and bow politely. Gulal Mangal walks steadily through the crowd, greeting the most important clan leaders and elders as he goes. Gradually, people begin to sit down and the speeches begin.

I've found a space next to the British brigadier, who sits taking notes during the speeches. The mayor speaks. The district governor speaks. I'm surprised at how direct they both are, particularly the district governor. Ahad Khan speaks out unambiguously against corruption, the Taliban and opium production. Nevertheless, he's still only warming up for Gulab Mangal.

The provincial governor has three main points: education, opium production and the fight against the Taliban. Education is an issue on which everyone can agree, but Gulab Mangal directs a major part of the responsibility back towards citizens themselves. Children shouldn't be sent out to work in the opium fields, they should be at school and it's the responsibility of parents to make sure that happens. How else can the Afghans hope to make a brighter future for the province? The assembly applauds.

The governor moves on to the next issue. Farmers must stop producing opium. Opium turns the youth of Afghanistan into drug addicts. Families fall into debt with the Taliban and the criminal drug network. Opium is anathema to Islam.

He speaks passionately about his wheat-growing programme, which is to be initiated in the coming months. He wants those who cultivate the land to dissociate themselves from the Taliban by their choice of crops. I can tell from the faces of many of those present that they know he is talking sense. And yet it's a dilemma.

Gulab Mangal concludes with a direct appeal to the assembly: 'I urge you all to assist our international friends, who have come to this country to help stop terrorism and benefit security, development and rebuilding. They make huge sacrifices and it is our duty to do all we can to assist them. This is our country. We own the land. And all of us must work together to bring about development and prosperity.'

His words are aimed not at us but at the crowd gathered on the floor of the hall. Only a handful of international representatives are present, a tiny splash of colour tucked away in a corner, a symbolic and rather exotic presence.

Following the governor's speech, a mullah takes the floor. Taking the Qur'an as his point of departure, he supports item by item what the governor has said. All four speakers have basically expressed the same views. Gulab Mangal is a governor who knows how to talk to people who are unable to read and write. No one can leave this assembly today and allow the Taliban to corrupt the message that has been put across.

We eat lunch served on great plates on the floor. The governor talks with clan leaders. After a couple of hours we break up and drive back to camp. It's all over as swiftly as it began. A couple of choppers land in quick succession and the governor and all the advisers from Lashkar Gah are gone. Now it's back to normal.

I have dinner with Gary. It's one of those evenings we can sit out and eat.

I find him alone at a table, more pensive than I've seen him before. He smiles as I sit down to join him. He and his team are going to Musa Qaléh in the morning. I heard in our evening briefing that there are four bombs waiting for them and that for some time patrols have been hampered by their presence.

We reminisce about Lashkar Gah, about people we know and what they're doing now. All we are missing is a bottle of wine, otherwise it could easily have been a date. A big camel spider scuttles about under the tables until one of the kitchen staff crunches it to death beneath his boot. We laugh a lot that evening. We're on an archaeological expedition in the Valley of Reminiscence and the tents of the camp are just a backdrop.

At the evening briefing of the battle group we congratulate ourselves on a successful visit.

As images from the *shura* slide over the screen, one of the officers from the intelligence section leans towards me and says: 'You were brave going into the hall without your body armour on. We had two suicide bombers in our sights outside.'

I'm speechless and can only stare back at him in disbelief. The true import of his words has yet to sink in.

'How come you didn't shoot them?' I ask, trying to remain calm.

'We never got the chance. The crowds were too big. On the other hand, they weren't able to close in on their target either. It wasn't you, I hasten to add. It was the governor. But it could have been you.'

I nod, trying to take it in. My body armour might not have saved me from a suicide bomber, but still … I'm not immortal. None of us is.

The colonel gets to his feet to round off the briefing.

'Yes, well. The governor has threatened to come again. We shall have to see. In any circumstances, we should be prepared for it to happen …'

Knowing glances are exchanged around the room at the prospect. The efforts that go towards making such a visit possible are enormous. ISAF 6 doesn't know it yet, but they are to be hit by more visits than any other ISAF tour during the Danish Army's brief but intense presence in Helmand.

In the evening briefings that follow in the coming days we are updated on the governor's successes elsewhere in the province. Governor Mangal has made himself visible to the people of Helmand. Many are afraid to express their support for him in public, but there remains a clear sense of new and brighter opportunities ahead. This is a man who has made things happen before.

Five days after the governor's visit I learn at the evening briefing that we have lost a British bomb-disposal expert. My first thoughts are with Hazel.

She lost two men in one operation. I remember how she fought back the tears.

The flags are at half-mast that evening as I make my way to yet another briefing. I'm following the reports of the governor's tour of the province closely. There are other news items too. The name of the British bomb-disposal officer is released and we are instructed to gather for a memorial ceremony for another Brit who died a couple of days ago. Once again, these ceremonies have become a part of my life. After the briefing I go back to the office. I just have time to run through my emails before attending the ceremony.

There's a knock on the door. 'Come in,' I shout.

It's Anders, our engineering officer. He lingers a moment in the doorway. Anders is a very enthusiastic person. Now, though, he seems ill at ease and the look in his eyes says that something is amiss.

'I'm not sure if you realize it, but it was Gary who died,' he says. 'Gary? My Gary?' I ask, confused.

'Your Gary, yes. The guy you knew from Lashkar Gah.' 'No, it can't be Gary.'

But deep down I know it is.

'I could see you didn't react when they said his name,' says Anders quietly. 'So I thought I'd better come and tell you that it was Gary.' He puts a hand on my shoulder. 'I'm so sorry. I know you'd known each other for a while. I know you were really fond of him. He was fond of you too.'

I weep uncontrollably through the entire ceremony for the British soldier whose name I don't know. For a moment I find myself thinking it's for Gary. But no, it's not Gary's name they mention. I don't hear the words they say in remembrance. All I can do is think of Gary and weep as though I'll never stop. I'm standing among the civilians next to Ted, an older British police adviser. He shuffles a little closer so his arm touches mine. I'm so grateful to him. I look across at all the soldiers standing to attention. How many more are we to lose? Please God, how many more?

The tears roll from my cheeks and when we reach the minute's silence I can hear them dripping into the dust. All the mad little moments with Gary pass before me. The Last Post is sounded. When it's over I run into the darkness, away from everyone else.

Anders catches up with me and pulls at my sleeve.

'Oh, God, he was too good to die,' I sob against his shoulder. 'I know. They all are.'

In the days that follow I learn things about Gary that I never knew. Gary 'Gaz' O'Donnell was always coy about his age. I always thought of him as an incorrigible 'lad', probably around my own age, maybe younger. I learn now that he was forty and had just been home on leave to be with his wife and their newborn son.

Gary's obituary is posted in HQ. He leaves behind him two grown-up children from his first marriage and two little ones from his second, the youngest only nine weeks old. Not surprisingly, Gary was one of Britain's most highly decorated soldiers, receiving numerous awards for bravery during his career.

Hazel and I exchange emails and I discover how incredibly well liked and respected he was by everyone in the little close-knit bomb-disposal unit. It's a phrase that's often bandied around. Seldom is it ever so true. Everyone, without exception, loved him, loved his sense of humour, his utter professionalism when it mattered, and his extraordinary ability to laugh in the face of form without content.

Gary disarmed all four bombs at Musa Qaléh in an operation that lasted hours. He was killed by a fifth, a so-called improvised explosive device.

The Taliban know that if we find a bomb, then sooner or later we'll send someone out to disarm it. The area was under observation. Bomb-disposal teams are always aware that more devices may lie concealed. But this time the Taliban succeeded.

For a long time afterwards I see Gary's face in front of me when I wake in the morning and when I go to bed at night, just as with all my dead. I hear him say to me: 'Hey, don't be so sad. We had dinner together the last night I was here, and it made me happy.'

In my mind, Gary keeps saying all the mad things he always said. There's a jaunty Gary-answer to almost everything, and Gary doesn't think I should be grieving on his account. Gary wants me to remember all the good times.

In the days following Gary's death I come to understand that it's not a question of how well you've known a person, but about what that person has meant to you. To me, Gary was someone who could never die. He died on 10 September 2008.

31

THE TOWN AT THE CROSSING

My first leave comes at the end of September. My boyfriend and I fly to London, where Sarah, Hazel, Andrea and I are finally reunited. Sarah is marrying her Danish boyfriend, Peter. It's a lavish wedding at an old castle complete with towers and spires. A sparkling Hazel tells us all that she's pregnant. We both got what we wished for when we stood outside watching the stars shoot across the night sky of Helmand.

When I again touch the sand of Camp Price I find myself unexpectedly on my own. Geoff's home on leave and Georg had to rush off the day before because his father had died.

I knew that I'd be coming back to a gruelling schedule of official visits.

Gereshk has been hosting an international delegation surveying infrastructure in the province, mostly roads and power supplies. Now a smaller delegation is on its way with a focus on economic development.

Georg hardly had a chance to pack. His father's death affected him badly.

In all the chaos, he has nevertheless managed to leave me a handwritten sheet of notes on plans for the visit. The programme that had been worked out relied on there being two advisers present. On my own, I'm going to have my work cut out. And on top of that, I still have only six weeks' experience as an adviser.

I put a note on the door saying I'm not to be disturbed unless it's urgent. Normally, soldiers and officers are in and out all the time to exchange ideas and generally have a chat, but in less then twenty-four hours I have to plan what hopefully is going to turn out to be a successful visit which in the long run is going to end up pumping dollars into Gereshk's germinating business community.

With Georg's notes in my hand, I attempt to unravel the threads with the guys from ArmorGroup. The next two days, I put in eighteen hours a day trying to pull the pieces together. At the same time, Geoff is stuck cursing the RAF at an airfield somewhere in the south of England. He's trying his utmost to get back here and lend a hand, but no one will fly him. The Brits are in the middle of rotating a whole brigade out so the next lot can go in and take their place. The timing is lousy.

I arrange meetings with Mayor Ali Shar and District Governor Ahad Khan at their offices in town. The delegation flies in and we drive them through the bazaar, which according to plan surprises them with its bustle and the relatively wide range of goods being sold. In the space of a year, Gereshk's bazaar has ballooned from some eight hundred shops to more than three thousand.

ArmorGroup takes me by surprise too when the guy in the front seat suddenly turns round and says: 'Do you want to go down and see the taxis, AC?'

'Taxis? We've got taxis now?' I ask, dumbfounded.

'Yeah. Sorry, I forgot to mention it yesterday. We just noticed them the other day. We can't stop down there because the place is packed, but we can drive through if you want.'

'Yes, let's see the taxis,' I say, smiling at the outrageous thought that there now are Afghans willing to pay to be driven rather than walk.

We ease our way slowly on to the little square where traders are selling fruit from wheelbarrows.

'You see, those decorated tuk-tuks over there, the motorized rickshaws, they're working as taxis,' our bodyguard says from the front seat.

I peer out of the car window. About nine or ten of them are parked, waiting two by two. There's probably room for two, maybe four people in them, protected from the dust by a wine-red drape, no expense spared.

'There are some little buses too. Servicing the villages further up the valley apparently.'

Our visiting economists beam.

We drive over to the other side of the river and up on to a ridge. The police checkpoint has become my preferred vantage point for giving visitors a view of the town.

It's a splendid sight. The river is lined by sculptural rocks rising dramatically to form a green plateau of cultivated fields and tall trees. Beyond the fields, houses fan out around the highway. Most of them have the same greyish-yellow hue as the clay dust. Far away in the distance, dwellings peter out and become desert. I glimpse Camp Price in the south, and in the north the jagged horizon of mountains.

CIMIC told me last night that a hotel has now opened by the checkpoint.

The owner makes his living mostly from selling tea and snacks to passengers on the bus routes that have recently opened between Gereshk, Kandahar, Kabul and Herat. As we take in the view, one of the buses pulls in and people stream into the café. The economists are impressed. A bus route all the way to Kabul and the other way to Herat. Kandahar is only an hour and a half away.

All traffic uses the famous Highway 1 ring road and no Afghan in his right mind would dream of travelling more than few kilometres without taking with him something he can sell. Every time I go out on to the highway I see buses filled with passengers; more often than not there are two cars and a pile of bricks lashed to the roof.

Gereshk is still dangerous compared to so many other places in the world. It's slap in the middle of a war zone. But Gereshk has something no other town in Helmand has. It lies at the point where the ring road crosses the Helmand River. Where there's water, there's rich soil that can be cultivated. Where there's a road, you can sell your wares.

The delegation is convinced. Gereshk's bazaar is already bigger than the one in Lashkar Gah. Gereshk is probably the most important town for trade in Helmand and should be connected with the province's political centre, Lashkar Gah. Together, the two towns and the surrounding area form a long cigar with the political dynamo at one end and the economic dynamo at the other. The economists say it's a familiar constellation in many countries.

The trick is to join them together.

The Town at the Crossing | 219

One of the delegation's ideas is to finance storage halls in which farmers can store corn and other legal crops so as to avoid them hitting the market all at once. The best thing would be to have cooling facilities too, so that fruit and other perishables can stay fresh longer, thereby saving prices from plummeting as soon as the harvest kicks off. The mayor's wish for a slaughterhouse is noted down too.

Power supplies, though, are a continuing issue. For fifty years, Gereshk has received its power from a hydroelectric plant the Americans built across the canal at the time of the irrigation project along the Helmand River.

Originally, there was room for a third turbine that was never installed. Today, finding parts for the two antique turbines is a difficult business.

While demand continues to rise, the plant is down to delivering only 1 per cent of its original capacity. Therefore, the town has been divided into sectors, each in turn receiving power for a couple of hours at a time. Many, however, are still dissatisfied. Some have paid for electricity they're not receiving, while others steal power for free by connecting their own wiring to the existing network. It's all something of a nightmare for the town's mayor. The situation now is that it will take about fifty million dollars to re-equip the plant with three turbines and dredge the canal.

Solar panels are being used experimentally. But they get covered in dust and are inefficient in the heat of the Afghan summer. An old-fashioned diesel generator is by far the most widespread source of power.

My criticism to the effect that we are unable to use development funds to support private initiative strikes a chord and matches observations made by the delegation in other towns. If we are to tackle things head on, we need to acknowledge the true extent of the opium economy in Helmand. All studies show what the man on the street already knows: opium money is sent out of the country to places like Dubai and Saudi Arabia. The authorities may try to confiscate funds, but the networks that generate them are hard to get at.

One of the members of the delegation, a prominent South American economist, points out that the most effective way of going about things would be to offer incentives to drug barons to invest in legal economies in Helmand. Money-laundering, perhaps, but it would provide the Afghan economy with a much-needed injection of capital. I agree, and from a cultural perspective too. Men who have gained power on the back of clan structures and opium money will remain powerful. To sit back and watch them move money out of the economy is to let an already impoverished country bleed. If, however, the opium barons can turn themselves around and gradually become law-abiding, wealthy businessmen and retain the power they have gained by virtue of culture and tradition, the opium economy will be smothered from within. In the long term earning money illegally will become less profitable as the Afghan police and the legal system continue to develop. Ten years from now, living a life of crime will be a lot more difficult than it is today. It's a state of affairs I'm sure the drug barons are aware of. As such, the process is similar to that which occurred in Russia following the Communist collapse. Some will become fabulously rich. It won't be fair, but it will be a huge boost to the economy.

After some intensive days touring Helmand, the delegation returns to Kabul. I've managed as best I could. A few days later Geoff finally turns up again. Once he gets the espresso going and is done bad-mouthing the Royal Air Force, he insists I take a day off.

In October, we three advisers are supplemented by six British soldiers attached as a research team and general run-arounds. It takes an enormous weight off our shoulders. They gather information and take care of some of our lower-level meetings. They make phone calls, table suggestions and maintain the forward momentum of our processes. In every conceivable way they are a much-needed help, immersing themselves with infectious enthusiasm and energy. It seems so obvious, but now we no longer need to spend time booking conference rooms and making tea and coffee we can concentrate on forward planning instead.

32

THE ROAD TO KANDAHAR

In the middle of October the commander of Bravo Company raises an issue at the evening briefing: 'Who is paving the highway east of Gereshk?'

We exchange empty looks. As a major civilian rebuilding project, the road is obviously our responsibility. The problem is that we're not the ones who got the work started. Truth be told, we have absolutely no idea who is out there surfacing Highway 1.

I know the stretch between Gereshk to Herat was done with US money. I vaguely recall having read somewhere that the stretch east of Gereshk to Kandahar was being funded by the Japanese. But I'm by no means certain.

'I think we should get in touch with them. There seems to be a pattern emerging out there,' the commander says.

I examine the map of Gereshk and the valley. The area is the scene of daily exchanges with the Taliban and roadside incendiaries are common on the stretches of road patrolled by troops. Now and again, soldiers are blasted; sometimes it's the locals on the receiving end. I haven't paid much attention to the fact that roadside incendiaries have been going off east of Gereshk this past week. No soldiers have been hit, though one or two civilians have been killed each time. The devices have all been placed where the road still needs to be surfaced. Maybe we can locate the firm doing the work and get them to speed up. We may even be able to help them in some way. The battle group might be able to do more patrols in the area or keep the road under observation at night.

I promise to ask the advisers in Lashkar Gah who is out there doing the work. The company commander will ask his people to enquire in the area. The locals might know where the Taliban are hiding out and where the bombs are coming from.

The next day, Lashkar Gah is able to confirm that the Japanese are indeed providing the wherewithal. The surfacing work is part of a larger project aiming to improve road networks throughout Afghanistan. The decision comes from Kabul and not even Lashkar Gah can say which firm is doing the job.

The company has already come back with the phone number of a man who is allegedly responsible for security along the road, but no one answers when I call. It seems we're stuck. At the same time I'm given a report saying that eleven Afghans have been killed by roadside incendiaries in the last fifteen days alone.

Back at the office I ask Geoff if he knows who's working on the road east of Gereshk.

'Yeah, a civilian firm.'

'You don't say. But how do we get hold of them?' I can feel myself becoming annoyed.

'What do you need them for?' Geoff looks up from his computer, where he's engrossed in some complicated diagram Lashkar Gah have asked for as soon as possible. I hand him a cappuccino and start brewing some more.

I explain the problem. Geoff looks at me in astonishment.

'Don't you lot ever communicate with each other? Didn't 5 and 6 go over this together? I mean, they're only here in the camp with us! Come on!'

Geoff gets briskly to his feet, overturning his coffee in the process.

I follow Geoff as he strides down the other end of our HQ, opening a gate no one ever uses and turning sharp right into the American area. We shouldn't be here at all. The Americans operate with wide powers under the Enduring Freedom mandate, whereas the Danes operate under NATO's mandate, with all the attendant constraints on the right to open fire in situations other than those involving self-defence. Collaboration worked well during ISAF 4, but it now seems to have deteriorated drastically. At the moment, it's an uphill struggle even to get the

Americans to inform the Danes of when they will be operating in the geographical area that merges with the Danish area of responsibility. I have spoken to Bob about it, but the American soldiers have now been stationed for up to two years and the best thing we can do is to wait for new faces to arrive.

Geoff and I walk quickly across the concrete and around some walls. The sun beats down on us and even our shadows are in a hurry. Inside a little compound fenced in behind wire mesh are some containers covered by camouflage nets. New Zealand's flag waves from the top of an aerial.

Geoff knocks on one of the containers. A guy sticks his head out for a moment while talking into a mobile phone. He nods, then closes the door again. He has the same black hair and wide, flat Maori features as one of our bodyguards.

I look around me. There's an outdoor stove with a chimney, a barbecue, benches and tables, even a little bar counter under a pent roof, all of it covered by camouflage net to filter the rays of the sun. It's like being in the shade of a tree. I sit down on a bench and wait. Geoff's impatient. He's got work to do.

The Maori guy comes out on to the concrete patio. 'Hey! What can I do for you guys?'

'Hi, I'm Geoff. You're the one in charge of work on the road to Kandahar, yeah?'

'Yeah, that's me. Tama,' he says, extending a hand.

Suddenly it all makes sense. The soldiers who were asking around came back with an odd-sounding name: Djama or Tima, they said. The locals described a man with Asian features. But Tama turns out to be Maori.

Geoff pushes his glasses back into place. 'OK. You two need to talk and I need to be off. I've got work waiting. Will you be all right?' he asks.

I nod.

'Sure you can find your way back?' 'Get lost Geoff,' I say, laughing.

Tama stands waiting timidly.

Leaning over a folded-out map, Tama explains to me that he heads up security for a civilian firm that won the contract to pave Highway

1 from Gereshk to Kandahar. He points at the map and shows me how far they've got. They're working out of both towns to meet in the middle.

'We're pulling up the old tarmac a stretch at a time and resurfacing. The problems arise where the tarmac's been pulled up and the soft gravel underlay is exposed,' says Tama.

'How come things are going wrong now?' I ask him.

'It's a long story. A month ago the Taliban kidnapped our chief engineer. The work just came to a complete standstill. He was the one with all the know-how and all the contacts. The labourers simply disappeared. Now the engineer's negotiated himself free. Bit of a miracle he's still alive, if you ask me. Completely unharmed and no money on the table. We're trying to get our labourers back, but some are in Pakistan and the rest are all over the place. Basically, it means things are moving very slowly at the moment, and the exposed area of the road is pretty extensive.'

I'm amazed by the plight of the kidnapped engineer. It really is a wonder he managed to survive. I make a mental note to check the story later, but first we need to sort out the business of roadside incendiaries.

'So what you're saying is it's too easy at the moment for the Taliban to dig holes in the road and conceal their bombs?'

'Exactly. I can only be in one place at a time. The devices are placed at night, when my local security guys can't see a thing.'

Tama lowers his gaze and stares blankly at the table. I can sense the pressure he's under. He drives out into the area every day. The locals know him and are most likely glad about his road and all the jobs he can give them. Now everything's been at a standstill for a month and people are being killed. It wouldn't surprise me if all of a sudden he's up against scepticism and reticence out there.

'The Danish Battle Group are concerned. I'm pretty sure the Danes would be more than willing to help you out if you have any suggestions,' I say.

'You bet I do. Two snipers would make a hell of a difference out there. I just didn't think I was welcome anymore.'

'Sorry?'

'Yeah. I mean, I used to be in on the evening briefings with ISAF 5, but then all of a sudden one evening someone said I wasn't allowed there anymore.'

I hesitate. Information given at evening briefings is generally sensitive and will often involve analyses of where the enemy is at, and so on. It's not for me to say if Tama can sit in or not, but I do know the battle group would like to speak to him.

'Tama, this is ISAF 6 now. I don't know what was going on before, but I know the battle group needs things to quieten down out there. I need stability too. It's very important that we maintain a relatively high level of security in the area for development to continue. If I set up a meeting, you and the Danes can discuss how best to re-establish security out there. It'll calm things down, the locals will be happy and you can carry on your work.'

Tama nods appreciatively and extends his hand. 'If you can do that for me, you've won a friend,' he says, and means it.

On my way back to HQ I ponder on the consequences of a contact like Tama disappearing out of our systems.

It's important to remember that the incendiaries and the killing of civilian road workers are the Taliban's work. But I can't help thinking that lives could have been saved if everyone had known from the outset who Tama was and what he does. Instead, he became a pawn who disappeared off the radar in the bigger picture of war.

That same evening Tama sits down gingerly on a folding chair. Opposite him is the second-in-command of the Danish Battle Group and a couple of others. I leave them to it. I'm here as a representative of the Foreign Office and am not even allowed to carry a weapon. The battle group is here on a completely different mandate.

A plan is devised. Tama knows the area; he's out there all the time and the locals know him well. The Danes make use of his knowledge and position a team of snipers where there's a good view of the exposed stretch of road.

That night, two of the Taliban are shot while trying to conceal an incendiary device. A couple of nights on, a new group tries its luck and is shot too. The Taliban soon tire of placing incendiaries in the gravel of Highway 1.

Work gradually picks up speed again. On a good day, Tama's firm paves eight hundred metres of road. Tama becomes a good friend and later comes to my aid when I'm in need of a favour.

Tama arranges for me to meet the kidnapped engineer. I'm mortified by what he tells me. The man is a Pakistani Pashtun hailing from the area here between Helmand and Pakistan. He looks old and frail but is mentally strong and unusually knowledgeable about the Qur'an and the history of Islam. The Taliban kidnapped him because they are against the road being surfaced and considered his working with Westerners to be a provocation.

The man's knowledge of Islam saved his life. The Taliban threatened to kill him every day. He countered with theological arguments, sowing the seeds of theological conflict among his kidnappers. After thirty days of captivity, one faction decided to set him free, dumping him on the same road on which he wished only to be allowed to continue his work.

He lived thirty days in constant fear of his life. Every day he prayed to Allah that he might see his son again. When finally he was released, he went straight back to work right under the nose of the Taliban. To his mind, the Taliban is an affront to Islam, darkened and misguided. How can development, trade and engineering be against Allah's will?

'Our God is good,' he says. 'He wants us to prosper.'

33

JOURNALISTS ON THE WARPATH

'I could kill them already,' the press officer splutters. She's an officer in the reserves and a journalist by profession.

We're standing waiting in the sun between the two buildings at HQ. In a few minutes, a group of Danish journalists will be arriving in the camp.

'One of them had his story ready before he even landed at Camp Bastion: medics working round the clock and field hospitals about to collapse under the weight. He wanted to go out to a field hospital so he could get some pictures. When my colleague starting asking him about his story it turned out he'd based the whole thing on a one-line quote from a doctor in Kandahar. One comment! One source! When the medics at Bastion were unable to confirm the story he'd written, he got really pissed off. They had a completely different take on things, but that wasn't the story he was interested in.'

She kicks at the dirt.

'Do you know what? That wasn't what I was taught when I trained to be journalist,' she says.

I nod. I know who she's talking about. I've had emails and phone calls from the embassy about a member of their staff being so grossly misquoted that they're considering making a formal complaint to the Press Council.

Journalism is a hard business and young journalists strive to make a name for themselves.

Army Operational Command arranges two- or three-day field trips for the press for each tour of duty. Most soldiers hate it. In their view, the press only cover the negative aspects, and every time the journalists have been here the troops go round biting their nails about the stories their wives, girlfriends and families are going to be reading, watching and hearing next. The constant pressure exerted by that same question: 'Is it all worth it?'

I personally wouldn't be here if it wasn't worth it. Those of us who are here are compelled to find meaning in it. But something happens when you shake a dirty hand and look into aged coffee-coloured eyes whose whites are no longer white but yellow. And even if the interpreter's English does leave a lot to be desired and the full meaning of what is said often blows away on the wind, there is always warmth and gratitude. Even if they do wear turbans and pray five times a day, they're not that different from us when all's said and done.

Many of the soldiers have been out here before. They say Afghanistan is better than Iraq. The Afghans are diligent and hardier. The Taliban are a problem, and the terrorist attacks, the opium and the poverty. But none of it is surprising.

The journalists arrive and are accommodatingly briefed by the battle group commander and his second-in-command. Then follows a tour of the camp. But the journalists are writing for five different and competing papers. They all want their own unique story, and in that respect politeness and a readiness to oblige often prove less than adequate. It might have impressed a sheepish reporter a year or six months ago, but now it provokes annoyance and suspicion. Our well-intentioned efforts to put forward our results are met with scepticism.

The situation in Helmand goes against their journalistic instincts. Outside the camp they are surrounded by soldiers. After a patrol, one of them comments: 'How do I know the farmer wouldn't have another story if there weren't thirty soldiers standing around him with guns?'

Security precautions lead to mutual distrust. The soldiers are afraid of what the journalists are going to concoct, and the journalists know they are only talking to one party in the conflict. Securing interviews with the Taliban, however, is no easy matter. The last Danish journalist to try ended up kidnapped and was lucky to escape alive.

I invite Christian Brøndum and photographer Søren Bidstrup from the Copenhagen daily *Berlingske Tidende* to come and see the women's centre in Gereshk. Gulaley doesn't mind journalists at all. She is proud of what she has achieved.

Before we go, I go over the ground rules: 'You can ask them whatever you want as long as you do so politely and with respect. These are my contacts. I've spent a year working with them and I want to be able to do so long after you've gone home.'

Christian nods. He exchanges a few words with his photographer. 'We've got some questions. You say this is a women's centre. Is it going to be a problem that we're men? Is there anything we mustn't do? And what about taking pictures?'

'Being men isn't a problem. Gulaley worked in Kabul under the Communists. She's used to men and women working together. You can take all the pictures you want, but ask the women first. They'll probably cover their faces, at least partially. It's important the women know you're from Denmark and that the article will be published in Denmark rather than Afghanistan or Pakistan, otherwise they won't say anything. And you mustn't try to shake hands unless the women themselves extend a hand first. It's an insult if you touch them when they haven't given their consent.'

Gulaley receives us with a big smile as always. She shows Christian and Søren the sewing workshop, where a dozen women are seated at their sewing machines on the floor. The women smile and giggle behind their colourful veils.

I watch the reactions of the two men, who both seem shy and overwhelmed by all this feminine energy. Sewing and smiling women without burkas provide a stark contrast to war, yet this is so very integral to what we are doing here.

Søren is allowed to take pictures. I exchange a few words with Gulaley. Her son, Hamid, is here too. I tell them that Bob, who started the clinic in the camp, has been killed while on patrol. Bob occasionally ordered clothes from Gulaley and gave her anthelmintics and other medication for the children. Only two weeks ago, I had two of Gulaley's shirts with me for Bob.

Hamid shakes his head and is clearly saddened by the news.

Gulaley is distressed: 'I've been so much looking forward to you coming, and now this,' she says.

I nod understandingly. Bob's death is a shock to me as well. I just didn't know what else to do. His name hasn't been released in the US yet, but I'd rather tell her now than risk her calling tomorrow to ask why Bob isn't answering his phone.

Hamid asks how Bob was killed. A Taliban stepped out into the middle of the road and fired off an RPG. They don't always impact on their targets and often they don't explode at all. But this one went straight through the windscreen of Bob's vehicle. He was in the passenger seat and was killed instantly. The driver lost a leg.

Gulaley tries to absorb this, then Christian takes over.

I let the two of them talk while I walk around with a glass of tea. Since Gulaley managed to persuade the then-governor, Sher Mohamed Akhundzada, to donate a plot in 2005, the women's centre has expanded dramatically.

The two buildings inside the white compound are used by up to seven hundred women in Gereshk. Gulaley's centre is now recognized by the authorities in Kabul as an independent organization primarily supporting widows.

Here women can learn to read and write. They can attend courses in midwifery. They can learn to sew. Forty women are studying English. Only half the women tell their husbands that they come for instruction.

Sharifa, the teacher, invites me into her reading class. Forty women aged from twelve to eighty are learning the alphabet and progressing on to simple words. There is an old-fashioned respect for the teacher, and classes are taken seriously. There are four classes a day, four days a week. Sharifa takes my hand. She points around the class.

'Thank you.'

She lowers her gaze. In front of us is a new class which by this time next year will be reading and writing at the level of Year 4 pupils. Running the course is cheap: the only things that are needed are the teacher's pay, notebooks, pencils, a blackboard, chalk, and a gift for the pupils at Ramadan. But for the women it means no longer being ignorant: no one will be able to call them stupid any more.

On our way out we pass a pile of shoes at the entrance to the centre. Indoors the women go barefoot, padding around softly on their fine feet with their henna-painted toenails. The sight of the shoes always makes me chuckle.

In all the time I've worked with the women of Helmand I have never once seen a woman in sensible shoes. I meet women wearing sandals in the cold of winter. I see all manner of cheap plastic shoes and all kinds of mended, decorated and embellished footwear. In contrast to what was intended, the Taliban sparked a boom in high heels and fine sandals. When you're shut up inside a burka, shoes are the only thing visible through which to signal personality and femininity. Afghanistan has become a nation of women who, although subjugated into wearing the burka, have decided never to let go of the will to be women—a nation of shoe fetishists.

As we head back to camp I notice there's an unusual number of police in the streets; small groups of them all over the place, partly uniformed and with guns visible. On the roof of a building directly opposite the police-army coordination centre is a bunch of men with long beards and RPGs slung over their shoulders.

'What's going on?' Christian asks. 'I'm not sure.'

'But this isn't normal?'

I shake my head and lean forward to the security guys in the front. 'What's going on, KK?'

'No idea, I'm afraid,' says KK.

He's Maori like Tama and a bit of an adrenalin junkie. When he's not working as a bodyguard in Afghanistan, he's generally on a snowboard in the mountains of Japan.

'Those are RPGs, aren't they?' says Christian. 'They are indeed,' says KK drily.

'What happens if we get hit by one of them?' 'Just pray it doesn't happen.' KK smiles.

There's definitely something wrong here, but I can't work it out. The men with the turbans and the grenades can't be Taliban or the police would have shot them. So who are they? What I do know, however, is what will happen if one of those RPGs goes through the armour of my car in the same way as happened to Bob. But that's something I prefer to keep to myself.

Back at Price I learn that the Taliban have been claiming for hours that they are in the middle of an attack on Gereshk. They're firing each other up on their Motorola radios and sounding off about how many tanks they've taken out. No one has seen tanks in the street of Gereshk, but the fear of something actually happening has prompted shopkeepers to close their shutters all through the bazaar.

The district governor is incensed. Every closed shop is a victory for the Taliban. The enemy is achieving exactly what it wanted, promoting insecurity, the sense of a town unsafe, yet another area in which the government has been unable to secure peace.

At the weekly security meeting a few days later, the commander of the local Afghan company apologizes for the fact that not all his men had time to get into uniform. Hence the bearded men on the roof, who had found a vantage point from which to engage an enemy without the courage to approach the town.

The Taliban have already demonstrated their lack of ability to lead Afghanistan. According to the local people, that's why support for the Taliban remains low. Now the Taliban are seeking to discredit the incumbent government by means of threats, suicide attacks and roadside incendiaries so the Afghan people never feel safe. If their strategy succeeds, people will blame the government for the lack of security in the country rather than directing their rage at the Taliban, who are actually responsible. It's a subtle power game.

Personally I find it ironic to have had a journalist and a photographer with me at the time. Imagine what one of the tabloids would have made of armed men on rooftops and the clear sense of insecurity in the town. The incident was also a perfect example of what lack of a free press can do to a society like Gereshk. Two thousand shops closed in two hours as panic spread; even the district governor called the shopkeepers cowards.

A couple of weeks later we're again visited by journalists. Jill McGivering from BBC radio and her producer, Caroline, are on patrol with CIMIC east of Gereshk when I receive a phone call from Robert, the British communications adviser based at Lashkar Gah.

'An Afghan drug combating unit has made a pretty big haul in your area.

Some storage building or other in Gereshk. Eighteen tons of poppy seeds. Have you heard anything about it?'

'No, I'm afraid not, Robert. I haven't heard anything at all,' I tell him. 'No, I thought as much. We just heard from the governor's office and apparently it's true. Eighteen tons. Did you get that? Ask Jill from the BBC to call me right away. Otherwise the story will go elsewhere, but we'd like them to get it first. This is a big one. Should be for them too. I'll see if I can get some more details.'

As soon as Jill and Caroline come back from the patrol I tell them about the haul. Either I'm not very good at selling the story, or else they're just not interested. They call Robert anyway and he manages to convince them. I watch as one of the girls takes notes.

'OK, and how many hectares did they burn last year? Three thousand hectares of opium poppies? So in principle you could say that with the eighteen tons of seed that's been confiscated there are going to be seven thousand hectares less opium this year ...'

She nods, then hesitates.

'Robert, I can't promise anything, but I'll give my editor a call and we'll just have to see what she says. Yes, I'll call you back. Yes, I understand that.'

She ends the call and looks up at me.

'He's so unyielding! He wants maximum coverage or he's going to give it to someone else.'

The BBC runs the story. On the other hand, Buzzard reports that the chopper the two girls are supposed to be flying out on has been cancelled due to technical problems. They're on a tight schedule and are to fly to Kabul in two days' time. This always happens when the British press are here. They're told to give themselves plenty of time for transport and set aside a day here and there, but they have no idea how difficult and time-consuming it is to travel in Afghanistan.

I call the press office at Lashkar Gah and together we work out a contingency plan involving land and air transport. Their best chance is for us to ask the Danish Battle Group to give the two women a ride with their logistics convoy.

Late that evening I follow Jill and Caroline out to the convoy and grab hold of Moe, the young sergeant who's leading it. He's one of those people who always puts you in a good mood, always friendly and ready to give you the time of day.

'They're not causing any trouble, are they?' he asks with a beam. 'Not at all, they're really nice.'

'Right then, they can come with me. That's mine over there on the far side.'

Moe points and says a three-figure number, the last digits of the registration plate of his armoured personnel carrier. I help the two women climb inside what for them must be a somewhat unfamiliar means of transport. We wave our goodbyes. I'm already walking away when I suddenly decide to go back. I can't help it, but I need to say thanks to Moe for always making me feel so good in the midst of all this tumult. He beams back at me, his smile bright in the headlights of the APC.

34

SEEDS OF TERROR

A few days later I'm standing at the helicopter landing area waiting. An icy wind howls across the barren landscape of the camp. My fingers are numb. This is a day we've been waiting for for a long time. Many man-hours reach their culmination today in what is hopefully going to be a peaceful inauguration of Helmand governor Gulab Mangal's wheat seed distribution programme in Gereshk. Seed has been distributed to all the major towns in the province. The Taliban and highway robbers have attacked two of the convoys and killed a driver in the process.

Far away in the distance I spot a little insect gradually increasing in size as it moves towards the camp in a straight line. A helicopter on its way.

The dark grey Sea King flies in low over the landscape before pulling itself up above the outer wall and settling on one of the three concrete landing pads. Instinctively, I turn my back before we're engulfed by dust and gravel sucked into the air by the force of the rotor blades. When I turn again, men in long robes and flapping turbans are already disembarking from the chopper.

I greet Deputy Governor Satar and the governor's adviser, Salem. In all, twenty Afghans from the governor's administration and three advisers from Lashkar Gah have made the journey. The deputy governor meets with the district governor and the mayor in the conference tent. A broadcasting crew from Lashkar Gah are here too and Radio Gereshk records all the speeches.

Five thousand farmers in the Gereshk district have agreed not to grow opium poppies in return for receiving free wheat seed to be sown at the same time as poppies otherwise would be sown. Politically, the programme has two aims: first, to reduce opium production; second, to demonstrate that the authorities are able to act dynamically.

The battle group has been instructed to keep a low profile. The task of providing security for the provincial administration's most ambitious attempt yet to reach out to the people, has been placed in the hands of the Afghan police in collaboration with the Afghan army.

Along with three advisers from Lashkar Gah I drive into town to see the inauguration. Police are gathered in force outside one of the warehouses lining Highway 1. They have blocked off the road and are patrolling the area. Today would be a good day for the Taliban to send in a suicide bomber. It would make for spectacular television and demonstrate police incompetence.

We climb out of the cars and thread our way through the crowd of waiting farmers. I glance at the police and decide I'll never get used to the sight of a bunch of RPGs casually carried around in a rucksack.

Several hundred farmers are seated on the ground and sit looking up at the deputy governor, Satar. It must be a strange moment for them. In the space of only a few months and after a thirty-year absence they've been visited by both the governor and the deputy governor. Satar speaks from the steps of the warehouse. I move a little closer.

'You should not be growing opium poppies at all. Seventy thousand of our young people today are drug abusers. If those seventy thousand were in the army instead we would not have need of the foreign forces here at all.'

I look around me. Children are playing and asking to have their pictures taken. Two little girls approach from the periphery and stand to stare at me. They're shy, but they won't let me out of their sight.

After a number of speeches, the first farmer is called up. Visibly proud, he walks up the steps, puts his fingerprint beside his name and walks away lugging a fifty-kilo sack of seed on his shoulders.

The names of the farmers who have agreed to the terms of the scheme have been put forward by the village elders. Along with an identity number and a guarantee issued by the elder responsible, all names have been approved by the district governor. Seed is evenly distributed between villages and individual landowners, and clan affiliation has also been taken into account. The farmers show their identity cards and sign for the seed.

We have spent a great deal of time working on this project and now we watch as the farmers disappear one by one with their sacks across their shoulders.

We drive on up the blue *shura* hall. The plan is for the deputy governor to meet with clan elders and hear their views. Afterwards, District Governor Ahad Khan and Mayor Ali Shar are hosts for lunch.

Since Governor Mangal was here, CIMIC has supplied furniture with the help of a local contractor. The big hall is now equipped with eight hundred chairs, while the small conference room has fifty. Shade from the sun is provided by colourful curtains made by the women at the women's centre.

I follow the debate in the hall. Twenty-five of the most influential clan leaders are gathered and the issues of education and overall future prospects for the province are eagerly discussed. Further back, even more sit listening. Across the assembly I catch sight of Gulaley. She is sitting at the front among the most important delegates, wearing a dark jacket and a bright green scarf to cover her hair. Gulaley asks for the floor and urges the deputy governor and town dignitaries to include women in their plans for the future. Satar thanks her for her input without commenting further. The subdued nature of his reaction makes no difference to me. A year ago it would have been unthinkable for Gulaley even to have been present at a meeting such as this. She and the other women will make themselves heard regardless.

After the discussion we're ushered into the smaller conference room. I make a beeline for Gulaley, who points proudly to the curtains. It's the women's first public commission. Gulaley's centre is now a bona fide workplace.

We sit down to eat: tender pieces of lamb, delicious flat bread and heaps of rice, tomatoes and cucumber, all topped by fresh coriander. Ali Shar sends me a smile and lifts a piece of meat.

'Good!' He laughs.

I think back to the first time I drove through Gereshk. It's a year and two weeks ago now and the town was considered so dangerous we would only pass through it at night. From that perspective what has happened here since is nothing short of a miracle. The battle group's second-in-command even stood alongside Satar on the steps today without a helmet. There are no guarantees in a war zone. There could always be a suicide attack tomorrow, but it's now almost five months since the last one.

With representatives of the battle group, three advisers from Lashkar Gah and my security, there are sixteen of us from the international community amid the bustle of Afghan politicians, police and soldiers. The governor's prestige project is under way and the inauguration day passed without incident. Fourteen days have been set aside to distribute the seed and I've a good feeling that everything is going to be fine.

After I get back to camp and the chopper has taken off with the deputy governor and his entourage, Gulaley calls me on the phone.

'AC, will you help me start a group for women's and children's rights at the women's centre in Gereshk?' she says.

I'm thrilled by the idea.

'Of course. What do you need?' I ask.

'I don't need money. I don't need anything at all. I ask only that you come. It lends so much importance to proceedings if there is an international person present.'

I call Fraser at Lashkar Gah and tell him the good news. He laughs and promises me all the support I need.

I write an article about the wheat seed programme that's published by *Berlingske Tidende* back home. The next day a letter to the editor from a chemical engineer harangues what he sees as my action-based prose and lashes out at us for not simply spraying fields from the air.

His criticism saddens me. It's so easy to sit at home in cosy little Denmark and on the basis of examples from South and Central America sound off about how the opium issue should be tackled in Helmand. Is it really that difficult to grasp that destroying the livelihoods of farmers is to send them directly into the arms of the Taliban? How else should the peasant population earn a living? As mercenaries of the Taliban? Is it really wrong of us to target the drug cartels and their backers rather than the farmers? Is it not reasonable to seek to convince farmers by voluntary means to switch to other crops, despite the fact they will suffer financial loss?

Other critical voices make themselves heard too. Twenty-six thousand hectares of seed covers only one-sixth of Helmand's approximately one hundred and fifty thousand hectares of agricultural land. I shake my head in amazement. Now we are being criticized for even trying. The project costs ten million dollars. Show me the investor who would put six times as much money into a project six times the size without first running a pilot project.

35

SPINNING IN A BURKA

After a month's preparation, meetings and poster production, the hygiene course is ready to go. Gulaley has selected sixteen women to take part.

Susanne from CIMIC has drawn up the day's schedule in detail. The chef has promised to make lunch for the women. Local police have provided a driver and we're footing the bill for a bus to fetch and carry.

Because of Ramadan, the course is getting under way after Lone's two-month stint of intensive medical duty in the camp has come to an end. I miss her, but having planted the idea she's here in spirit, and the course will continue long after I too leave Afghan soil.

For a few hundred dollars the course opens up a whole new world for the Danish women soldiers and nurses and, not least, for the Afghan women who suddenly find themselves with their own forum in which they may approach, however gingerly, issues such as sex, health, childbirth, breast-feeding and hygiene.

The women take all of it in, giggling with veils drawn up in front of their faces when matters turn to subjects of an intimate nature. They feast on the good food and are thrilled with the little goody bag containing toothbrush, shampoo and other necessities each receives at the end of the day.

As the course takes shape and the women get used to the idea, it becomes easier to broach subjects deemed particularly difficult. One woman weeps with relief when she realizes it is not necessarily her fault that she can't get pregnant. She won't tell her husband, but now she feels she has been given strength to resist his reproaches.

Because the doctors and nurses taking part are women and foreigners to boot, they are allowed to touch on the many taboos that religion and culture through the centuries have combined to shroud in shame.

One day, when the police come to drive the women back to the women's centre, I'm stopped by the policeman who drives the bus.

'Thank you for teaching our women,' he says, and shakes my hand vigorously.

I'm not sure exactly what Gulaley has told him, but it's clear that in his view we're doing society a service.

In November we are able to open the new gym at the women's centre. The female press officer and I are there and are allowed to film some footage for the national news programmes back home. The woman officer from CIMIC is an aerobic instructor and puts the women through a series of exercises on treadmills and exercise bikes. The women are eager, pedalling away and even trying to do sit-ups while balancing on the big exercise balls. They laugh like I've never seen them laugh before. The news desks back home love it: lovely ladies full of life, casting off their burkas and giving it all they've got in the gym. It's an instant hit.

The next few times I visit the centre I'm anxious to see if the women are still as enthusiastic. But I've no need to worry: the gym is in constant use. I'm not sure why they like it so much, but many of them are really determined to get into shape. To others, it's the best playground they've ever had. One of the severely overweight women slims significantly and thanks me every time she sees me. I can't help thinking about that afternoon over a year ago when Gulaley explained to me how important it was for the women to exercise given that they were unable to go for a run in their burkas. The solution was so obvious. Yet the results have a wider impact than I could ever have imagined. The gym allows the women to improve their health, gives them a renewed sense of their own bodies, and last but not least, means they've something to laugh about.

In mid-December I'm back home enjoying a much-deserved reunion with my boyfriend. My brother is home on a short leave too. He's now spent over a year in the Golan Heights, Lebanon and Israel. Both of us feel equally out of place in Denmark.

Two weeks later I'm sitting at Kabul's airport on my way to Helmand when news reaches me. Three Danish soldiers killed at once. Rumour has it they burned to death.

When I get back to camp, I learn that one of those killed is Moe, the good-looking, smiling sergeant from the logistics convoy. His APC ran over a mine. It's only four weeks since I piled Jill and Caroline into his vehicle so they could make their connection. Dear Moe, so full of energy, so full of life. I didn't know those who were with him. All I can think now is how terrible Christmas will be for those three families. Every Christmas will remind them of their loss.

A few days later I run into a senior medic I know well. He saw the bodies and made them ready for their journey home. He is angered by the rumours that the three soldiers burned to death. The story hit the front pages back home without there being a grain of truth in it. The thoughts and emotions it must have given rise to in the families affected don't bear thinking about.

'They were killed instantly. But they were in relatively good shape.

Nothing missing and most certainly recognizable,' he tells me.

The information comes as a relief. For some years I worked as an emergency service counsellor and having dealt with a number of traffic accidents I soon learned how difficult it is for families to deal with the death of a son or daughter if they are unable to see the body. Seeing the person dead allows closure. You don't forget the person living, but seeing them dead means understanding that death is final.

On the morning of Christmas Eve I visit the women's centre again. For my British bodyguards, Christmas isn't until tomorrow whereas for the Danes Christmas starts on Christmas Eve. I look out on the streets as we drive through the bazaar. Four old men sit drinking tea under a pent roof. One is explaining something to the others. Their conversation is momentarily interrupted as the three armoured Land Cruisers pass slowly by. They lift their gazes, but they know us now.

Once in a while I'm thankful the windows are tinted so they can't see me and rumour doesn't spread about how often I'm in town. As it is now, they never know if it's me or Geoff or Georg or some of our run-arounds.

Mostly, though, the tinted windows annoy me. They close me off from the locals. Women and men are no longer able to see a Danish woman at work with their own eyes.

At ten o'clock, Gulaley inaugurates the group for women's and children's rights. She is to head it up, assisted by Hadja, with Fatima as secretary. All three took part in the seminar in Lashkar Gah and as such are natural choices to run a similar group in Gereshk. Seven women in all are present.

More arrive as we get under way. If things proceed in the usual manner, then next time anywhere between five and twenty-five will show up.

Through the Foreign Office at home I've received an enquiry from a Danish documentary film-maker who would like to follow some of our meetings. The women say it's OK by them.

The three women leading the group have divided the seats between them.

There seems to be a better balance between Hadja and Fatima than ever before. Nevertheless, I know it's a fragile constellation. Competition between Hadja and Fatima will be a problem. But my thought is that at least it's a start. Hopefully the group can run itself when my contract expires in three months. Maybe I can find someone to keep an eye on them when I've gone.

Back in my container home I open a parcel Hazel has sent me. Inside is a whole supply of necessities, including warm socks and fairy lights for Christmas. There's a luxurious shampoo, lotions and all sorts of other things we loved back when we were together in the girls' room. There's even a pair of red panties too. I laugh so much I cry.

At the joint Anglo-Danish Christmas dinner, the Brits serve traditional Danish duck and pork. In a corner of the mess tent is a Christmas tree with all the decorations, and three long tables have been set up running through the middle of the tent to seat everyone. The Brits are all wearing bow ties made out of black gaffer tape and cardboard, so the waiters look suitably smart. The food is good, though the alcohol-free red wine is a testing experience. The young soldiers are full of beans, laughing and joking.

They're here with their mates and are used to making the best of things. Even so, I can't help feeling sad.

After dinner I open the so-called square stocking we've all been given by a British charity that sends Christmas cheer to servicemen and women overseas. It's a shiny metal box packed with little things: a compass, a collapsible Frisbee, a pocket mirror with a ruler, a deck of cards, that sort of thing.

At the bottom of it all I find a little note telling the story of how the charity started. It's folded in the middle and when I open it all I can do is burst out laughing. Accompanying the story is the famous picture of Sarah and Hazel wearing reindeer antlers and red noses taken last year at Lashkar Gah.

36

THE MONEY GAME

New Year's Eve brings an unexpected visit from Lashkar Gah. The global economic crisis has also impacted the development funding. Almost the worst thing is the British pound's nosedive against the dollar. The UK–Danish development fund receives its capital in sterling but pays out in dollars. Added to that, funding now has to stretch further in geographical terms, with the high-crime village of Nad-e-Ali having been given its own adviser and a district centre. All districts are to be hit hard by spending cuts. The budget for Gereshk is being cut by 50 per cent.

The adviser from Lashkar Gah is well liked by everyone in Gereshk, but we fight against the proposals all we can. The projects Georg, Geoff and I have put out to tender, all the things we've promised to implement here, are stopped immediately. It may be necessary, but the message is so sudden and the consequences out in the districts immeasurable. It is one thing for advisers like us to go back on promises and lose face. We'll get over it. It is quite another for Ali Shar and Ahad Khan to lose credibility in the eyes of the local Afghan people on our account.

For some time I have been working on my American connections in Lashkar Gah. The US aid organization USAID is a major player and has suffered less as a result of the weak pound. Although USAID also cuts back on its involvement, its coffers remain an attractive proposition for us in so far as we have never before bothered USAID for funding and we need to find other avenues if we are still to be able to direct development efforts towards Gereshk.

For months, Georg and I have felt that the time is ripe to bring non-governmental organizations into play in Gereshk—charities, development funds and human rights organizations would all be significant players here. Some have worked in Helmand before, while others have woken up to the need as a result of press coverage, an upswing in media attention that in some cases has even prompted governments and funds to bankroll increased activity despite the ongoing crisis.

Gereshk suffers badly from its own reputation in previous years.

Convincing NGOs to come here is an uphill struggle. The majority still think Gereshk is Helmand's most dangerous town. But Georg and I plug away. All of us are feeling the pressure. Geoff's gone home to London, Georg will soon be at the end of his long stint, and I can't keep going much longer either. Other people will take our places, but if we can 'sell' Gereshk and attract new players and new money from outside, then the initiative is no longer going to be confined to what three lone advisers can cope with.

Maybe our successors will even be able to last longer than eight or nine months before they're whacked.

We know we're on the right track when an independent organization appears on the scene granting micro-loans to people wanting to start a business or increase agricultural production. Like many of the NGOs, the people behind the micro-loans don't want to be associated with the international forces, so we don't actually know where they're operating from, only that they're here. The Taliban are already threatening the organization in both Lashkar Gah and Gereshk, but so far the new player is holding out and is apparently operating in close collaboration with local police.

The situation motivates me even more in my efforts to pull in new players. I pinpoint organizations already involved in collaborations with the Americans. One of the biggest has a man called Johnny in Kandahar. He wants to take a closer look at Gereshk and has already been booked on to a chopper several times, only for his visit to be cancelled at the last minute because the mother organization feels that Gereshk is still too dangerous.

But I'm not giving up.

Georg has a similar challenge on his hands. For almost half a year he has been trying to attract the interest of UN Habitat, an independent organization under the auspices of the United Nations specializing in urban planning. Each time a visit has been arranged they've pulled out, seldom even featuring on the choppers' passenger lists.

In principle it doesn't matter what NGO we manage to get in here first. The main thing is to convince one so the others will see it can be done. Johnny's organization claims 3 per cent of the project budget for itself, but gets things done, implementing projects in war zones. It operates on a global basis, but prefers to remain as anonymous as possible since the Taliban bombed its offices in Kabul. Johnny is especially interested in projects involving young people, sport in particular, but he's in no way dismissive of projects for women.

After working at it for months I receive a call one day from Johnny's colleague, Ken, who takes care of security matters for the organization. We've exchanged a few emails, but this is the first time we speak on the phone.

After a while listening to his voice I decide to take a chance: 'You're from New Zealand, aren't you?' I ask.

'Yes, Ma'am. Maori and proud of it too.'

'Do you know Tama?' I ask, flicking feverishly through the pages of my address book to find Tama and his lengthy Maori surname alongside his phone number.

It turns out they're old army buddies. It's been ten years since they've been in touch. I give him Tama's number. He even knows KK from ArmorGroup too.

Following our casual discussion in which I praise the virtues of Gereshk and highlight his chances of hooking up with old friends here, I call Tama immediately.

'I need some Maori magic,' I say, then put him in the picture.

'Don't you worry,' Tama says, laughing. 'I'll bring Ken to Gereshk.' Half an hour later, Ken calls me back. Johnny's trip is booked and Tama has promised a barbecue. I plan the visit down to the minutest detail.

Buzzard owes me a favour. He promises to do everything he can to make sure Johnny and Ken get in and out of Camp Price with an absolute minimum of friction. I know from personal experience that being stranded somewhere for days on end with no helicopters available is going to make you think twice next time around. Desks pile up regardless of whether choppers are flying or not.

Johnny, Ken and I tour the town together, stopping off at relevant places along the way, including the women's centre, a sports arena and an old playground in desperate need of repair. I've also set up a meeting with Mahmoud, a local official responsible for sports and leisure.

Sports activities generally are booming. Lashkar Gah has several judo and karate clubs and a number of football teams. To our amazement, bodybuilding is popular too. I know some of these clubs from my time with CIMIC at Lashkar Gah, but the same trend is now becoming apparent in Gereshk as well. The town has ten football teams and five school teams.

Clubs for martial arts are mushrooming, two bodybuilding clubs have started and there's a chess club too.

After two days of meetings and outings on patrols, Johnny has drawn up applications to the tune of half a million dollars. I don't expect them all to be approved, but if only a few of the projects can be implemented, Johnny's organization will have put Gereshk firmly on the map for all the other NGOs to see.

Tama throws a big barbecue. During a grenade attack on the camp, a hole was blasted in the wall next to Tama's barbecue area. No one was injured and only a corner of the camouflage net bears further witness. Tama has decided to leave the hole as it is: it leads out on to one on the roads through the camp and saves him a long detour through the American area.

Tama's food is fantastic. The three Maoris do the traditional dance. I'm very pleased with how things have gone. I feel I've given it everything I've got and used all my cunning. Now we just have to wait and see.

I go a few rounds with Lashkar Gah about the budget. I know it's hopeless, but I'm angry nonetheless. Shutting off all investment can do irreparable damage, regardless of the fact that, in the wake of visits by a couple of international delegations, Gereshk now looks set to become a major fulcrum of future investment in Helmand.

There's only one thing I can stubbornly continue to point out: the principles of war prescribe that victories must be exploited and advanced reinforced if the stalemate is to be broken.

Thanks to the unremitting efforts of the Danish Battle Group in Gereshk and its outlying areas since ISAF 4, Gereshk has been transformed into a success story. It's not a Danish county, but by Afghan yardsticks it's an astonishing achievement indeed.

37
THE MAYOR AND THE JOURNALIST

General Mhajadin is surprised to see me. Once, his glasses almost fell off his nose when he saw me striding through the camp at Lashkar Gah in full battle dress. Today he is standing in HQ drinking coffee and smoking a cigarette. Mhajadin is in charge of the Afghan forces spearheading a major operation to flush the Taliban out of Malgir and Spin Masjed in the northern parts of Babaji.

I've a trump card I can play. General Mhajadin received his military training in the Soviet Union.

I greet him in Russian.

His expression runs the whole gamut in seconds. I can tell he recognizes me from somewhere and in a moment he'll probably place me.

'You speak Russian,' he blurts out in surprise. 'Yes, I do.'

'We met once before at Lashkar Gah. But you were in uniform then.' His eyes sparkle now he's got things sorted out.

'I'm an adviser for the Foreign Office now,' I explain. 'Yours or ours?' he asks, and laughs.

It feels a bit like one of the old Soviet jokes. Perhaps the general isn't quite convinced I'm not a Russian spy.

We talk about the impending operation, the first step towards a new goal three years further on. A surfaced road is to be built between Gereshk and Lashkar Gah, running through the densely populated Babaji district. The operation is intended to remove mines from the area as well as the Taliban.

Governor Gulab Mangal himself has requested the area be swept and a road built along the canal where most of the people live. Whether people need to get their sons to hospital or goods to the bazaar, the existing roads are so poor that from the middle of Babaji it takes two hours to reach Gereshk or Lashkar Gah. We're talking thirty kilometres as the crow flies at most.

The decision to build the road is definitely the right thing to do from the perspective of economic and social development opportunities. But it will cost lives.

Mayor Ali Shar and General Mhajadin have presented the operation to clan leaders and leading representatives from Babaji so that local inhabitants can leave the area before fighting commences. The local people support the operation wholeheartedly. The prospect of finally being able to get rid of the Taliban and the mines, and the promise of easier access to Lashkar Gah and Gereshk, are just what the doctor ordered in terms of hopes for the future of the area. Rumour has it, though, that the Taliban are intending to go all out and fight to the last man.

Afghan army command is reckoning on four days. The Danish Battle Group has warned that four days will not be enough, six or eight being more realistic because of the time-consuming nature of sweeping for mines and roadside incendiaries, finding them and blowing them up.

I hint at the discussion, but the general is a born optimist. In the unexpected event of having to spend a couple days more on the operation, he believes the powers that be will bend.

The atmosphere at HQ is tense. The operation goes ahead that same evening.

The Afghan troops lead the attack. The Danes follow on behind, supplemented by British military engineers. Fighting is intense for four days under inhuman conditions. The area is heavily mined and the Taliban have dug in with battle positions, trenches and ammunition depots.

I'm able to follow progress on a map at HQ. Cleared mines are marked by frighteningly tight clusters of dots. The Afghan units fight hard and tenaciously. Four of their soldiers are wounded. No Danes are seriously hurt.

After four days, Afghan Army Operational Command orders the Afghan battalion out because it is needed elsewhere. The operation is only half-complete.

The Danes take the new situation in their stride. They were aware of the risk that the Afghans might be pulled out. Half a victory is better than none at all. A huge number of mines and roadside incendiaries have been cleared and the locals are now better able to move freely around the area. Fewer children and adults will die and fewer limbs will be amputated.

Nevertheless it is a source of annoyance. We feel we have promised the people more than we were able to deliver and the Afghan army command has pulled the plug on us.

We drive over to the weekly security meeting. We know it's not going to be easy.

Author and journalist Carsten Jensen has been with the battle group for some days. The second-in-command has decided Jensen can be present at the meeting as an observer.

I've never before seen the mayor so exhausted or so dejected. He strokes his white beard. There are dark rings under his sad eyes. The district governor has been away for weeks taking part in official meetings in Kabul and Ali Shar is looking after the district on his own. He hasn't the energy for yet another meeting. In particular, he hasn't the energy to sit listening to the police and the army. Especially not the army.

Ali Shar levels a devastating broadside against the operation that has just been carried out. The timing was wrong and pulling out halfway through was a mistake. The Afghan battalion has long since made itself scarce and the Danes must bear the brunt of his attack.

After the meeting I find the mayor outside venting all his frustration and anger on Carsten Jensen. Ali Shar is enraged. He feels he has been left in the lurch and that the government is pulling the wool over the eyes of Helmand's citizens. He is bitterly disappointed about continuing corruption and feels that in all the years that have passed nothing good has come at all. The air is thick with accusations and reproaches.

I'm completely speechless. But I'm also saddened. Why should Ali Shar's pent-up frustrations be heaped upon a foreign journalist? Does the mayor have any idea at all that he is in the process of pulling the rug out from under all of us, himself included, by sounding off so angrily?

But for me personally there's more to it than that. I have laid my life on the line as a soldier here and I am working my guts out in the face of diplomatic bureaucracy in order to bring further development and prosperity to Gereshk. I've seen with my own eyes the enormous progress that has been made there since I left the town one cold day in February 2008. And now the mayor is telling Carsten Jensen that nothing has changed whatsoever. Carsten Jensen isn't just anyone. As a world-renowned author and opinion-former, he has enormous clout and is capable of shaping public debate.

I try to calm Ali Shar down. I try to make him see at least some of the more obvious improvements that have occurred. But it's no use. The old mayor has lost his head and is letting off years of accumulated steam in one go.

I turn and walk away. It feels as though I've just been stabbed in the back by a man I've been doing everything in my power to help. I can do no more than what I have already done. I'm angry about what we are doing not being good enough and about the lives we have lost being completely forgotten.

Back at camp I ask my interpreter to call the mayor. I watch Waheed's chubby face, his sad eyes as the phone rings at the other end. Waheed can see how dejected I am, but he doesn't know why yet. Ali Shar will be able to tell from Waheed's tone that something is wrong. I never know how much goes into the lengthy introductory pleasantries, but I do know that as an interpreter Waheed feels responsibility for preventing and ironing out any misunderstandings that might arise between the two cultures. He is clearly on edge now.

'I understand your anger at the operation in Babaji not being completed,' I begin. 'You have lost face and we are the ones responsible.'

Waheed quietly translates. I hear a mumble at the other end.

'I am calling you now because I am unhappy about the way you expressed your feelings to a journalist. I had hoped that you were my friend, and as your friend I cannot understand why you did not choose to come to me with your grievance.'

Waheed translates again and nods to say Ali Shar hears me. I hold back tears and am embarrassed that Waheed can see how upset I am, but it can't be helped. Things would only be worse if I were unwilling to open my heart and say what has to be said.

'There are many good things about the society from which I come. But of course there are other things about it that are less than good. For one thing, we place far too much trust in what the media tell us. You have no idea how much influence you as mayor of Gereshk have on public opinion in a country such as Denmark. No one there will listen to me when the mayor of Gereshk has said that we do nothing here and that nothing is worth our efforts. We are a fragile nation. When the mothers and fathers of our soldiers read in a newspaper that you do not believe their presence here makes a difference, they will begin to discuss among themselves. They will complain and lobby our politicians and ask why their sons and daughters must die on foreign soil for such a worthless project. The debate might even escalate to the point that the politicians will feel compelled to bring the soldiers home. That happened in the case of Iraq. We withdrew before we had finished the projects we had started. The same thing can happen here.'

Waheed translates, sentence by sentence. Suddenly he stops and looks up at me. His face is pale, as though all the blood has drained away. I know that the full meaning of the words he as an interpreter has just translated mechanically has now hit home.

He asks the mayor to wait a moment, then says softly to me: 'Does that mean that the people can ask your politicians to order that you should not be here any more?'

'Yes.'

'That would not be good. That would not be good at all,' he whispers, and fixes his gaze on the floor.

'No,' I say. 'I know.'

Waheed translates my words on the power of the press and the people. 'The mayor is devastated,' says Waheed. 'He says there will be a bloodbath if you leave us.' Waheed looks at me despairingly.

'Yes,' I say. 'I know. And you know too. Unfortunately, journalists only very rarely ask what would happen if we were to pull out. At least, I have never heard one yet. They ask if progress is fast enough. And of course it never is. There are always things that could be better.'

Waheed looks up at me: 'The mayor is very sorry about what he said. He was not aware of the consequences.'

'I understand that. The only thing I ask of him is that he respect our friendship and our working relationship and in future come to me if he is angry or disappointed before telling a journalist who may turn his words into a front-page story. Many mothers and fathers will read that story and conclude that their sons have died in vain.'

Waheed translates again before answering: 'But they did not die in vain. The mayor has never said that.'

'No, he has not. But the same misunderstanding occurs time and again,' I mumble in reply.

'What misunderstanding?'

'Afghans and Danes work on two different timescales. You saw the Taliban removed in 2001 and for a long time after prospects were bright. But the international community made the same mistake as always. We won the war and yet we were unprepared to invest massively in development.

Many international observers have pointed out that Afghanistan should have received massive aid before the Taliban had a chance to regroup. We should have helped on a grand scale while we had the chance. Had we done so, you might now have had the kind of society you wanted, or at least the beginnings of it. But aid didn't come. I have spoken to many who worked here in the years immediately following the collapse of the Taliban and they all say that security was better then than it is now. They initiated small local projects, but nothing of any scale. The mayor is right inasmuch as the Taliban had not yet gathered its strength. We could have done something.

But the international community was unwilling to pay the cost. The feeling was: the Taliban are gone, the rest is up to you. We Danes think differently. Out timeline begins when we arrived in Gereshk in the autumn of 2007. In the time we have been here, security has greatly improved. Does Ali Shar recall what it was like in Gereshk one year ago?'

Waheed translates a shortened version of my lengthy explanation and then listens to the mayor's reply.

'Yes,' he says. 'The mayor had just been released by the Taliban. Gereshk is a better place now than it was a year ago.'

'Indeed. And every time we talk about security we are talking about two different things. You are right in so far as the international community ought to have achieved much more in eight years. But these are the sins of the past. We are paying the price now with our own blood. The Danes came in after the Taliban had regained its strength. We have killed many and initiated many worthwhile projects. But we are still a long way from making up for what has been lost.'

The mayor apologizes again. He explains that he lost his patience. He had spoken with a lot of angry people from Babaji and promised them that the Taliban would be removed, only for the whole thing to stall when the Afghan battalion was called back on another mission. Now the people of Babaji are disappointed in him.

Waheed and I end our discussion with the mayor. All of us are dejected, but it's too late now. I can't ask Carsten Jensen to talk to Ali Shar again. If he changes his story now it'll look as though we've been telling him what to say. That's not what I want. All I want is a fair say.

Carsten Jensen writes four lengthy pieces for *Information* back in Copenhagen. The essence is we're doing too little. That the troops are manoeuvring in a landscape they don't understand. The mayor's outburst is included, though Carsten Jensen is fair enough to say he's in no doubt that it was later regretted.

In many respects I'm inclined to agree with Carsten Jensen. But I'm tired of how easy it is for observers to fly in and then put on the garb of experts after only a couple of days in Helmand. Their snapshots engender opinions that may later give rise to serious political decisions.

Two weeks later, on 22 January 2009, we are visited by members of the Danish parliament's Foreign Affairs Committee. The committee has expressed a wish to meet some of the local officials and people of particular significance in local society. The district governor is still tied up with meetings in Kabul and Ali Shar must again shoulder responsibility. I have also invited Gulaley, whom the committee's women members in particular are looking forward to meeting. Unfortunately, she calls to cancel because of illness in the family.

As I stand waiting outside the conference tent, Ali Shar comes hurrying towards me.

'Hello, how are you?' he asks in English as always. 'I'm fine, thank you. How are you?' I reply.

'I'm fine, thank you. How are you?' he repeats. After the satisfaction of being able to day the right things in English has subsided, the look in his eyes saddens: 'What am I to tell them? I'm afraid of saying the wrong thing.'

I kick myself. I've ended up muzzling the mayor.

'There's no need to be nervous. These people are politicians. They are the ones who make the decisions. You must tell them everything you know. Not just the good things but the bad things as well. They'll be asking you a lot of questions and you must say what you think. They're perfectly aware that mistakes are made, but they also want to help. The more you tell them, the better they'll be able to do their job.'

'Yes, but I am afraid they will pull the soldiers out. I have had terrible nightmares since you told me that. I had never thought it could happen and now I can't think of anything else,' says Ali Shar, who is clearly concerned.

'Then tell them. Ask them if they intend to pull the soldiers out.' 'Are you sure?'

'Yes, I'm sure.'

Ali Shar strokes his long white beard. These past weeks have taken their toll on him. He's doing the job of two men, and unlike the district governor he's never before been anywhere near a journalist. The idea of being able to speak frankly and profitably with politicians at a national level is a complete mystery to him.

I leave the mayor in the conference room together with the Danish parliamentarians and walk over to my office feeling dejected. We are like a giant with impaired vision and hearing. We fumble around and make mistakes. Our muscles are big and our punch is hard, but we have no idea where to aim if the Afghans don't tell us and lend us their eyes and ears.

All of a sudden my phone rings and it's Gulaley. She's at the main gate and wants to meet the Danish politicians after all. I don't ask questions.

I've no idea if her sister's illness was just a story she came to regret, or if she has paid her visit and simply found she had the time after all. I've long since come to understand the folly of pointing to error and exposing white lies, unless in the case of men who refuse to take me seriously.

I run down to meet her. Hamid has driven her as usual and Gulaley is in the back, looking extremely nervous.

Perhaps she was just afraid. Perhaps someone tried to prevent her from taking part. Perhaps she's unsettled by the prospect of meeting some of my country's most important politicians. Whatever the reason, inquisition would serve no purpose. If Gulaley told me a fib, she's perfectly aware of it herself and there's no way I'm going to cause her to lose face. If she's been threatened or if there's any danger involved, she'll most likely tell me herself.

I jump into the front seat next to Hamid and point him in the right direction.

'I'm glad your mother could come,' I tell him. 'Yes, we are here now,' he says solemnly.

We tumble out of the car by the conference tent. I give Gulaley a hug.

She takes a deep breath and adjusts her clothing, and then we go inside. Ali Shar is seated in front of the committee. I explain to them that Gulaley has been able to come after all. She sits down next to Ali Shar and I leave them all to it.

Gulaley makes a strong impression in the Danish politicians. Ali Shar is able to vent some of his frustrations and thankfully receives the kind of assurance he has been hoping for. The Danes have no plans to break off relations with the Afghan people.

38

DEMOCRACY AND FEAR

One day in January 2009 I realize the true extent of the women's network. Three women from a village in the valley north of Gereshk suddenly turn up at the women's centre. They've come to find help to sort out the documents needed for them to be able to register to vote in the coming election. One of the women at the centre immediately gets to her feet to accompany the three women to the district governor's office to receive confirmation of their identity. The female polling officials in Gereshk are all actively involved in one of the women's *shura*s.

The impending registration of voters is a major security challenge for the police. The Danish Battle Group and civilian advisers are asked by Lashkar Gah to keep a sharp eye on proceedings. Paradoxically for the troops, the international forces have at the same time been requested to keep a low profile. The election is an Afghan event and security is rightly a matter for the Afghan security forces.

Through my contact with the women I am able to follow the month-long process at close hand. The district governor regularly issues bulletins about how things are going, and British units training the Afghan soldiers and police also report back from their sporadic visits to the three registration points. The same locations will be polling stations when the election takes place. The women register at the Girls' High School, where last year I met Hadja's *shura*.

Governor Gulab Mangal decides to visit Gereshk again and the speeches are to be given at the school. I drive to the meeting with the Danish TV documentary film-maker, who is now following the women's rights group.

A number of advisers have also come up from Lashkar Gah.

The governor is highly aware of his public profile. The risk of a suicide attack is considered to be great, but that doesn't worry him. He takes his time until sufficiently large numbers have gathered in the concrete yard in the middle of the school. About four hundred in all, a figure the governor seems to be unhappy about. In the former Taliban stronghold of Musa Qaléh, more than eight hundred men turned out to see him for his second-time venture into the town where the Taliban had twice fired rockets at his helicopter.

Gereshk is a different matter. People want to vote, but they know too that the risk of being wounded or even killed increases dramatically the closer they are to the governor. Four hundred people is as good as it gets.

ArmorGroup have pulled their vehicles right into the yard, whereas the military police remain outside on the street. Today, I'm with them. I join the other advisers to hear what they have to say about 'my' town. Derek, who was here with Fraser, is full of praise.

'I've been to at least two hundred *shura*s in Helmand and this is the first one I've seen with women taking part. Just look at how many there are,' he says, throwing out his arm.

The governor, the district governor and the mayor are seated together with a number of clan elders on a row of chairs behind the microphone. To the left of the microphone sit ten women in burkas. Just about opposite is a small bench on which I can see four women, two in blue burkas and one in green, as well as a very slight woman, or perhaps just a young girl, wrapped up in a big shawl. Close by, another two women are sitting in the ground.

The other advisers' comments about seeing women at a political rally makes me realize that Gereshk really is special in that respect. For me it seems normal that they take part to the extent they do.

I'm sure things would look different elsewhere if there were more women advisers. It's not that I'm particularly fanatical. It's just the fact that I'm there. I'm proof that women are capable. Unfortunately, though, I'm the only woman adviser operating in the rural districts.

Women keep coming in from the street. Ignoring the speeches, they turn directly to the nearest corner, where an elderly lady sits waiting on a bench with a metal detector in her hand. We gave detectors to the women's centre last year at the time of the ridiculous scare about women suicide attackers, having ordered them before Fatima discovered that her and Gulaley's antics on a borrowed moped had sparked panic. Now the women line up by the old lady to be checked with the detector before going into a low building to be registered. I approach gingerly. The old lady nods.

I step inside the low building. In one room, some women are standing looking out of the frosted pane as they listen to the speeches. In the next, registration takes place. I have to communicate by gestures and the few sentences I'm able to utter, but with smiles and nods we understand each other. I'm allowed to take a photograph of the woman as she fills in the registration form.

The atmosphere is pleasant. The women are proud of their work registering new voters. I thank them for letting me have a look and go out again into the yard to listen to District Governor Ahad Khan's speech.

Suddenly, a shot rings out.

People leap to their feet. Old people become agile. But the district governor calls to order, gesturing for everyone to sit down. I find I've moved instinctively closer to ArmorGroup's bulletproof cars.

A couple of policemen come hurrying in from the street. Hardly a minute later I learn what's happened from one of ArmorGroup's bodyguards posted on the street. A policeman with a defective handgun found he was unable to remove a round from the chamber and decided to fire it into the tarmac instead.

The bloody fool, I think to myself. Doesn't he realize how jittery people are today? The Taliban have got nothing to lose and everything to gain by spreading fear and terror on a day like this.

As I stand cursing the unthinking policeman my gaze falls on a little girl standing beneath the microphone. She's about ten years old and is watching the district governor as he delivers an impassioned speech to the crowd. A little later, she approaches me. I smile to her. She looks at me intently before going over to the women's bench with a rather solemn expression.

One of the burkas turns slightly in my direction.

Shortly afterwards, the girl comes back. She waves me towards her with an encouraging look and offers me her arm. I jerk my head at the nearest military policemen so he understands I want to move further into the crowd. I hear him click his radio as I follow on behind the little girl.

She takes me by the women's bench. I look across to those seated on the front row next to the other dignitaries. I hazard a guess that the burkas conceal a couple of members of the provincial council together with Gulaley, Hadja, Fatima and other teachers.

Someone takes my hand. I should have recognized the curve of her back and the colours of her clothes. The slight figure on the bench belongs to Khanumgul. She lets the veil fall from her face. Her big brown eyes smile up at me. Khanumgul has always been fond of blue and hated the burka.

Today she is among the crowd with only a big shawl to cover herself.

The fuller figure next to Khanumgul lifts the veil of her burka slightly, making sure to remain hidden for all but me.

'Hello. We met last year. I am in the English class,' she whispers in unhesitating English.

I can't remember her at all, not for the life of me. But she smiles, and I smile back and nod. Khanumgul squeezes my hand as we sit on the bench and listen. The air is thick with tension.

Someone screams. The crowd is on its feet. Khanumgul reaches for my hand and we run. I leap over the upturned bench. Khanumgul grips my hand. As we run, I count the seconds. Three. Four. Five. When will the explosion come? We run beside the wall.

No shots have sounded. No explosion. We stop to catch our breath by the wall. People are gripped by panic. Chairs are overturned and there's a shuffling of feet against concrete. The governor's voice rings out across the yard, a metallic crackle in the microphone. One of the military police grabs hold of me.

'I've got AC, I've got AC,' he yells into his radio.

Khanumgul is chuntering away at my side. I can sense she's frightened, yet in doubt. I smile cautiously, point to my ears and shake my head. We give each other a hug. I can see now that she is scared. I clench my fist into a ball at my heart, pound my chest and make the sound of a pulse.

She laughs and nods as she tries to catch her breath. I point towards the yard and throw up my arms. What's happening?

Khanumgul exchanges a few quick words with some bystanders. A sense of embarrassment spreads among the crowd. Someone shouted '*Bomb!*' and we ran. But it was a false alarm. Khanumgul takes my hand and we make our way back again. People laugh with relief. ArmorGuard have had their charges prone on the ground and have now bundled them into the cars. KK is incensed that I'm not their 'parcel' today. He's afraid something will happen to me.

I stay until the speeches are over and most of the invited guests have gone home. A woman approaches me slowly. She turns her back to the others and lifts her fashionable beige-coloured burka. It's Hadja. She's been sitting on the podium.

I repeat my pounding gesture and my imitated heartbeat, and she nods her understanding. She chirps and strokes my cheek. I give her a hug. I understand she's on her way to the women's centre and that the governor has promised to stop by.

Before she goes, Hadja bends down to the little girl at her side. I understand now it's Hadja's daughter. Hadja lifts the girl's face gently with a finger under her chin. She looks up and smiles proudly. The little girl's eyes are bright blue.

I get to the women's centre in time to catch the incredible sight of Hadja cheerfully and with enthusiasm showing the governor around the centre in Gulaley's absence, telling him about what the women do here, how much they have learned and how significant such opportunities are for half the Afghan population. The Danish documentary film-maker follows in their footsteps and Hadja is now performing for two rolling cameras.

After the speech, the women stride directly into the gym and proudly show off the facilities.

The governor turns to me and exclaims: 'What a marvellous idea! I think you should do this for all the schools in Gereshk, don't you agree?'

I kick myself at the thought of the empty coffers. It would have been so good to have been able to extend my hand and say: 'Do you know what, Governor, I think we'll do just that. And while we're at it, I reckon we should lay a couple of kilometres of tarmac going up to the hydroelectric plant, and of course erect some solar-powered street lights so people can feel safe after dark, don't you think?'

Instead, all I can do is tread water and assure him I'll be working on it.

We pass through the corridor, past all the shoes, and get back into the cars. The governor is a master of the lightning visit. An hour later, he and his entourage are already in the chopper on their way home.

39

ALL CHANGE

ISAF 7 is rotated in. ISAF 6 is out. I'm no longer 'the girl who used to be a captain attached to CIMIC, then landed a nice little earner working for the Foreign Office'. Now I'm 'the girl who's been in Helmand for more than a year'.

Rotation is in February and coincides with me having just been home on leave and bringing two new advisers back to Camp Price to replace Georg and me. The camp is full of people on their way in and others on their way out.

The new soldiers arrive well prepared, full of good ideas and with an abundance of enthusiasm. Like those before them, they're here to do a job of work and to do it at least as well as their predecessors. This time, the new ones have got a lot to live up to. ISAF 6 was led by an extraordinarily clear-sighted commander.

The new arrivals try to slip into the routines as quickly as possible. When they're confused by a whole stack of reports all saying something different and yet vaguely similar, they appear at my door to ask questions whose answers appear to me now to be obvious. Persistent rumours have been going around about the general election being brought forward. But no one is fooling me into believing any election in Afghanistan is going to be held six months ahead of schedule. I know exactly what kind of a logistical challenge an election in this war-torn and mountainous land presents.

I no longer need to write endless emails. I know exactly who to call to confirm or discount rumours about a new police chief being appointed for the town. The recurrent whispers about an imminent attack on the camp leave me cold too. Even in Lashkar Gah I'm taken more seriously now. I'm the adviser for the rural districts who has been here the longest.

But I've been burning the candle at both ends. There have been nights when I've cried myself to sleep. Not because I thought I wasn't doing things well enough. I cry because I'm exhausted and because there's nothing left inside me. For eight months I have worked between seventy and a hundred hours a week. I've passed the threshold of what I can do. Bringing development to Helmand has cost the life of one Danish soldier a month and I've been more than keenly aware of my responsibilities.

I've a month and a half left, and in the last few weeks I try my best to act as an experience bank and guide so the new guys feel they've got some support. I tell them about the history of all this and about the long-term ideas; about how Gereshk has gone from scraping the bottom to being the economic capital of the province; and I tell the soldiers about the work with the women, because all of them have a girlfriend, a mother or a sister who can't understand why they've gone to war.

The soldiers are angry that we haven't done a better job of getting the positive stories across. All I can do is express my regret. But my regrets don't help a young man who has to queue up for twenty minutes at the welfare phones to call a girlfriend who is reproachful and feels she has been abandoned and accorded low priority.

I don't know what to do. Selling the advances we've made to the media back home is just as hard as selling them to Kabul. As far as the southern provinces go, the suspicion exhibited by the capital borders on disdain, and journalists are deeply distrustful of politicians and their wars.

In some cases, journalists come here astonishingly unprepared. A journalist gets out of a car in front of the district governor's office and concludes immediately that it's unsafe when he sees two armed guards standing outside. How safe does he think it would be if they weren't there? I feel like sending him on holiday to Ecuador, where there are armed guards outside every McDonald's and Kentucky Fried Chicken. Or to South Africa, where there are twenty-two thousand murders a year. Or to Copenhagen's Nørrebro, for that matter, where sometimes there's more shooting and more killed than here in Gereshk.

Generally, though, press coverage tends not to be marred by poor research or poor journalism. What characterizes it more than anything is the fact that the well-written account highlighting the struggle for life and death sells more than the equally well-written account of schools opening and teaching going on.

Journalists are only human. Give them a ticket to Helmand and their boyhood dreams take charge. They want to go to war. Why sit around in Helmand writing about a school whose pupils can't wait to get started in the mornings when you can pen a dramatic account of bullets flying around your ears so your male colleagues go green with envy?

It's about eight one evening and I'm in the middle of giving a talk about development initiatives in Helmand. In front of me are thirty soldiers on folding chairs. They're worn out but pay attention anyway. I can inform them of things they hardly ever hear about. What plans there are for development. Where we are at right now.

I show them a picture of the Tom Bridge, which most of them have crossed a hundred times. I explain how the bridge panels of the sixty-year-old Russian construction no longer join together as they are supposed to but float freely along the length of the bridge. I've inspected the bridge myself on foot. It shudders violently every time a truck passes over it. The soldiers don't notice inside their vehicles because most of it is taken in by the shock absorbers, the rest being attributed to the vehicle itself.

The Danish Battle Group has long since mapped alternative crossing points if Tom should collapse. Building a new bridge would cost around fifty million dollars, but no money has been found yet. The diplomats are fishing in a number of the big development funds, but so far without luck, I tell my audience.

Suddenly there's a brief hiss, followed by an explosion and a blast wave. All thirty soldiers are prone on the ground in front of me. I'm still on my feet.

'What the fuck's going on?' one of them yells. 'Mortar! Who's firing?'

'It's ours,' I shout with my fingers in my ears, glancing down at the soldiers lying there between their overturned chairs. They're used to being a target. They've been through this so many times before that their first reaction is to throw themselves flat on the ground, share information and get ready to fire back. My reaction is to put my fingers in my ears. At Camp Price the norm is that it's us firing at them. Only very seldom is it the other way round.

I imagine Checkpoint 8, three kilometres south of the camp. Most likely it's now bathed in the light of tracer shells falling slowly through the sky. Ever since the police took on responsibility for the checkpoint, the Taliban have been trying to break their moral by launching attacks just after dark. And each time, the Danish Bravo Company comes to their aid with its armoured personnel carriers, the mortar section simultaneously casting light over the area so the police can see what they're doing.

The mortars are launched quite close to the briefing tent and the explosions are ear-shattering. A couple of the lads leave the tent and receive confirmation that Checkpoint 8 is under attack. For me, it's a recurring incident.

'OK, is this something we need to react to?' one of the soldiers asks. 'No, just sit down. Usually, Bravo get out there and pull the plug on the party,' I say.

They sit gawping at me. It's absurd. I'm standing here in a pair of Fjällräven trekking pants and one of the sequinned shirts the women have sewn for me, and I'm telling a bunch of hardened soldiers from a Green Zone outpost that they've no need to worry.

They do as they're told and sit down again. I carry on with my talk, interrupted only by the occasional hiss that sounds every time a shell leaves the mortar barrel, then the ear-splitting blast that demands we fall silent and wait.

40

A PRAYER FOR GULALEY

USAID has approved a much-needed renovation of the women's centre, as well as a number of trial projects. Though the funds are from elsewhere, the women see it as thanks to me that the place is being injected to the tune of two hundred thousand dollars. Similar funding has also befallen a number of sports projects, much to the delight of Mahmoud, the local official with responsibility for sports and leisure. In all, USAID is investing almost half a million dollars in Gereshk.

The rights group is still running. Things go up and down because of personal tensions between some of the women, but they're open for new discussions at least.

During the last meeting at which I'm present before leaving Afghanistan, we speak for the first time about girls hurting themselves in order to avoid enforced marriages or because they simply can't cope with life any longer. Most suicides among young girls are committed by means of consuming large quantities of opium. Suicide and self-mutilation are subjects fraught with shame and grief. Putting things into words is a help. I've no idea where their discussions will lead, but I do know that no action ever comes without words first.

We're sitting together in a tight group when Gulaley sits up straight and looks me directly in the eye.

'AC, will you pray that I win the election?'

Everything stops for a moment. Her candidature is news to me. A district council is to be set up and five of the seats are reserved by law for women, though I doubt whether they will actually be filled. But not only has

Gulaley announced her candidature, she is now asking a Christian woman in Muslim company to pray for her.

I nod. 'Yes, I will,' I tell her. 'I will pray for you.'

Gulaley nods back appreciatively.

She was taken aback the first time I said I would pray for her and the women. We have never discussed religion. We fight for the same things. Our God is the same, only the packaging differs.

Gulaley doesn't know it, but I've been praying for her and the other women for a long time. I have done my best for the women. They have changed my life and I have changed theirs. I will never be able to forget them. Not even those first four women who peeked through the gate at me on a patrol so long ago have I forgotten. I have seen them all. I have seen the lost widows begging on the streets who are beyond my help. I have seen the young women teachers who may perhaps already be building the future of Afghanistan. I have seen the midwife who patches up the women of her town and who now wants to be elected to office.

When our soldiers die and we send them home, we gather in prayer. The prayer begins thus: 'They do not grow old as we who are left grow old.' And ends thus: 'At the going down of the sun, and in the morning, we will remember them.'

I may not be able to keep in my memory all the many soldiers we lost in my fourteen months as a soldier and civilian adviser in Helmand. But I will remember the women of Helmand until the day I die.

Saying goodbye is strangely unreal. We did it once before, last winter. The women were surprised when I came back. The way it happened and the time at which it occurred surprised me too. But this time my feeling is I won't ever be coming back.

I take Gulaley's soft hands in mine and kiss both her cheeks. I feel more confident leaving her this time. She is by no means the last one to whom I must say goodbye. I still have a few days left. The illusion is there still.

My final meeting is the weekly Tuesday session with the district governor and the mayor. During the two hours it lasts I say practically nothing. The two new advisers are already finding their own approaches, their own ways.

District Governor Ahad Kahn glances at me now and then with sorrow in his eyes. I know he's going to miss my company. There are people we get to know and of whom we grow fond because they speak their mind and do things their own way. But it's clear to me now that I must let go. I know I'm exhausted and need to go home. But I don't want to leave. When I say goodbye to Abdul Ahad Kahn, the first tears begin to fall. He looks me straight in the eye and clasps my hand tight.

'Don't cry, Miss AC,' he says comfortingly in English.

I'm unable to speak. All I can do is look at the floor and blink through the tears.

I say goodbye to the mayor of Gereshk, Ali Shar. The tears roll down my cheeks. I think of how he comes to us each week, tenacious with his long list of projects, and of how he has been able to cross them off one by one.

He has given so much to the town. He was held captive by the Taliban for a month along with his son, until Ali Shar had borrowed enough money from shopkeepers in the town to pay the ransom. And still he keeps on.

He takes my hand in his and looks me in the eye. Waheed translates for him: 'It has been such a pleasure working with you, Miss AC. I wish you happiness and a long and good life.'

I nod and try to stem the tears.

'May I have your telephone number, Miss AC?' he asks.

'But Ali Shar, you don't understand my language and I don't understand yours,' I mumble.

Waheed translates.

Ali Shar looks at me and holds an imaginary telephone to his ear. 'Hello, how are you? I am fine. Hello, how are you?'

I laugh through the tears.

41

HELMAND AND HOME

What I come home to is unfamiliar to me.

One afternoon I drive up the ramp of the underground car park at Copenhagen's Israel Square and hear children scream. My heart pounds and sweat appears on my brow. I never heard children in Helmand scream like that. In my mind's eye I see torn limbs and wounded bodies lying motionless and waiting for help. But this is not the war in Helmand. These are children from the school close by. They're playing on Israel Square. A screaming game every time a car appears from the depths.

I feel the grip of anxiety and am prepared to react in any way. I'm angry and begin to cry. What do they think they're doing? I feel at odds with a country in which people scream just because they can.

I get angry with homeless people begging for money. I'm offended by people who neglect themselves filling the aisles of public transport with their alcohol and dogs. I have met far more impoverished people in Afghanistan who nevertheless have fully retained their self-respect and their instinct for self-preservation. I know I'm not supposed to think like that.

But all of it fills me with contempt.

One day, five months after my return home, I pull into a car park. Two young men stop alongside a black car, prise open the petrol cap and snap back the windscreen wipers before stuffing kitchen roll into all available crevices. It looks like the start of some major vandalism.

I ask them what the hell they think they're doing. Don't they have anything better to do with their lives? They call me a stupid bitch and tell me to mind my own fucking business.

I feel like I've been stripped naked. I've come from a place where I can mobilize an army and have landed in a society in which I am an idiot. If someone wants to destroy someone else's property in front of me, it's none of my business and I'm supposed to look the other way.

On my television news I see a society increasingly obsessed by itself. Distance is short between citizens and politicians. Every time someone bleats, they trigger an interview with some politician who promises to do something about it. Nothing is too small that it can't get a government minister on the screen to assuage potential voters.

Where are the people with the will to do something themselves about the things they're dissatisfied with? Where are the narratives about these people?

Anxiety has left a mark on my body and soul. A mark surfacing only now after I have returned and have let down my guard. It comes in the night or in the sudden fits of sobbing. My boyfriend is fixing a lamp when there's a sudden spark and I burst into tears. I have an irrational fear that he will die in front of my eyes.

In all the frustration over things no longer in my power, I try to forgive myself for being so vulnerable. I try to protect my fragile emotions and to accept that I am no longer able to cope with life on less than nine hours of sleep and a nap during the day. I, who have slept in the desert, armed to the teeth, and gone hundreds of kilometres on coffee and biscuits without tiring.

All of us encounter fear at some point, some day out there where anything can happen. But we ignore it. Otherwise we would break down and malfunction. We pull our helmets on tight and roll out through the gate, because someone has to be out there on patrol. We do it because our comrades need us, and because there is a major goal to be achieved.

Afghanistan must be able to fend for itself someday.

The goal can be achieved one difficult step at a time. Every patrol is a step. The road is long and we know some of us will die along the way. But we're out there. Every day we're out there, even as you are reading now.

Since leaving Afghanistan in April 2009 I have spent my time writing this book. The debate on Afghanistan pains me. My country's involvement is not just about statistics, development projects and loss of life. It is about people in Afghanistan for whom the conclusions reached in our own domestic debate have very tangible repercussions. We have failed to convey the results we are having. We have perhaps also failed to convey exactly what the goal is and the conditions in which we are trying to achieve it.

That failure is not for lack of trying on the part of those of us who have spent time in Afghanistan.

Large areas of Afghanistan are today relatively calm and developing towards lasting stability and progress. Schools have been reopened and teaching resumed. Life has become normal for the first time in thirty years.

And yet the only results most people know about are flag-draped coffins sent home on planes. It seems to me that the picture of what is happening in Afghanistan has become increasingly distorted and forms an increasingly inadequate basis upon which to make decisions that affect our involvement in a war that continues to cost the lives of our soldiers.

If as stand-ins for the Afghan police and armed forces we pull out of Afghanistan overnight, only the Taliban will be there to fill the vacuum.

In a short space of time, a Taliban regime would have serious repercussions for the peoples of Afghanistan and Pakistan. Most likely the men would survive, sticking to the religious precepts, allowing their beards to grow and keeping their wives indoors.

The real losers in that scenario would be the women and children. If the Taliban come to power, women will be forbidden to work, to earn money and to move freely of their own will. They will not be allowed to go to school.

Imagine you are a woman. Imagine you are forbidden to learn, forbidden even to learn to read and write. Imagine you become ill or pregnant and are forbidden to seek medical help.

If the Taliban are given free rein in Afghanistan, their violations of power can become a threat to us all. Terrorist attacks perpetrated by the Taliban and al-Qaeda have an impact far beyond the borders of Afghanistan and Pakistan.

Hazel, Sarah, Andrea and I still keep in touch. They've all been promoted now. Hazel is Officer Commanding of an Engineer Squadron and the mother of a little girl named after the constellation Cassiopeia. Sarah has been promoted no less than twice and now holds the rank of colonel.

Andrea tours the UK giving talks about Afghanistan. She dreams of going back to Helmand.

Following the election, Helmand's governor, Gulab Mangal, has been offered five different government ministries and will doubtless soon become a member of the Afghan government.

District Governor Abdul Ahad Khan has been offered a place in the provincial administration at Lashkar Gah, but wishes instead to continue his work in Gereshk. Ali Shar continues to be a popular mayor of the town.

Gulaley was voted on to the district council together with four other women. The group for women's and children's rights still meets regularly to discuss relevant issues. A new women's centre has opened east of Gereshk with support from CIMIC and other players. On its inauguration the women held emotional speeches thanking the international forces for their help.

'Yesterday, we had the Taliban. Today, we know our rights,' one said. But the women also know that the war is far from over.

ABOUT THE AUTHOR AND THE TRANSLATOR

AUTHOR

Anne-Cathrine Riebnitzsky is an award-winning bestselling Danish writer with an unusual background. She graduated from the Copenhagen Writers Academy in 1998 but joined the Army. Having completed training as a Foreign Language Officer she worked at the Danish Embassy in Moscow in 2003–2004 before going to Afghanistan in 2007–2009 first as a soldier and then as an advisor to the Ministry of Foreign Affairs. In 2010, she was awarded the Anders Lassen Award by His Royal Highness Crown Prince Frederik X for her "significant military and civilian achievements during deployment". Only then she began her career as a writer which to date includes four novels and three nonfiction works.

TRANSLATOR

Martin Aitken is a full-time translator of Scandinavian literature. Working mainly from Danish and more recently Norwegian, he has translated the works of writers such as Kim Leine, Helle Helle, Peter Høeg, and Karl Ove Knausgaard. His recent translation of Hanne Ørstavik's *Love* was a finalist for the 2018 National Book Award.